*past, present
and future*

contents

:
introduction

by Lloyd Siegel, M.D.

Robert Mitchell Lindner's *The Fifty-Minute Hour* has endured as a work of psychological writing since its first appearance over half a century ago. But one may well ask, Why has this book remained so appealing while the purported science underlying it has been seriously and effectively challenged? The obvious pulls are the storytelling skill of the author, the spirit of the writing, and the nature of the five extraordinary cases reported. I believe, however, that more compelling and decisive factors account for the book's staying power and appeal. These factors encompass the times in which *The Fifty-Minute Hour* was written, the boldness of Lindner himself, the tradition to which the work belonged, and the fuller expression of its themes, which followed shortly after its publication.

The book's first edition was published in 1955, during the heyday of American enthusiasm for the Freudian enterprise. Many of Freud's followers and disciples had fled Europe in the late 1930s and settled in England and America. Many had been analyzed by Freud himself or were members of his inner circle. They carried with them the founding father's immense belief in psychoanalysis as a treatment modality. It is this type of treatment, with extensive modifications, variations, and additions that Lindner presents to the reader.

The reporting of psychiatric cases has a long and rich tradition. Freud and Breuer's seminal *Studies in Hysteria* was written in the 1890s and stood as prelude to the great flowering of Freud's genius in *The Interpretation of Dreams* (1900). Freud presented some of his most original thinking in the form of case studies, including "The Wolf Man," "The Rat Man," and "The Case of Schreber." Nor was Freud alone in famous case reporting; Ludwig Binswanger's almost-novella "Ellen West" appeared in the same era (1944). In this work, Binswanger presents a wider scope for the genesis and progression of mental illness.

Parenthetically, Freud's only formal recognition—aside from a postage stamp issued by the Austrian government in 1981 with his image imprinted to commemorate the 125th anniversary of his birth—came in the German-speaking world by way of the Goethe Prize for literature while Freud's great rival in Vienna, Julius von Jauregg, received the Nobel Prize in Medicine/Psychiatry for his malarial treatment of syphilis. In this way, Freud cut a literary figure rather than a medical one. At the same time, Freud himself had the dubious distinction of declaring as his doppelganger the salacious and overwrought writer and playwright Arthur Schnitzler of *La Ronde* fame. Schnitzler and he were almost exact contemporaries, were similar in appearance, were familiar with the intellectual and social scene in Vienna, and, most important, sought to explain the nature of human sexuality. Freud was in continuous communication with writers such as Arnold Zweig and Thomas Mann, conducted beautifully written exchanges with numerous eminent men of letters and science, and was meticulous in monitoring English translations of his oeuvre, standing by the Stracheys and Joan Riviere, while remaining critical of his American translators. Freud's prose style was precise, energetic, graceful, and limpid; leaving aside his monumental psychic discoveries, his uncommon command of language would ensure him a place of honor in the literary world.

Lindner was undoubtedly influenced by Hervey Cleckley's textbook on sociopathy, *The Mask of Sanity*, which appeared in 1941. In this textbook, the author presents the phenomenology of what was then called the psychopath. Dr. Cleckley as well wrote another well-known book about the symptoms of severe mental illness, namely, *The Three Faces of Eve*. Many years before *The Fifty-Minute Hour*, Lindner had written *Rebel without a Cause*, again a work dealing with psychopaths. He had also produced a scholarly paper called "The Equivalents of Matricide" for the *Psychoanalytic Quarterly* (Vol. 17, number 4, 1948, p. 453), well before *The Fifty-Minute Hour*, once again dealing with the psychopathetic personality and its origins. A great deal of Lindner's interest in this topic derived from the fact that he was a prison therapist. This entrenched interest in psychopathy, loneliness, and rebellion adds still more features of interest to Lindner's magnum opus. In his case studies, he carefully and extensively elucidates all of the signs and symptoms of the psychopathic (sociopathic) personality. He also goes further than Cleckley in offering various forms of treatment for this disorder.

Lindner himself was followed by the efforts of R. Laing and his group in London, who described in penetrating detail their extraordinary endeavors with schizophrenic patients (see J. Berke, "The Case of Mary Barnes," and M. Schatzman's exquisite exposition of the Schreber case in "Soul Murder"). These developments in psychiatric reportage were quickly followed by American literary lions who turned their attention to such material for writing exegetic and new-style masterpieces: See Truman

Capote's *In Cold Blood* (1965) and Norman Mailer's *The Executioner's Song* (1979). Strikingly, these two literary innovations also dealt with psychopaths in an extremely engaging and compassionate manner.

Thus the time directly following Freud's death in 1939 saw a proliferation of psychiatric and psychoanalytic endeavors in therapy and writing by physician-therapists and men of letters. Consequently, many observant and keen minds rushed in to explain and deal with mental illness. Flaws in scientific method and quixotic adventures should be, and were, expected in such a time and climate. Between 1900 and 1960, the Western world stood dazzled in the light of Freudian illumination and the majority of European intellectuals and prominent writers on both sides of the Atlantic anticipated "analytic cures" and / or amelioration of neurotic suffering.

So it was into these frothy waters and expectant times that Lindner launched his sleek and staunch vessel of therapeutic adventure. That he and his voyagers returned safely home is measure enough of his craft, ingenuity, and therapeutic artistry.

As Lindner wrote in his foreword, it is "the self of the analyst" that is "the common element in all of the tales . . .," which carries the day. Lindner died at the age of forty-two in 1956, one year after the first publication of *The Fifty-Minute Hour*. It was impossible then in ensuing editions to emend this claim. Nor was a correction necessary. Lindner was again following Freud, if we allow "the self of the analyst" to include recognition of transference and countertransference phenomena, with which Lindner was of course familiar. It appears, however, that Lindner went beyond these considerations, and was willing, as it were, to take on the patient *mano-a-mano*, going outside and beyond transferential development issues. Freud himself had gone outside these parameters often, traveling with patients and engaging in interchanges outside the "fifty-minute hour" and the office sessions at Berggasse 19.

We must keep in mind that Lindner's patient population—often encountered in prison settings—differed very greatly from the Freudian cases, most all of which came out of middle-class, *fin-de-siècle* Vienna. In a bold and imaginative transposition, Lindner sought to apply Freud's theories and methods to psychopaths, criminals, and murderers. He obviously saw the common strand of humanity that runs through every man and undertook to apply his very generous and empathic nature to the alleviation of psychic anguish without prejudice. He was compelled by the stories of his patients and scrupulously applied himself to the decoding of their histories in an effort to help them understand and find themselves. Today, this might be regarded as a noble, if unscientific, effort. Indeed, his patients would be treated at a more objective and distanced remove with medications, cognitive therapy, and behavior modification, and in so doing the drama of their lives might not even come into play.

Moreover, very few of today's psychologists and psychiatrists would accept Lindner's subjects as patients. Two of them demonstrated clearly sociopathic personality disorders. Another became a bullying ideologue in session, revealing severe character pathology. Yet another combined chronic debilitating depression with pseudocyesis (an imagined pregnancy). And the last, most appealing and convincing of all Lindner's subjects—the eccentric scientist from "The Jet-Propelled Couch"—displays a vast encapsulated delusional system.

In the first of Lindner's five presentations, the case of Charles ("Songs My Mother Taught Me"), he preludes the tale with a quote from Troyat's *Firebrand: The Life of Dostoevsky*: "We are all responsible, defiled, unhappy. We have stolen with the burglar whose face we do not know, we have murdered with the parricide about whom we read in the newspapers, raped with the lewd, cursed with the blasphemous . . ." Lindner was able to see, crystallized in the psychopath, unconscious traits that exist in all of us. Thus, in this case, he demonstrates his overarching acceptance of the human condition. He commiserates with and looks through to the etiologic core of a dangerous and feral psychopath who experiences command hallucinations to commit murder, and does, in fact, kill a young girl. Via a fascinating Pentothal interview, Lindner elicits vital information needed for a considered approach to treatment. He presents Charles, in the light of an abusive and traumatic past (e.g., repetitive, painful abandonment by his biological mother), and uses this perspective to reach out to the boy and help him to tame his inner demons and then deal more reasonably with the world.

Lindner, in this very first case, introduces the reader to the use of intuitive methods to treat patients on an individual basis. He also exhibits his steadfast commitment to find a way into the inner pathological life. Then—skillfully, painstakingly, artfully, and with considerable danger to himself—he enters the depths of the patient's world and forms a therapeutic alliance that acts as the fulcrum point of inner discovery and the chance for positive change. Lindner pushes the treatment with Charles to its limits in poignant revelatory interchanges, but in the end must bow to social forces that limit continued therapeutic work. Charles was released from prison and there was no further contact between him and Lindner.

In the second case, "Come over Red Rover," Lindner again gives the reader an example of his unique treatments with the introductory quote about cure by travel on the Volga. "'A calming influence on the nervous system,' they say, 'can be obtained by travel on the Volga,'" (this taken from *Soviet Psychiatry* as quoted by J. Wortis). In this inspired case description, Lindner leads Mac through a labyrinth of understanding Mac's own overt behavior as a devoted member of the American Communist Party, through exploration and elucidation of a past hitherto unconsidered by the patient. It is by making connections between a brutal past that is suppressed and then repressed into the unconscious that Lindner provides Mac with a key to his redemption. The reader is treated to a vivid application of the psychoanalytic technique. This delineates precisely what Freud enunciated in his famous dictum, "Where id is, there shall ego be." Freud believed that by bringing to conscious awareness unconscious memories, wishes, and fantasies, a cure of neurotic patients could be achieved.

Finally, in the case of Anton ("Destiny's Tot"), Lindner, with his quote from Orwell's *Nineteen Eighty-Four*, prefigures his willingness to see psychopathology in the context of personal and social misfortunes. He deals with Anton's generalized misanthropy, his specific anti-Semitism, and his generalized grievances with authority figures in a neutral and disarming treatment approach that finally compels Anton to reconsider his life-long oppositional state. Once again, Lindner employs his highly empathic methods to produce a clear unfolding of a treatment that reaches to the core and origins of the patient's illness.

Lindner concludes Anton's case with a modest and sensitive coda: "We terminated treatment when it was agreed that analysis had taken Anton as far as he could go while in prison. His symptoms had disappeared and his personality was altered to the extent that I, at least, would no longer have diagnosed him a psychopath. How permanent the 'cure' was, I will never know. After all, time is the test—and in Anton's case, time ran out on us. Shortly after the conclusion of his analysis, he was given a parole into the Army. I had a couple of letters from him, one from a P.O.E. on the West Coast, another from an undisclosed Pacific island. Two years later I learned he had been killed in action during the recovery of the Philippines . . ."

In this we are able to feel the author's most sincere and unique combination of stoicism, compassion, and deep understanding. In 1955, all of this was heady and eye-opening material, and felicitously introduced readers into the inner sanctum of analytic uncovering. For the first time readers were exposed to the thought patterns, motivational wellsprings, and feelings of criminals, murderers, and generally anomic people who, without Lindner, never would have crossed paths with those living in so-called normative society.

Lindner, armed with his strong and unique personality, a sense of mission and compassion, and employing the entire panoply of Freud's precepts and teachings, went confidently forward with his work. To this the author added a compelling style of writing—"tale-telling," as he termed it. He was clearly a maverick therapist: an independent thinker who set great store by his confrontational and even combative style, especially when presenting his own idiosyncratic treatment themes. He ventured out upon unknown waters and returned with unfathomable tales to tell.

It must also be added that Freud, in his profound wisdom and prescience, foresaw and stated that his formulations would ultimately be replaced by physical, biological, and chemical-physiological explanations; in this way, Freud recognized his system as a bridge to the day when deeper scientific discoveries would confirm or disprove much of his purely psychological ideas. For example, depression was once explained genetically and dynamically in terms of loss and depletion. It is now considered a physical illness, not much different in form from, say, diabetes. Both conditions will respond only to medicinal treatment, with talk as adjunctive help.

At this distance, we may examine more objectively the enduring fascination with *The Fifty-Minute Hour*, the nature of the cases presented, the analytic (i.e., Freudian analytic model *qua* therapeusis) endeavor as it is here displayed, and the interplay of science and imagination, fact and fiction. It is not inadvertent that many of these cases are psychopaths, for their lives often involve bizarre circumstances and the communication of these events is often skewed and suspect. Fantasies, hopes, desires, realities, and make-believe often meld and are then reified and refracted in the minds of such aforementioned notables as Laing, Lindner, Capote, and Mailer—a potent combination bound to produce memorable written fireworks. But as the Italian proverb would have it, "se non e vero, e ben trovato" ("at least if it is not true, it is well conceived"). Thus we are faced with extraordinary minds plunging into speculative seas all tethered to the tenuous anchor of Freud's universalizing system. This cannot help but make good reading, but minimal science and questionable therapy.

A marvelous example of such melding occurs conspicuously in the tale labeled "Solitaire," in which Lindner, following Freudian dicta, concludes that Laura's bulimia is the outcome of her unconscious wish to have her father's baby. Omitted in this reckoning are the facts that Lindner himself presents: that the hated mother is obese and Laura gobbles up her candies to torment her; that Laura's first gift from the runaway father is "a box of salt-water taffy from Atlantic City"; and that Laura is chronically depressed and persistently intrapunitive. In plain terms, the analytic explanation is dogmatic and fits the case into the Procrustean bed of oedipal theory while also satisfying the poetic needs of the author. The more parsimonious explanation, conforming to the logic of Ockham (Sir William of Ockham was a medieval philosopher who propounded the rule that if a number of explanations are offered to fit a scientific problem, the simplest explanation should be accepted rather than more complicated interpretations), is discarded to fit an elemental Freudian belief. Lindner consistently repeats this analytic sleight of hand, but his results are still relatively good, because, as he truly says, he throws himself heart and soul into the plight of his patients.

The final tale, "The Jet-Propelled Couch," is clearly the most successful foray into treatment, as Lindner adopts the methods of P. Rosen. Paul Rosen was a psychiatrist who entered into the psychotic delusions of his patients for the sake of breaking down these delusions from the inside, that is, believing the patient to such an unqualified extent that the patient was forced to renounce his fabricated system. In this case Lindner abandons the Freudian approach altogether, and cleverly pushes the delusional system of Kirk off the mental stage. *The Three Christs of Ypsalanti* fits exactly into this mode of therapy. At Ypsalanti State Hospital in Michigan, three patients who all believed they were Jesus Christ were brought together and after long arguments between them two eventually renounced their claims. As well, Chekhov, obviously more remembered for his eternal short stories than for his powers as a physician, had written just such a tale, "Ward Number 6," quite a while before 1955. In this masterpiece, a psychiatrist, after many, many visits to the cell of a psychotic patient, chooses to believe the delusional ravings of the patient who then is freed of his psychotic creation and leaves the cell in which the psychiatrist remains.

To conclude, Lindner's achievement is one of humanity and daring and spirit rather than an accomplishment of sound theory or reasoned practice. The constant interest in this pioneering effort is a tribute to and recognition of a sincerely committed man who, above all, wants to relieve human suffering. To this end, he gave himself license to use his heart and soul.

: foreword

I have written these tales from psychoanalysis to share with my readers some of the experiences I have had in pursuing what must surely be one of the strangest of all occupations. From a literally inexhaustible storehouse of material that increases each day, I have chosen a handful of stories that seem to me to illustrate something of the adventure of this fabulous profession, something of its romance, and much of its practical detail.

Around psychoanalysis there has been built a fence of mystery and something resembling awe. Its practitioners, if not the objects yet of veneration and fear, are well on their way to elevation as priests of a certain kind; and the initiates —those who have lain on couches, that is—threaten to become a confraternity of the saved, a latter-day community of saints whose cancelled checks comprise a passport to heavens denied those less (or more?) favored by fortune.

This cabalistic climate which today surrounds the practice of psychoanalysis has had some weird and, I think, harmful effects. Not the least among them has been the conversion of the psychoanalyst—in the public mind, at least— to a kind of devil's disciple who works with means arcane and mystic to secure the transformations of character or personality he desires.

Nothing could be further from the truth. Neither the science of psychoanalysis nor the art of its practice depend upon extraordinary agencies. As a matter of fact, the only medium employed by the analyst is the commonest instrument of all—his own human self, utilized to the fullest in an effort to understand its fellows.

The gradual replacement of men by machines to execute the functions of life is a characteristic of our time. Everywhere, devices are being substituted for the human hand, the human eye, all of the senses and even the brain. Very likely the day is not too distant when the remarkable animal we call man will be only an attendant of the vast products of his invention, concerned solely with the command and care of appliances that do his work. But there is one area where no machine, no matter how complex, no matter how inspired, can act for its maker. This is the area of understanding, of sympathetic comprehension, of intimate, knowing communication between one being and the next. Now and forever, only man will fathom men.

Psychoanalysis is that branch of knowledge which formalizes the study of man in all his aspects so that he can be understood. Founded upon observations of human functioning and behavior, grounded in the laws of interpersonal communication, it has raised understanding to an art so fine that it can actually be practiced as a legitimate occupation, and its workers instructed in the development and exercise of the talent each of us possesses for comprehending others. A psychoanalyst is, therefore, nothing more than an artist at understanding, the product of an intensive course of study and training which has—if it has been successful—rendered him unusually sensitive to his fellow men. And it is this sensitivity—in short, the analyst's own person—which is the single instrument, the only tool, with which he performs. Only on himself, and on nothing else, does he depend.

The common element in all of the tales that follow is the self of the analyst. Each story, while it tells of a specific "case," deals finally with the deployment of that self in the therapeutic enterprise, the adventures that befell it, and the effects exerted upon it by the actors and situations described. Because the self in question is my own, and my intention far from confessional or biographical, I have exercised a certain degree of discretion; but the portrait I have drawn is on the whole a quite honest one and delineates, to the best of my ability, the personality of the agent of therapy involved. That this agent is a mere human, just another person with his own hopes and fears, goals and anxieties, prejudices and pretensions, weaknesses and strengths, is really the heart of the matter. . . .

R. Lindner

songs my mother taught me

CHARLES

"We are all responsible, defiled, unhappy. We have stolen with the burglar whose face we do not know, we have murdered with the parricide about whom we read in the newspapers, raped with the lewd, cursed with the blasphemous . . ."

—Henry Troyat, *Firebrand:* the Life of Dostoevsky.

If you had seen Charles on the street in your city, you would not have known him for a vicious killer. In prison, he still has a freshness of face that belongs in a choir stall. When I last saw him he was scarcely twenty-one. Even then, his eyes were blue and innocent, and he seemed to look at you with a perpetual questioning, as if to ask why a fence of steel must always stand between him and the trees he could see through the bars of his cell window.

Before Charles came to prison I had read about him in the newspapers. The case had made headlines for many days: it was composed of elements that were "naturals" for arousing public interest—a boy, a pretty girl—"Not so pretty," says Charles—an empty apartment, an ice-pick.

On a certain day in a certain city (according to the press) a young girl stood in the hallway of an apartment house. In one hand she carried a brief case with samples of religious books and records, in the other a purse and a portable phonograph. She hesitated before the panel of bells at the mailboxes, then rang one. There was no answer, so she rang a second, then a third, finally a fourth. At last a buzzer opened the lock of the inner door. She pushed against it with her shoulder and came into a narrow foyer with a staircase in the center. As she started up the steps, a youthful voice inquired who was there. Before she reached the first landing she saw a young man. He was standing by a partly opened door, looking at her. Recognizing by his youth that he could not be the head of this household, she smiled and asked if his mother were at home. He nodded, then waved his hand vaguely toward the interior of the apartment.

"She's in there," he said, and moved aside so she could pass.

"Can I see her?" she asked.

"Sure," he replied, "go on back. . . . She's in the bedroom."

The girl entered, turned to her left, and started down a passage. Midway, she passed a small kitchen. Near the door was an ice-box. On its porcelained top lay some tools. Ahead of her was the door to a bedroom. Just as she crossed the threshold she heard a noise behind her. She turned. As she did, the youth struck her on the head with a hammer. Then he stabbed her sixty-nine times with an ice-pick. Then he flung himself on the corpse and raped it. . . .

When Charles rose from the girl he had murdered, he left the apartment, closing but not locking the door behind him. He strolled out on the street. It was a bright, sunny day in the fall of the year, just right for a pleasant walk. Accordingly, he meandered down an avenue, crossed the long bridge over the river, and sat for a few minutes on a parapet watching cars and people go by. After a while he felt hungry and searched through his pockets for money. He found a nickel. With it, at a stand by the end of the bridge, he bought an ice-cream cone. Leisurely sucking at the cone, he stood in the roadway. With his free hand he signaled to cars until one of them pulled up and he got in.

"Where're you going?" the driver asked.

"Just across the bridge," Charles said.

"What's that red stuff you got all over you?"

"Where?"

"On your face and hands. Some on your clothes, too."

Charles raised his palm and brushed it across his face. It came away flaked with dried blood.

"Oh," he said, "I've been doing some painting. Looks like I got it splashed all over me."

He laughed.

At the end of the bridge Charles got out, thanking the driver for the lift. He walked to a nearby filling station and inquired for the washroom. Inside, he washed his face and hands carefully, combed his hair, scratched the rustlike stains from his coat and trousers. He could not remove the blood from his white shirt but his coat covered the red spots. On leaving the station he walked slowly down the avenue toward his home. Halfway, he stopped. For some moments he regarded the police station across the street. Finally he crossed over and climbed the steps between the green-globed pedestals. Inside it was dim, musty, cool. A sergeant was bending over papers at a desk. Charles stood opposite, quietly, until the policeman looked up.

"There's a dead lady in apartment 2-B in the Gaylord Apartments across the street," he said.

The officer scratched his beard. "Yeah," he said. "And how d'you know?"

5

"Because I killed her. . . ."

The same nonchalance and emotional flatness was shown by Charles during the first days of his imprisonment, and I can recall nothing remarkable about the reports that reached me concerning him. However, toward the end of the first week one of the medical officers admitted him to the surgical ward on the complaint of lower abdominal pain and nausea. Three days later his appendix was removed. He was, therefore, a hospital patient at the time his initial interview took place.

This preliminary examination was conducted by a colleague of mine, so that the only knowledge I have of it comes from an official report prepared for the record. It reads as follows:

> The subject is cooperative, although somewhat tense, during the interview. He answers all questions readily but sometimes reveals a rather silly grin, not appropriate to the content of thought. Stream of speech and mental activity show no marked abnormalities, no blocking or similar defects. He is emotionally immature. Affect and mood are appropriate at times; however, his grinning when he discusses the murder which he is charged with, is not appropriate. He is very cool emotionally.
>
> His content of thought is not very clear at present. He states that he knew nothing about the person who was killed, although later on he says that it must have been temporary insanity. First he does not want to say whether a man or a woman was killed and seems somewhat suspicious of the examiner, and then states that the prosecution said it was a woman. There seems little doubt from the way he talks that he knows very well what occurred. It is difficult to evaluate whether this is evidence of mental abnormality or whether he is acting. Since his admission to the hospital here he has had a number of dizzy spells and weak fainting attacks which cannot be explained on the basis of his operation. He is well oriented. General knowledge and

intelligence are average. Insight and judgment are difficult to evaluate at present and further reports will be made in the form of Neuropsychiatric Progress Reports as soon as more information is available.

In summary, this is a cool, immature individual who shows some inappropriate affect at times. He may be acting the part of an insane individual although he has some characteristics suggestive of dementia praecox. A definite diagnosis cannot be made at present. He is being placed under observation for dementia praecox, paranoid type.

When this report came across the desk, it naturally attracted my attention and I asked the doctor who made it to bring the case up for discussion at our next staff meeting. He did, and after some debate it was decided to transfer Charles from the surgical to the psychiatric ward where he could be brought under close and constant surveillance. Here I saw him daily and followed the notes on his behavior prepared by nurses and attendants. Actually, Charles gave them little to comment upon for the entire month during which he was a patient on the ward. He co-operated well with officials and inmates, was neat about his person and belongings, spent his time reading or working at small occupational therapy projects, and behaved no differently from what one would have expected of a boy his age. Twice he complained to one of the nurses about dizzy spells; once he was involved in an argument over a game of Chinese checkers. When the thirty-day period of observation ended, it was generally assumed that, since Charles had given us no reason to hold him longer on the psychiatric ward, we would have to discharge him to the general population. But when the matter came up at staff, none of us was willing to commit himself to a clear-cut opinion. The colleague who had made the original examination expressed the indecision and confusion of all. He put it this way:

"I'm damned if I know how to dispose of this kid. All I have is a 'feel' about him. While he's been here I've talked with him every day, but I get nothing out of him. He's got a wall around him a yard thick. He gives you the right answers for everything, but there's no depth to them. Something's missing. Sure, he's schizzy, flat, a little silly—but maybe he's just a kid with a lousy background and a lot of practice at keeping his thoughts to himself. Sometimes he tells you about things that other guys would laugh or cry or show some kind of emotion about; but he does it with that silly grin on his face and you can't get through. He's not hallucinating and he has no delusions. All we've got is a vicious crime, a rotten history, a few dizzy spells that could come from anything, a stupid grin, and a feeling when you talk to him that something's rotten somewhere. We can't hold him on that!"

"Why can't we just continue his observation?" someone asked.

"Space," I answered. "And, besides, we've got to be able to justify continuing observation beyond thirty days according to regulations. We have to have evidence and all we've got is intuition."

"I should think the combined clinical intuition of all of us would be enough justification," the same speaker commented.

"It should be but it isn't," our Chief said. "The institution's on a war-production basis. They need every employable man they can get for factory work or maintenance. If you psychiatric boys can't give the custodial people a better reason for prolonging observation than a clinical 'feel,' we've got to turn him out of the hospital."

"Can't we invent a reason?" another doctor asked.

The Chief shook his head. "No; that's not possible, because we'd have to go back and alter the daily reports. We can't start doing that kind of thing."

"There's one thing we haven't done that we ought to," said the psychiatrist who had seen Charles at the initial interview. We all turned toward him expectantly. "Before we let him go into population we ought to get a pentothal interview. Maybe that'll turn up something we can put our hands on."

The suggestion was accepted immediately. That afternoon, while all of us bent eagerly over the cot on which he was lying, the pentothal sodium was fed slowly into Charles's veins. We listened as he counted backwards—"100-99-98 . . ." his voice trailing off sleepily as he continued. Then the numbers came thickly and in a meaningless jumble. Finally a snore replaced the boy's voice, and he settled into a drugged sleep. At this point, my colleague motioned me into the chair by the head of the bed.

"You take over," he said.

I seated myself and began.

"Can you hear me, Charles?" I asked.

His head moved in a nod and his throat contracted with the effort to force air through to his dry lips. A slow "Yes, I hear you," became audible.

"This is Dr. Lindner speaking to you, Charles," I said. "I'm going to ask you some questions. Will you try to answer them?"

"I'll—try," he said.

"Just say whatever comes into your head. It will be easier to talk in a moment. Why are you here?"

"Because . . . because I—I—killed her."

"Who did you kill?"

"Girl."

"Why did you do it?"

9

"Voice. . . . Kill. . . . Kill."

"Did someone tell you to kill her?"

"Voice. No one tell. . . . Just voice. Kill."

"Where did the voice come from?"

"Heard voice. Don't know—where—where it come from."

"Was it the voice of someone you know?"

"No."

"Had you ever heard it before?"

"No."

"What else did it tell you to do?"

"Nothing. Just—kill."

"Did it tell you how to do it?"

"No."

"How did you do it?"

"Hammer. Hit with hammer. . . . Then ice-pick."

"How many times did you hit her?"

"Don't know. Hit—lots of times. Hit . . . hit. Couldn't stop. Hit lots of times."

"Why did you stop hitting her?"

"Hammer fell—on floor. Under girl. Full of blood. . . . Slippery."

"What did you do then?"

"Ice-pick."

"Why?"

"Don't know. Saw—ice-pick. Couldn't stop."

"Did the voice tell you to use the ice-pick?"

"No."

"Did you hear the voice all the time you were hitting her?"

"Yes. Loud. Kill . . . kill."

"Where did you stab her?"

"All over."

"Any special place?"

"Breasts."

"Why her breasts?"

"Make milk."

"Did you want milk?"

"Don't know."

"How many times did you stab her?"

"Many times."

"Did you hear the voice all the time you were stabbing her?"

"No."

"When did the voice stop?"

"Don't know. . . . Just stopped."

"What did you do after you stopped stabbing her with the ice-pick?"

At this, Charles moaned but made no answer. In a moment I repeated the question. This time he whimpered and a sweat broke out on his face. One of the doctors leaned across and wiped the boy's forehead with a tissue. Charles sighed. My colleague whispered to ask the question again.

"Can you hear me, Charles?" I asked.

His parched lips parted and a "Yes" like a sigh came through them.

"What did you do after you stabbed the girl with the ice-pick?"

"I—I—don't know. . . ." Now he twisted on the cot and his face expressed the pain of a memory.

"Can't you remember?" I asked.

"I—I—pulled—down her pants—and I—I—put my— it . . ." Here great sobs racked his body as if they were being forced from him by torture.

"Don't you want to tell me, Charles?" I asked.

11

He nodded slowly and licked his lips. "I'll—tell—" he said. "I couldn't find—her—the—place—so I—I put it between—between her legs. . . ."

"You didn't put it in her?"

"No."

"You're sure?"

"Yes."

"The coroner's report says she was torn. Did you do that?"

"Yes."

"How?"

"With—my fingers. . . ."

"Why?"

"Because—because—I was—angry with her."

"She was dead then, wasn't she?"

He nodded again. "Yes," he said. "She was—dead. I—I killed her." His sobbing shook the cot now. His fingers tore at the sheets.

"You were angry with her even though you knew she was dead?"

"Yes."

"Why were you angry?"

"I—couldn't—I couldn't find it."

"Her vagina?"

"Couldn't find it. . . ."

"But you found it with your fingers later."

"Yes."

"Did the voice tell you to do that?"

"No. No voice."

"Did you ever hear the voice before that day?"

"No. . . . Never."

"Have you heard it since?"

"No."

I looked up at the men standing around the bed and asked if there was anything else to be covered. They shook their heads, one by one. I turned again to Charles.

"You're tired, Charles," I said. "Go to sleep. When you wake up you'll feel better."

Back in the staff room we discussed what we had just heard. The interview had altered the picture of the case significantly. We agreed it would be folly to send Charles into population, that we now had enough evidence to hold him on continued psychiatric observation. The most convenient diagnosis for this purpose, we decided, was *Psychosis in remission, schizophrenia, with auditory hallucinations and homicidal trends.* We shared a further feeling that the boy had been insane at the time the murder was committed. A search of the records, however, disclosed that a plea of guilty had been entered and the case heard before a judge in closed chambers without a jury. The possibility that we could urge that it be reopened was mentioned, but we decided that the evidence from this single interview would not be sufficient and that, in any case, our prerogatives did not extend so far. Finally, we were in agreement that the case required further study and that the boy was in desperate need of treatment. Since, at the time, I was the only one with a free therapeutic hour, the matter was assigned to me.

The following morning I saw Charles in my office. He greeted me cheerfully as he came in and settled in the armchair with a cigarette to which he helped himself from the pack on the desk. I asked him if he recalled the interview of the previous afternoon.

"I remember some of it," he said. "The doctor gave me an injection and I got very tired. Someone was asking me questions. When I woke up my throat was sore."

13

"I asked you the questions," I said. "Do you remember what they were about?"

"They were about my crime, weren't they?"

"Yes," I said. "They were about your crime."

"What did I tell you?" he asked.

I summarized the interview while he listened intently. When I finished, he said, "That's about it."

"Do you want to add anything to it?" I asked.

He shrugged. "I guess there's no more to add."

"Why didn't you tell them this at the trial?"

"I didn't get a chance to," he answered with some feeling. "My lawyer said I'd just better plead guilty and get it over with. He said I'd get a lighter sentence. I guess he was talking with my mother and they decided to do it that way."

"Did your mother know everything you told us yesterday—about hearing a voice and so on?"

"Yeah," he said. "I told her most of it—not about the rape part, though."

I was puzzled. "Why," I asked, "didn't she let you plead insanity if she knew about it?"

"We talked about that," he said. "She didn't want the publicity. She's a buyer in one of the big department stores and she was afraid she'd lose her job. She wanted everything kept quiet. She was afraid to have her name connected with it."

"But the newspapers were writing about it."

"Yeah. But, you see, she has a different name than mine and so nobody connected her with me."

"How do you feel about being here?" I asked, and then added hastily, "I know that sounds like a foolish question because nobody wants to be in a place like this. But what I mean is, do you feel as if you belong here?"

14

Charles ground out his cigarette before answering. Then he folded his hands and leaned forward. "I think I was crazy when I did my crime," he said. "I don't think they should have sent me to the penitentiary."

"Where should they have sent you?"

"To a hospital, I guess."

"What for?"

He thought a moment. "Well," he said, "maybe in a hospital I could find out why I did it and would get fixed so I wouldn't do it again."

"Do you think you might do it again?"

"I don't know. I can't say. I guess it could happen again."

"If you could find out about why you did it while you're in here," I asked, "would you like that?"

"Yes," he said.

"Suppose you and I study this together," I proposed.

"That would be fine." He paused, then regarded me with his innocent eyes. "Would that keep me from doing it again?"

"It might," I said.

"I'd like that."

"It takes time," I said.

"I've got lots of that," he said.

Is it enough to say that a murderer was born on a day in April in a certain calendar year in a city in the North? Can a destiny be triangulated? No; for the roots go deep, and the ancients may have put it better when they wrote that, for such as Charles, the fault lies with the stars.

Long before Charles was born the marriage between his parents was falling apart. They had not wanted each other nor the two children that followed. Under religious compulsion they maintained a semblance of harmony for over

15

two years, but in the first month of their marriage both had known it could not last. So Charles and his brother were marked before birth. In Charles's third (his brother's second) year, a religious dispensation permitted the parents to separate, and the figure of their father disappeared from their lives. For a few months their mother tried to maintain the home, but since she herself was a harassed, conflicted, easily disturbed person, she found the task too great. On the advice of her confessor the children were placed in an orphanage. For fifteen years thereafter the two boys were to live in homes and institutions.

From the outside, the places where Charles spent most of his life appear pleasant. One has really to live in them to learn the truth: that for all but a handful the swept floors, the neatly made beds, the pots that gleam on pantry shelves, even the smiles of matrons and pseudo-parents, are designs on a façade. By and large, the children consigned to the care of such places are the victims of the emotional impoverishment of their keepers. They grow as weeds in a desert, stretching this way and that for sustenance, twisting themselves out of their natural design, mocking Nature's blueprint. They are exposed, more than others, to the vagaries of the human elements, now stifled in the heat of emotional suns, now frozen under loveless snows, now drowned, now parched.

Charles's life in one institution and home after another was miserable and shocking to learn about. He lived in constant fear and terror. He was brutalized beyond description. In the first "home," a religious one, even at the age of four and thenceforward, he was beaten unmercifully for the smallest infractions and made to do extravagant penances for expressing the ordinary playfulness of a small boy. Supervisors, who by their faith alone should have been

16

obliged to give him affection if not love, handled him—
and all of their charges—as if he were not a child but a
species of animal. In small sadisms these governors reflected
their own frustrations, and it often seemed as if they acted
under orders to grind out the lives committed to them.
Existence was regimented under the pretense of piety.
Before long Charles found himself regarding his person
and his being with guilt; for under the warped codes and
philosophies to which he was exposed he was forced to
accept the idea that what was happening to him—his exile
from normal life, his abandonment by his family—was
somehow his own fault.

It was not long before Charles donned the only armor
available to him. After a few years during which he had
been the recipient of brutality, the target of assaults sexual
and physical, the butt of sadisms that make a small boy's
life a hell, he associated himself in spirit with his tormentors.
The process of this identification began with a change in
the fantasies he had so long employed for comfort when
he nursed his wounds in the dormitory at night. In analysis,
we learned that these first fantasies were heroic in stamp,
epic with poetry and, though mean and pitiful from such
a distance, panoplied with the glory that life lets us
know only once. But they did not help against the harsh
realities of his environments. The heroes in his mind could
not hold out against the inquisitors in his real life, nor
could their gleaming swords avail against the sticks and
blows of his masters and fellows. Into his reveries, then,
there crept a new note. Richard Coeur de Lion was replaced by Genghis Khan, the Dragon Slayers by Bluebeards,
and instead of dreams of chivalry he came to cherish
fantasies of revenge. As the character of his inner life
changed, so did Charles. Growing meanwhile, and acquir-

17

ing physical strength, he was soon able to express the vengeful hate in him. Toward those smaller and weaker he behaved as he could not toward those larger and stronger. He passed on his hurts: he became an afflictor, delighting in giving pain. Also, he learned shrewdness and cunning; and soon he was accomplished at diverting hurt from himself to someone else. In sexual activities, where he was once the target he became the arrow, and on the vainly protesting forms of others he discharged the venom of his frustration. By the age of ten he had become perverted in every way to the roots of his being—already his soul had been twisted into that of a murderer.

During these years, when Charles was undergoing the changes described, he saw his mother only infrequently. Her occasional visits on his birthday or a holiday were always hurried. They left him with a feeling of something incomplete, undone and unsaid. Always laden with gifts, she made a small, excited flurry in his colorless life. He said to me, "She was like a fairy princess when she came. She smelled so good." But at the same time that he looked forward to her visits and dreamed of her after she had gone, part of him hated her, too, for having placed him in the purgatory of his daily life. It was this that made of her visits the incomplete episodes they were. He wanted to ask her to take him with her when she left, but he feared to ask, knowing her reply in advance. So an emptiness would seize him when she went away. At such times he would cast about for victims on whom to vent himself, and the record I have of his life shows that every visit was followed by a display of aggression. In it we read a tale of his acts and the punishments received: it is a story of small violences, swift retributions, long and hard penances.

On special occasions there were visits to his mother's

home. Brief exposures to normal life, these were more confusing and destructive than solacing, for all they gave Charles was a taste of what he should have had, and they increased an appetite that, under the circumstances, could never be satisfied.

At the age of eleven Charles ran away from the Home he lived in at the time. One day, on his way between buildings, he saw a group of boys who had been dismissed from the public school across the road crowding aboard a streetcar. Unthinking, he joined them, somehow in the press managing to avoid paying a fare. He rode to the end of the line and got off by railroad tracks that ran along a river. Until nightfall he sat on an embankment, watching the trains, dreaming of their destinations. As evening came on he became aware of a small fire and voices nearby, and he drifted toward it. Some hobos were cooking a stew, which they invited the boy to share. As he recalls it, there were three men, and when he first joined them they were cordial and understanding. He told them about himself; until a late hour he listened to their tales. They promised that in the morning they would show him how to hop a freight, that he could go with them to a distant city. Later one of them produced a bottle, and they all drank from it. The liquor dazed Charles and numbed his body, so that when they began to toy with him he was semiconscious, almost paralyzed. Through the night, all three of them used and abused him. He remembers laughter and sweat, but nothing of the blows that bruised him or the things they did that tore the cavities of his body and awakened him to the sight of his own blood.

A trackwalker found Charles. He was sent to a hospital. When recovered, they returned him to the Home, where he was disciplined with even more than usual thoroughness

19

and held up as an example to the orphaned community. But this and the fact of his adventure served only to enhance the new conception of self that was assuming a lasting shape in him; and when the punishments and penances had run their course, Charles emerged from the chrysalis of childhood an antagonist of all values.

In the following year he was completely unmanageable. He lived in a perpetual orgy of self-indulgence and his mischiefs were no longer small. Finally the authorities at the Home were unable to handle the problem they had shared in creating. To his mother they wrote: "He is having a bad influence on the other children. We can no longer keep him here."

Placement in a foster home was arranged for Charles, and in the opening of his thirteenth year he was sent to live on a farm with a middle-aged couple whose only recommendation for parenthood was the fact that they had once raised a prize bull.

Between the ages of thirteen and fifteen Charles lived a life comparable to that of a farm animal. The people whom the boy was now expected to regard as his parents were dull and uncommunicative. After the first week, when talk was necessary to demonstrate their expectations and his duties, words were rarely used between Charles and the taciturn couple. Grunts, gestures, an occasional command— these sufficed to convey what was essential, and what was essential always had to do with the sixty acres enclosed by a stone fence. Apart from them, and Charles's tasks involving them, it was as if he did not exist. Awakened by a heavy hand tugging at the bedclothes, the arduous days began before dawn. They ended in the dusk with "washing up," when Charles smoothed the soggy dishcloths over the back-porch railing, muttered a "good night," and climbed by the back stairs to his room on the third floor of the old farm-house. Here, in the dark, he would lie on the bed and wait for sleep to overtake him so that he could respond again in the morning to the pull at his blankets.

Years later, when we worked together, I asked Charles about the silent months he had spent on the farm. I wondered at his passivity during that time, his inaction, and this curious acquiescence in a discipline of labor for which his former existence had certainly not prepared him. Had he, I asked, undergone some kind of personality change around this time? Was he not lonely? What had he thought of, dreamed about, during this period of isolation?

To these questions, Charles had good answers. "I didn't mind it much," he said, "because I didn't feel like I was alive most of the time. I got to thinking of myself like one of the horses or pigs around the place. That's the way they seemed to think of me, so that's how I thought of myself. They told me to do something and I did it—that's all. For that whole time there wasn't much in my head. I didn't seem to care about anything. So long as they left me alone—didn't bother me—it was fine. I was like a block of wood. Oh, sure, I'd get a little lonely once in a while. I'd want to see some of the kids I knew, or something. But until I took off I guess I was too busy during the day and too tired at night to try anything. When I did any dreaming at all, I'd remember things about what happened before, or maybe think what I was going to do someday, but this was usually at night when I was starting to fall asleep."

The manner of Charles's leaving the farm was unceremonious. Apparently on a whim, without forethought or plan, he simply walked off one morning, cutting across the fields to a highway where he flagged a truck that took him to the city in which his mother lived. When she arrived

21

home from work that evening she found him sitting on her doorstep. Her greeting, Charles told me, was not very cordial. Almost immediately she began making plans for him to return to the farm, and when he refused she became angry. He couldn't stay with her, she said, she couldn't afford to keep him, and besides, the apartment was too small. Moreover, she had a job to do, and if he remained at home she would be worrying about him every minute, worrying about where he was and what he was doing and what new mischief he was up to. No; it was out of the question: he'd have to go back to the farm; or if not there, somewhere, someplace where he'd be safe and "out of her hair." But somehow, after much discussion, Charles prevailed on her to let him stay for a few days. He assured her he'd be no trouble, that he'd get a job. He was almost sixteen and big for his age: he would work and help out with the expenses; after he "got on his feet" he would move to the Y. . . . Please!

It was a week, however, before Charles got around to looking for a job. For some reason he couldn't "get going." He would awaken in the morning full of good intentions, fix his mother's breakfast, straighten up the apartment after she left—and then "just sit around all day, look at some comic books, listen to the radio, maybe go for a walk." One day he picked up a prostitute and spent the afternoon with her.

In the second week after his home-coming Charles found a job as office boy at the local headquarters of the Red Cross. His employment there lasted less than three weeks. To a routine inquiry made after Charles had been imprisoned, the Office Manager recalled that ". . . we let him go because he was never available when needed. He

22

seemed to be in a trance most of the time . . . very vague . . . impressed us as probably feeble-minded . . . completely incompetent even at menial tasks."

At loose ends once more, Charles resumed his accustomed mode of life—until his mother discovered he had lost his job. This time his pleas were unavailing. After a tearful scene, she telephoned her religious counselor, who immediately made arrangements for Charles to be sent to another Home. This time it was one where the legend "Industrial School," following a saint's name, hid the fact that it was only a way station for youths who were expected to become criminals—if they were not such already.

It required no effort for Charles to fit himself into the routine of the institution that was to be his home for the next two years. By now it was all so familiar. From the moment he put his comb and toothbrush on the shelf above his bed it was as if he had been there all his life. Without thinking he slipped once more into his usual character of vicious castoff, tormentor of those beneath him in the pecking order, fawner and appeaser of those above. With a practiced eye he surveyed the situation. Before too many days had passed he established himself as a "wolf," a bully, a swaggering tough whom no one could "push around"— established himself by an act calculated to move him at once into the inner circle of boys who, whether the Brothers and Sisters knew it or not, really ran the School. It happened this way.

The institution consisted of two large buildings joined by a passageway. One of the buildings contained classrooms, offices and an indoor gymnasium; the other, two dormitories, a chapel, two dayrooms for recreation, quarters for resident Brothers, and a few "private" rooms for the elite

23

of the school who were granted the special privilege of living in them because of their positions as monitors or assistants to the supervisory staff. In this inverted society, however, the elite was not made up of the better element of the School but of the worst and the most unregenerate. It consisted— as it usually does in such places—of the "hard guys," each of whom had won his right to belong by demonstrating qualities of cruelty, lack of sentiment, ability to withstand pain, sexual perversion and proficiency at every kind of knavery and thievery the environment offered.

It was to this group that Charles wanted to belong, and he accordingly made plans to obtain an "invitation." Because all the rooms were filled when he arrived—hence the inner circle closed—he knew that his only hope lay in displacing someone. For some days, therefore, he did nothing but observe the chosen few, coldly estimating his chances against each in turn, and devising a plan of attack. After he had selected his victim, with the intensity and caution of a general on whom the fate of armies depends, he plotted his tactics, chose his terrain, and even, in imagination, rehearsed his plan to the merest detail. When he was satisfied that he could not fail, he acted.

The site Charles chose for his debut was the corridor beneath the passageway between the two buildings of the School. Here, he had learned, the clique gathered after supper each day to smoke forbidden cigarettes, barter the products of their thefts, horseplay, exchange smutty stories, and hatch the plots that maintained them in power. The corridor—a narrow, ill-lighted hall with a cement floor, whitewashed walls, and pipes crowding the ceiling so that the tallest boys had to stoop to avoid them—was reserved by School tradition to the "roomers." No one who was not of the inner circle was permitted to linger there, and the

24

authorities, who of course knew the uses to which it was put, closed their eyes to its existence and gave tacit approval to what went on by carefully avoiding the place during the after-supper hour—thinking, perhaps, that this was a small price to pay for the real service the group rendered in keeping the rest of the population so well in line.

When Charles, in accordance with his plan, appeared during the holy hour on this sacred territory, all activity ceased, and the dozen or so occupants of the smoky corridor regarded him with silent, surprised hostility. Not in the memory of the oldest among them had this ever happened; no one had even dared approach the corridor—they called it, Charles said, the "Hatchery"—and to invade its fastness was something unheard of. Momentarily caught off guard, they seemed immobilized as Charles sauntered over to the boy he had chosen for his victim. Facing this lad, Charles took a crumpled cigarette from his pocket and said, "Gimme a light."

The boy stared. Charles repeated his request, this time more loudly: "I said gimme a light!" Still the boy stared.

Suddenly Charles reached out, grabbed the hand in which the boy was holding his own cigarette, and pulled the other toward him. Aroused by this, the boy freed himself with an abrupt movement.

"Watch what you're doin'," he said. Then, "You ain't supposed to be down here."

"You own this joint?" Charles asked belligerently.

By now the other "roomers" had gathered round the antagonists. From their presence the boy took heart. Slowly, deliberately, he dropped his cigarette and ground it out with his toe before answering.

"Yeah," he said. "We own this joint. Now scram before you get hurt."

25

"Make me," Charles said, dropping his own unlit cigarette and crushing it with his foot in imitation of the other.

The boy looked around at his fellows, then back at Charles. "Look, kid," he said, his tone an amalgam of contempt and reasonableness, "you're new here. You don't want no trouble. Maybe you don't know your way around yet. You better get outa here 'fore you get hurt."

"Make me," Charles repeated.

The boy shrugged. "O.K.," he said, "if that's the way you want it."

"Yeah," Charles said, "that's the way I want it," and leaped at the boy's throat.

Overborne by the swiftness of Charles's assault, the other fell to the ground. For some moments they were locked together, thrashing about on the cement floor, each seeking a firm hold. But Charles had chosen his victim carefully, and the fight had scarcely begun before it was over, with the boy pinioned face down and arms pressed against his sides between Charles's thighs. Now, holding his victim securely, Charles took a penknife from his pocket. With one hand he pressed the boy's head to the floor, with the other and his teeth he opened the knife. Swiftly, he inserted the blade beneath the collar of the boy's shirt, and in one movement ripped the material from top to bottom, exposing the flesh. Then, while the "roomers" looked on too horrified to interfere, and to the accompaniment of the screams of his victim, Charles carefully cut his initials into the boy's skin. When it was done he wiped the blade clean of blood, closed the knife, replaced it in his pocket, and stood up.

"Now," he said as he took another cigarette from his pocket, "who's gonna give me a light?"

Within an hour the entire School knew what had taken

26

place in the "Hatchery." The next day, as if by magic, Charles found himself quartered in a "private" room.

After this Charles rose rapidly in the secret government of the institution and before long was the undisputed leader of the School. A virtually unopposed dictator, for the remainder of his two-year stay he lived the life of a young potentate. His every whim was catered to, he was able to gratify almost every impulse, even the Brothers feared him. For a time his life was a delinquent's idyll.

In about the middle of his seventeenth year Charles ran away from the Industrial School. Bored with an environment that offered him every satisfaction but the freedom to leave it—although Charles told me about many occasions when he and his friends made forays into the city at night and returned the following day with spoils of tobacco and whisky—he conceived a plan for a mass exodus of the "roomers." The details of this plan were ingenious but need not detain us here. Suffice to say that Charles, after a month on the "bum," turned up again one winter's morning on his mother's doorstep.

This time his mother's insistence that he return to the same or another "Home" was unavailing. Because of his age she could not enlist the help of authorities in ridding herself of this "burden," and Charles was adamant, refusing to move. He insisted on remaining with her, made vague promises about finding a job, and turned a deaf ear to all her pleas, tears and protestations. Eventually she had to resign herself to his presence while he, in turn, fell into the familiar pattern of aimless existence for which he had, apparently, been longing all these years.

Out of sheer boredom, after he had been home a few months, Charles applied for and got a job as a Western

27

Union messenger. Once again this employment proved to be only temporary. His superiors soon tired of an employee who took his duties so casually, who could never be found when wanted, who was never wholly "there."

It was just before noon on the third day after he had been fired from his Western Union job that Charles heard the doorbell ring. From the landing he watched the girl climb the steps toward the open door of his mother's apartment.

The analytic task that stood out more sharply than any other during the first weeks of Charles's treatment was the problem of making contact with him. His was a childish nature, and to insist that he follow the "basic rule" of psychoanalysis—that he associate freely while lying on the couch—was to make an impossible demand upon him. Like a child, he was incapable of following instructions to report his free associations, his dreams, his memories, and his current states of feeling. For weeks, therefore, until I realized that orthodox technique was out of the question, we got nowhere. Characteristically, when his hour for therapy arrived, Charles would present himself at my office. He would lie on the couch and reel off long reports on his current daily activities, his relations with fellow inmates, the petty details and gossip of his present prison life. When I tried to get him to relate these matters to his past, or to examine them closely for clues to the dynamics of his personality, I faced what seemed to be an insurmountable barrier. It seemed as if this youth lived "off the top of his head," that his personality was a two-dimensional structure, lacking depth, and functioning only in the "now." Indeed, I almost came to this conclusion as hour followed hour and the stalemate persisted. In vain I looked for signs to indicate that our time, at least, was not being wasted. Our relations remained casual, too casual—not only did Charles fail to develop the slightest indication of a positive relationship with me, but the hidden, negative response was also missing. He came to his hours automatically, because he had agreed to do so. But beyond lending his physical presence to the business, he was not involved at all.

I have already said that I had begun to think of Charles and his personality in two-dimensional terms. This impression grew stronger with the passage of time and led me to consider abandoning therapy. Had the case developed this way I would not have been surprised. Before this I had encountered such people, people without a recoverable past, people who lived entirely in the present moment. Many, of course, were feeble-minded; but more of them had been traumatized personalities, persons who had lived through crucial and shocking experiences which their minds, in an effort at self-help, had mechanically sealed off; and all too often the sealing-off process did not stop with the traumatizing incident but spread to create a virtual amnesia, leaving the person in many respects an individual without a past. I am sure my reader knows many such people. They are the ones who have great difficulty in recalling things most of us remember without effort—the names of schoolteachers, the locations of former residences, the small and large events that orient them to their present by establishing continuity with the past. In every such case one is justified in assuming some cruxlike, traumatic incident, followed by the self-preservative reaction of memorial isolation I have referred to.

I thought, for a while, that Charles belonged to this group of traumatized people without pasts. After all, he had lived the kind of life anyone would want to forget. The incident leading to his confinement was certainly to be thought of

29

as traumatic—only under the influence of pentothal had he been brought to speak of it, and even then with obvious reluctance. Thus I was prepared to write him off as therapy-fast, when an incident occurred that made me change my whole approach to the assignment of treating Charles.

Before I describe what happened, it is necessary to answer the question that must be in the mind of the reader. Why, he wants to know, did you not use hypnosis? Or narco-analysis? Surely either of these methods might have broken the dam and given access to the abundant store of memories, to Charles's unconscious, to everything you were looking for.

The best answer I can give to this question at such a distance in time from the problem is that I was afraid—and, as events proved, justifiably afraid—to employ any but tested and dependable therapeutic technique with the patient. I could not have formulated my reasons so clearly then, but I think I "knew" intuitively that to force the lock at that time would have been disastrous. Recall that Charles had been diagnosed as a remissed schizophrenic psychotic. This meant that his insanity—I use this strong nontechnical term purposely to impress the reader with the nature of the case we are discussing—his insanity was always potential, just over the horizon of his behavior, likely to reappear at any time and without warning. I could not afford to run this risk, the risk of precipitating psychosis, which is implicit in the use of hypnosis with pre-psychotic, incipiently psychotic, or remissed (temporarily stabilized) psychotics. Hypnosis—and the various methods employing narcotics to induce hypnosis—is often too sharp an instrument; sometimes it penetrates into the unconscious too quickly for safety. At such times, and particularly with the near psychotic, it dredges the hidden recesses of the mind before the patient is prepared to receive and digest what is brought up. Confronting an unprepared ego with these unconscious contents may, in these cases, unhinge the precarious balance of the mind. No; with Charles it was better to go slowly, or not at all.

The incident that changed the entire picture and enabled me to continue treating Charles was a small and otherwise insignificant one. During the period of which I am writing, Charles was quartered on the psychiatric ward. He was assigned as a "patient-attendant" with the object of keeping him occupied while at the same time ensuring that he would be under constant observation by the psychiatric staff. His duties were domestic, for the most part, but he was also required to assist the ward nurses and to be helpful with other patients. A thing he was asked to do—and did well—was to fill in where needed in the recreational activities of the ward. In the afternoons, therefore, Charles played games with ambulant psychiatric patients, organizing and managing contests in checkers, chess, bridge, model-construction and whatever else was used for the diversion of the hospitalized men. This assignment exactly suited Charles's temper, of course; to be always "playing" something accorded well with his childish nature. If anyone could be said to love his "work," it was Charles. When the custody of the game closet was given him, he beamed with pleasure, and no hero ever received a medal more proudly than Charles accepted the key to the closet from our Head Attendant.

Late one afternoon I was preparing to go home. As a matter of habit, just before leaving for the night I made final rounds, a hasty and casual inspection of the ward to satisfy myself that everything was as it should be. For some reason I was in a hurry that evening, so I hardly noticed

31

Charles on his knees before the open game closet as I entered the security unit of the psychiatric service—a series of rooms separated from the rest of the ward by a strong steel-and-glass door. On my return, however, I was momentarily diverted by sounds coming from Charles, still on the floor before the cabinet. Curious, I paused, watched and listened. Over the boy's shoulder I could see that he had set up three or four chessmen—I recall the king, the queen, and one or two other pieces. Behind them he had made an arrangement of checkers in three sides of a square, and in this enclosure with the chessmen he had placed various items from other games in the closet. While I watched, he moved the chess pieces to the accompaniment of noises and sounds which I took to be conversation in differently pitched voices, although I could not hear what was said.

For a few moments I observed Charles at this occupation, amused and mentally comparing him with my two-year-old daughter whom I had often seen doing the same thing. Then some involuntary movement or noise betrayed my presence to the boy. He turned and saw me standing there. As I recall, it took him a while to recognize me. When he did, he blushed, then smiled.

"Hi, Doc," he said. "Goin' home?"

I nodded.

"When are you gonna take me with you?"— This was a convention between us, to which I was supposed to answer, and did, "When hair grows on the Warden's head."

As usual, we both laughed. Then I asked, pointing to the things on the floor, "What's that, a new game?"

"Nah," he replied. "I was just putting things away and got to playing with the stuff."

"Playing how?"

He nudged the king with his toe and it fell on its face. "Oh," he said, "pretending these were people I know, and this"—with his foot indicating the three-sided arrangement of checkers—"this is a house they live in. . . . Spare a smoke?"

I gave Charles a cigarette and we said good night.

It was only when I was driving homeward that the meaning of this incident struck me. Of course! *That* was the way to establish contact with this boy. Play technique—psychoanalysis through play!— Treat a child like a child. How could I have been so dense?

It was difficult to wait until the next day. When morning came I rushed to the dime store. There I bought almost everything in sight on the toy counter—dolls, guns, miniature autos, furniture sets, animals, paints, clay, anything I found that could be used for what I planned to do. When I arrived at my office, ignoring everything else, I called for Charles. On that day his analysis began.

There is no need to recount the details of the method I used to probe Charles's unconscious and to expedite his treatment. Because Charles was, after all, not a child, I naturally had to compromise with orthodox play-therapy technique. Instead of following the rules, I had to improvise as we went along, to play by ear as it were. Consequently, my notes on the case resemble the pieces of a jigsaw puzzle: they make sense only when assembled, but otherwise consist of random observations of my patient's behavior; snatches of his history as it emerged through our discussions following and during his manipulation of the toys; reconstructions of significant events in his life and their accompanying attitudes as these were inferred from his actions in our sessions; and various jottings concerning the ever-changing relationship that existed between Charles and myself as he "transferred" his feelings upon me, his therapist.

One of the earliest important accomplishments of the method we now used to analyze Charles was the discovery of the two-sided nature of his feelings about his mother. By the time we arrived at this point I had extracted the gross details of the history I have already delineated. We had discussed her rejection of Charles, and he had given expression—both by projection on the toys and in his behavior toward me—to a considerable amount of the resentment and hostility his mother's consistent refusal to permit the boy to live with her had engendered. He was gradually beginning to understand that this rejection had inspired much of his past aggressive behavior, and we had been occupied for a few days with establishing the almost one-to-one correspondence between rejective experiences (by his mother or such substitutes for her as his various environments had provided) and the long series of aggressive, sometimes vicious, acts they inspired.

A drawing Charles was working on during one of our sessions gave me the opportunity to confront him, for the first time, with the reverse side of his attitude toward his mother, and to open up the topic Charles had been avoiding since we began our work. The drawing was no more than a sketch. It depicted a rather large building topped by a cross, a lawn in front of the edifice, and what I assumed to be a wall surrounding the whole. While Charles was working on it we talked. It represented, he said, one of the Homes he had lived in when he was about nine. As he remembered this place it was a dingy, depressing institution. Life there, he said, was tough, mainly because it was run by members of a religious order outstanding for its strictness. The discipline was hard and cruel. A passionate note crept into his voice as he recounted some of the penances he had been

34

forced to undergo for small infractions of rules, and the whippings administered him for breaches of discipline. In the midst of his tale he ripped the paper from the drawing board and flung it to the floor.

"To hell with that joint," he said.

I picked up the drawing and inspected it. "Are you finished with this?" I asked.

"Yeah," Charles said. "I don't even want to think of that place again. It stunk!"

I continued to examine the drawing. "It's incomplete," I commented.

"Sure," Charles agreed. "I left out lots of things."

I handed him the drawing. "What did you leave out?" I asked. He recounted a list of details he had omitted.

"What about the gate?" I asked. "Didn't the Home have one?"

"It sure did," Charles said, "only I never used it." He replaced the drawing on the board. "Here," he continued, "I'll show you." For some minutes he busied himself with his crayons. While he worked he chuckled, and as he handed me the finished drawing, he laughed loudly.

"That's the way it really was," he said.

I inspected the revised drawing to see what Charles was enjoying so hugely, then joined in his laughter to show him I appreciated the joke. What he had done was to transform the drawing into a surprisingly subtle cartoon. With a few dozen strokes he had sketched in a heavy gate secured by great hinges and a giant padlock, and above the wall roughed out the figure of a boy soaring on angel's wings over the barrier, smiling ecstatically and blowing kisses.

"I guess I busted outa that place a dozen times," he commented. "It got so one of the Sisters said I probably had wings."

"Where did you go when you ran away?" I asked.

"Home, of course."

"You mean to your mother's place?"

"Sure. . . . Where else?"

"I don't know," I said, "but isn't it kind of strange that you kept going back there? Especially when she'd never let you stay very long and always turned you back in?"

The laughter disappeared from Charles's face. It was replaced by that sullen look I had begun to recognize as a signal of his withdrawal into regions of self that were still closed to me. "Where the hell else could I go?" he asked. "What's a nine-year-old kid supposed to do? Starve?"

"That's just the point," I remarked. "You knew she wouldn't let you stay home once you got there, and you knew you had to go there. You also knew they'd punish you when you came back. So why did you persist in busting out time after time?"

"I guess," Charles said, "I guess I always expected it to be different. . . ."

"Different how?"

He picked up some clay and began to roll it between his palms. When he spoke again his voice was softer than I had ever heard it.

"I remember I used to dream about how it would be," he said. "I'd think every time that this time I'd get there and she'd ask me to stick around, stay with her. Maybe I'd go to school like the other kids." —Now I noted his hands were still and his eyes clouded over; while a small and bitter half-smile played about his lips. "Like the other kids," he continued to muse, "kids who lived in houses." He paused again. "Then, I even used to think she'd take me to a store and buy me things—things I could try on. . . ."

I was puzzled. "Try on?" I repeated.

"Yeah," he said. "Try on." He laughed, and the ruminative mood was gone. "You know," he said, now looking at me, "I never tried on a goddamned thing in my life. I never had a chance to pick out something and see if it fit. Ain't that funny?"

"I don't think it's funny," I commented.

"No, I guess it ain't," he said; then, philosophically, "Kids should have a chance to try on things. If they don't get to do it, somehow it never feels like it belongs to them. I never felt like a goddamned thing was mine, nothing belonged to me. It always felt like I was borrowing it. She'd bring stuff to the Home—shoes, pants, shirts, all sorts of crap— and I'd take it. When she left I'd put it on. If it fit, O.K.— but it hardly ever fit so I'd have to get somebody to fix it or just wear it like it was. Sometimes I'd trade it with a guy for something else, something that fit better." He paused. "That feeling," he said after a moment's silence, "that feeling that nothing's yours . . . it's lousy. This is the first time I thought about it. Is it important, Doc?"

"I guess so," I said. "Tell me more about it."

"Well," he continued, "it's hard to say what I mean. If what you got—I mean—if you feel nothing belongs to you, then maybe you don't know who you are. . . . I mean, it's always someone else, like wearing a costume in a play. Especially if it's like it was with me. You see, I never had nothing that could—tell me who I was. Even my bed wasn't mine. I was just a name. —Don't you see what I mean?"

"I think so," I said. "But knowing who you are doesn't come from *things*, Charles. It comes from inside yourself."

"But how's it going to get inside?" he asked.

"It emerges," I said. "A person gets his sense of self in his relations with others. When he's small and helpless they

37

take care of him. First he feels he's part of them, then. . . ."

"I know," Charles interrupted. "I heard the talks you doctors give the attendants. (He was referring to the mental-hygiene lectures by which the psychiatric staff indoctrinated inmate personnel.) But with me it was different. I couldn't find out about myself from inside because she got rid of me too fast. So I had to have things to—to tell me—who I was, and," he concluded bitterly, "I didn't even have that."

I was amazed, I confess, at the psychological acumen this naïve boy disclosed that day. Of course, he was right! Unknowingly, he had hit upon an important psychodynamic not only in his but in other cases; a basic cause for delinquency and mental disorder. He was, to put it more clearly, tracing and defining the sense of "alienation" so prevalent in our society, and, obliquely, pin-pointing a reason for the gross materialism all observers speak of as the curse of modern times. Rejected either actually (as he had been) or by parental attitudes of neglect, self-preoccupation, fear or anxiety; or, on the other hand, apprehensively clutched too closely by emotionally starved parents, the infantile ego never achieves independent identity or that emergent sense-of-self necessary for individual and social maturity. It then is forced to seek selfhood from without, from "things" that serve as referents. And this is a tragic affair, both for the person and the world. As it applied to Charles, the tragedy was compounded by the lack in his life even of "things" by which he could come to know himself. So he became, for all intents, ego-less, an individual without a separate identity, hence a creature—not a person. His role, that is to say, was never a stable one; it shifted from moment to moment as instinctual pressures (and societal demands), lacking the mediation normally provided by a balancing "I," fought for dominance in action. No wonder, then, that he was psychotic; for, beyond all technical subtleties, psychosis is that state wherein the ego has disappeared, wherein identity is lost (as illustrated so well by the not-so-funny prevalence of Napoleons and Christs in our mental institutions). The key to Charles's therapy, therefore, must be to provide him with an ego: otherwise he was doomed to remain a robot whose sanity could only be imposed on him by authoritarian controls, by rigorous external checking devices that we know to be undependable.

Charles had given me—as all patients, I have since learned, do—the clue to his treatment and the first major insight I had obtained thus far into the unconscious dynamics of his disorder. Many others, I knew, remained to be isolated. In a certain sense the session I have described was a diversion—a productive one, to be sure—and I was eager to return to the material we had begun to develop, the material having to do with his ambivalent attitude toward his mother. It was not until a few days later, however, that the play technique I employed gave me the opportunity I was seeking to develop this theme further.

My patient, I recall, was building a boat model and talking about an excursion some Ladies' Auxiliary had arranged for the children of the Home. He was lampooning these matrons with a good deal of humor, but also with a certain malice. In the midst of his tale, while reaching for a pot of glue he was keeping fluid over a Bunsen burner, he upset the pot and the sticky contents spread over my desk. Apologizing, he quickly mopped up the mess and returned to his task and the tale he was relating. He had hardly begun to talk again when I noticed he had neglected to clean a small area of the stuff, and I called this to his attention. Annoyed, he put down the tools, rubbed at the spot I

39

indicated, and flung the rags at me with an exclamation of disgust. "Christ Almighty," he swore. "You make me sick— just like my mother!"

Now I cannot tell the reader why I took his word "sick" in a literal sense, why I did not choose to understand it idiomatically as a common expression of irritation. The only instrument with which the analyst works is his own unconscious. Through this, he comprehends the unconscious of his patient. Call it intuition, if you like, or telepathy, or anything you wish: the fact remains that the analyst, when he is functioning correctly and well, is somehow attuned to his patient's unconscious and, with his own, "understands" what is going on in the other person. In this instance I suppose I could trace the "reasons" why I knew immediately that the word "sick" was to be taken literally and not figuratively, but these reasons are afterthoughts, and I was not aware of them at the time. Charles had been talking about the excursion, which was the first and only time in his life he had been aboard a boat. He mentioned something about seasickness. Then he caricatured the matrons of the Ladies' Auxiliary. He spoke contemptuously of their "female" smell, their big bosoms, their officious, bustling manner. A moment later he had upset the gluepot. Perhaps these minor elements of his talk, condensed into significant action when he threw the rag, now led me to inquire, "Did your mother *really* make you sick?"

Charles hesitated. "Come to think of it," he said, "I was always a little sick when I saw her."

"Sick how?"

"In my stomach . . . like I was going to throw up."

"What do you think made you feel that way?"

He shrugged. "I don't know," he said. "Maybe it was

40

excitement, or something like that. Or maybe it was the way she smelled."

Again I experienced that curious leap of the unconscious that Reik calls "surprise"; that shocklike response within the analyst that indicates perfect attunement. Seasickness, female smells, glue-pot, the rag—each assumed its place in a pattern, making it possible for me to conjecture the story Charles now began to tell—not, however, in its details, but in its psychological outlines and overtones.

"Always," he began . . .

Always when he thought of his mother Charles would feel a little sick; not actually sick—perhaps nauseous was the better word. It was as if something deep within him, something indescribable but real, was slowly turning. He would have this feeling about other women, too, when he thought of them. It was as if rather than merely thinking of them, or looking at them, or even being near them, he had swallowed a live thing that squirmed and twisted in his organs. By now it was an old feeling, something to be expected in the presence of women; but each time it appeared he would regard it with mingled disgust and bewilderment. At the very edge of his mind—he said, "on the tip of my tongue"—he could identify it as a familiar sensation, but it remained elusively nameless.

The first time Charles had felt it was on his ninth birthday. (Here the reader will remember that when we began to study his relationship with his mother, Charles reverted to his ninth year in the drawing of the Home he lived in at that time.) The boys were playing in the yard when one of the Sisters called to him that his mother had come. A few minutes later he stood before her, his face flushed and his cheeks feeling as if branded with the imprint of her

41

gloved hands where she held them while she kissed his lips, his senses overwhelmed by her sweet perfume and the thick softness of the fur coat she wore. As she was telling him she had come to take him home for Christmas, he first felt the small, sick squirming inside, and he thought for a moment that he was going to vomit. Because of it, he could not trust himself to speak until they were in the taxi and the thing within him had subsided.

Although Charles knew there had been other Christmas holidays at home with her—she made a practice of alternating holiday visits with the two boys so that both were never with her at the same time—the one near his ninth birthday was the first he was able to recall fully. It had many landmarks.

The apartment his mother lived in then was the same she had occupied in those distant days. Little had been changed in the intervening years, so that now, when Charles reconstructed these repressed events in therapy, he was able to move memorially among familiar landmarks. There was the living room with bright curtains and gas logs in the fireplace, the carpeted hall with the kitchen gleaming whitely off to one side, and then—then his mother's bedroom with its odors and softnesses, the drawers of the bureau full of feminine secrets he feared somehow even to guess at, the mysterious vials and bottles on the mirrored dressing table always flecked with pink flakes of powder, the trunk under the window covered with a shawl and colored cushions, and in the middle of the room the bed with the cold satin spread over which he loved to run the tips of his fingers.

When his mother had gone off to work for the day and Charles had washed and dried the breakfast dishes, he would often tiptoe down the hallway and stand at the door of her bedroom. For some unknown reason he always expected to find someone there in the room. Always surprised to find it empty, and never quite believing his actions went unobserved, he would look beneath the furniture, turn back the spread and peer under the bed, open the door to the bathroom and search behind the shower curtain. Assured then that he was, indeed, alone, he would finally throw himself on the bed. Lying there, his face pressed in the cleft between the pillows, the "sickness" would begin. What twisted inside him seemed to grow, and with its growing turn more and more rapidly until he became dizzy and faint. Then, abruptly, it would cease; and in a moment his self seemed to dissolve. Now he would feel as if floating in an odorous cloud, exhausted but exhilarated while the noise of his own rapid breathing and the rush of his blood quieted. Soon he would arise and carefully smooth the satin spread.

There was another reason for remembering this holiday near his ninth birthday. On New Year's Eve of that year his mother had given a party. She had told him her friends would arrive late and that he would have to sleep in her bed that night instead of on the couch in the living room. After his bath he lay between the sheets and watched her as she dressed, sharing her obvious excitement. But when she left him, he could not sleep. The curious sickness, preceded by the thought that sometime during the night she would return and share the bed, filled Charles with panic and sent him from the bed to the trunk. Seated on the cushions and hugging himself against the cold, he fought sleep by listening to the merry sounds from the next room and staring fixedly at the line of brightness beneath the door. After an hour or more, chill and drowsiness overcame his turmoil, and he stumbled to the bed as if in a trance.

43

Toward morning, in the midst of a warm and dreamless sleep, Charles felt himself lifted by strong arms. Sleepily, he opened his eyes and saw a face he would never forget but never quite remember. There was a voice, too, and some laughter as if from a distance. In the morning, however, there was only the dimmest memory, lost beyond recovery but teasingly persistent, as he surveyed a litter of empty glasses and stub-filled ash trays from the couch in the living room. He knew without knowing that the door behind him—the door to his mother's bedroom—was locked.

Everything changed for Charles after that visit. When he returned to the Home it was as if a new and ungovernable force inhabited his body. A demon, the Sisters said, possessed him. There was no rule he did not break with wild and scornful disregard of consequences. He even seemed to relish the punishments and penances that became his daily lot. Defiantly he bent to the birch, and there was no one—not even the Sisters—who remained longer on his knees on the floor. Once he fainted in the Chapel; when they undressed him a shower of stones and broken glass fell from his knickers and the cloth had to be torn from his bloody legs. It was at this time, too, that with charcoal and a pin he painfully tattooed the words TRUE LOVE on his fingers—a letter to each finger just below the knuckle.

More and more, as the days went by, we probed even deeper into the twisted structure of Charles's relationship with himself and the world, unraveling the strands of his incestuous preoccupations and identifying the significance of this as a dynamic force in his life. As before an inexorable tide his repression gave way, and the memories he had exhausted himself denying rose to the surface of consciousness. Sometimes our meetings were stormy, and occasionally I got a glimpse of the violence that was in this boy. For me, it was like looking into a deep pit where wild and hungry animals howled for release. But for the most part the kind of therapy we were using seemed to drain his aggression, or at least to divert it. For during all these long months—and particularly at this time—Charles was tractable and mild in his institutional life. With the ward patients he showed great consideration, even tenderness. Somewhat isolated from companionship because of his youth, he nevertheless found a few acquaintances with whom he spent his hours off duty. But in our sessions he vented his accumulated hatred both on the objects he manipulated and on me. My office became a shambles as jars were overturned, paint spilled, dolls broken, fires were lit, and toys destroyed by "accident." As for me, on my head fell torrents of abuse.

The therapist's role, wrote Dr. Suttie, "is not the technical one of doctor nor even the godlike one of perfect parent. It is much more that of sacrificial victim upon whom all hates, anxieties and distrust are worked out, so that he is the mediator, the catalyte—whereby the separated psyche is reintegrated in its society." So all the privations Charles had known were now laid upon me, and into our daily meetings there flowed a continual torrent of complaint, blame and indictment fed by streams from the past. Not only to release his aggressivity, but also to test my patience and—yes—my love, Charles destroyed almost every object I brought into our work. If I showed the slightest trace of annoyance or impatience, he was quick to seize on it, to castigate me for it, to accuse me of unfairness, lack of understanding, and a dozen other "crimes" of feeling against him. Progressively, as I almost continuously exercised tolerance, acceptance, forgiveness and understanding, his testing of these qualities became more severe. One after another he arranged small trials for me—and always from the corner of his eye he watched intently, ready to pounce should I somehow by word or gesture show the vaguest and most fleeting change from an attitude of utter acquiescence in all that concerned him.

Thus tension mounted between Charles and myself until a session when the last barrier to his deepest and most intimate secret fell. As is usual in such things, an extraneous incident held the key to the unconscious.

In the prison hospital during the last war the Officer of the Day was charged with many duties. After the routine business of the evening was completed, he usually retired to O.D. quarters on the top "deck" of the hospital to read or write letters until bedtime. Since he was on call during the night, almost his last act before retirement was to remove the drug box from the pharmacy, dispense therefrom the necessary hypnotics, sedatives and medications to appropriate nurses' stations on each "deck" as he made his final rounds, and check the drug records against the contents of the box when he reached his quarters. Thereafter, and until he was relieved on the following day, the box—a formidable metal container—never left his sight; its precious contents were in great demand, of course, and the care of the box was one responsibility that weighed heavily on all of us.

At about ten o'clock of a night when I was O.D. I removed the drug chest from the refrigerator in the pharmacy and started on my rounds. On the way to Ward A, I passed a group of inmates standing by the Hospital Admissions Desk. They were engaged in that weary, never-ending small talk confined men substitute for the social life withheld from them—chatter and gossip interlarded with sex. In the group was Charles, who eyed me in a friendly-curious way as I said good night to the men and walked on. Halfway to the door of the Ward, I heard footsteps behind me. I turned and waited for Charles.

"Something wrong?" I asked.

He smiled slowly. "No," he answered.

"Want to make rounds with me?" I asked.

He nodded assent and fell in with me. After another moment he put out his hands.

"I'll carry the box for you," he said.

The rule that the chest was never to be entrusted to an inmate flashed through my head and I was about to refuse; but almost at the same time I reflected that Charles was very likely trying to make amends for some of the things he had said in our session that day, and that to deny his offer of this small service would be misinterpreted by the boy as counter-aggression.

"Thanks," I said, and handed him the box.

At Ward A, I made rounds, signed charts, and prepared to dispense the required drugs to the night nurse in the usual manner. At my request, Charles set the chest on the table before me. He observed the procedure very intently as I unlocked the box with a key from the O.D. ring. While I rummaged in it and made the necessary dispersals, I became aware of a growing tension in him; soon I could actually feel his excitement as he leaned over my shoulder. When I closed the box the sharp, hissing sound of his breathing caught my attention, and I looked up at him inquiringly. Catching my gaze, he smiled disarmingly. When I stood up he lifted the box from the table and held it closely to him. Together we left the ward and started for the next floor.

On Ward B the same performance was repeated. Charles watched fascinatedly while I went through the routine. He never took his eyes from the box, and when I locked the chest he grabbed for it convulsively, possessively.

The patients on Ward C were a special lot, confined there voluntarily for purposes of a medical experiment. They required no attention from the O.D., whose only duty respecting them was the checking of fever charts. Accordingly, I signed the graphs the nurse set out for my inspection and rose to go. Charles, who had been standing by silently, one hand on the box where he had set it down, inquired as I stood up, "Don't you want the box?"

"No," I explained. "These boys don't need anything."

"Aren't you even going to open it?" he asked.

"What for?"

"Well"—he hesitated somewhat lamely—"I thought you might want something from it."

It was only then that I looked at him more closely. His eyes were bright, his face drawn, and his whole body trembling.

"Is there something wrong with you, Charles?" I asked.

He shook his head. "No," he said.

"Maybe you ought to hit the sack," I suggested. "You look tired."

"I'm all right," Charles said.

I reached out for the drug box. "You'd better turn in," I said. "I'll finish this myself."

Charles literally wrenched the box from under my hand. "No . . . please," he begged. "Let me go with you."

D Ward was the last and longest stop in the O.D. routine. Here the surgical patients were kept, and both the chart work and the drug dispensations took considerable time. After making a check on the patients—bed by bed and room by room—I sat at the desk in the Nurses' Station under a gooseneck lamp carefully shielded with strips of green blotting paper. It was by now well after ten o'clock and quiet as only a hospital in a prison can be. The silence was heavy, eerily broken only by an occasional cough or the moan of someone in pain, while in the background, as a menacing undertone, there rose and fell the breathing of two thousand confined men. In the circle of light cast by the lamp, the three of us—the white-clad male nurse, Charles in his prison denims, and I in my uniform—made a weird, Kafkaesque tableau. The nurse and I talked in muted tones as I worked over the papers before me. Charles stood by, staring fixedly at the open box from which bright gleams were reflected to his face by the vials, capsules, and boxes of varicolored pills.

Engrossed in my work, I at first paid little attention to the inching movement of Charles's right hand as it crept forward like some live thing toward the open box. It was only when the fingers had crawled up the sides and the whole hand had disappeared into the chest that the movement registered in my mind.

"Charles!"

He seemed not to hear my sharp call. His hand remained in the box on which his whole attention was fixed. The lines of his face and body were rigid.

I grabbed his wrist. The skin was clammy with a cold, oily sweat. His hand jerked spasmodically as I pulled it from the box;—and then I could feel his whole frame relax as if some spell had been broken by my touch.

"What the hell are you doing?" I asked.

"Nothing," he said. "I was just trying to see what's in the box."

I was puzzled and angry. "You know what's in the box," I said, "and you know you're not supposed to fool with it."

"I'm sorry," he said. "I . . . I guess I forgot."

49

Still angry, I slammed the lid of the box, locked it, gathered my belongings (including the chest) and walked off toward the staircase leading from Ward D to O.D. quarters. By the time I began to climb to the "top deck" and my room, my anger had given way to curiosity about what had happened. So engrossed was I in my thoughts that I failed to hear Charles's footsteps behind me until I stood on the last landing, fumbling to find the key for the grille at the head of the stairs. Just as I opened the gate Charles called my name and I turned to find him standing directly behind me. Now, however, I faced him not with anger or curiosity but with fear. It came to me suddenly that we were completely alone in a part of the hospital forbidden to all save members of the medical staff. Behind and below us was a long staircase, ahead was the unlighted corridor terminating in the O.D. suite. Ordinarily this situation would not have inspired fear; but Charles was, after all, a dangerous potential psychotic, his behavior of the past hour most unusual, and my relations with him, for the time being at least, highly equivocal. More than this, his aspect would have been enough to arouse apprehension under the most ordinary of circumstances. Sweat beaded his whole face, his breathing was rapid and shallow, his lips dry, his skin drawn in taut lines suggesting an extreme of tension. Looking at him, my insides tightened, but I faced him with what I thought was a disarmingly casual manner. Now I know that to one less excited than Charles was at that moment, my fright would have been plain.

"What do you want?" I asked.

His tongue flicked out over parched lips. Staring at the chest I was carrying, he put out his hand. In a shrill and tremulous voice, he said, "The box. Gimme the box."

"Why?" I asked.

"I want to see what's in it."

"But you know what's in it," I said. "It's just drugs for sick people."

"I want it," he said, and moved toward me.

I backed away, holding the box behind me by the handle on its cover.

"You can't have it," I said. "You know I'm not allowed to give it to you."

"But I gotta have it," he said.

Senselessly, I asked again, "Why?"

"To see what's inside."

"You've already seen."

"Not all of it . . . not down at the bottom. Please!"

Because the last word was uttered in a tone halfway between the pitiful urgency of a plea and a command, I was reassured of my safety for the moment. My own mind, released from the fear that had seized me at the sight and sound of this obviously distraught boy, was now able to cast about for a way out of this awkward situation. I moved toward him and put my free hand on his shoulder. The trembling of his body seemed to quiet under my hand where it rested on his damp shirt.

"Charles," I said softly, "why don't you turn in? You're not feeling well and it's late. We'll talk about the box tomorrow."

For the first time he raised his eyes and looked into mine.

"You don't understand, Doc," he said. "I just *gotta* see what's in that box."

"What do you think is in it?" I asked.

"That's why," he said pleadingly. "I don't know. Something . . . I don't know what."

"If I show you what's in the box will you go to your quarters?"

51

Eagerly, he responded, "Will you let me see everything?"
"Sure," I said. "Come on. We'll go where it's light."

With this I started back down the stairs toward Ward D, moving quickly, acutely aware of Charles behind me. At the desk in the Nurses' Station, within the circle of light from the shaded lamp, I opened the box and removed everything it contained—tubes, vials, boxes, syringes, needles, capsules, clamps, pills, bottles. Then, conscious of the male nurse's silent astonishment, I handed the box to Charles. He took it, glanced briefly into the now empty chest, then at the array on the desk, finally at me. Slowly, and with relief, he set the box down. "Thanks," he breathed, and walked swiftly away.

The sleep I managed to get that night was troubled. Charles's behavior had disturbed and puzzled me. The questions I asked myself could not be answered, and each led to a dozen more. What had all this been about? What did Charles expect to find in the box? What caused his excitement? Had I done the right thing in allowing him to see into the box? In letting him go? Should I have notified the guard on duty where Charles quartered that he was acting strangely? Should I have checked him into the hospital again? Was he really psychotic again? What did this mean? What? . . . What? . . . What? —The more I thought, the more the questions multiplied. Tiredly, I resigned myself to waiting for the day to bring its answers.

Charles reported promptly for his session with me the following morning. Before he arrived I had set the scene for this interview by clearing everything from my desk, putting away and locking in the cabinet all the materials we had been using in his therapy, and removing from the walls where they had been stuck with Scotch tape the drawings and sketches he had made in the past weeks. I had also obtained permission to empty the drug box of its usual contents; and now it and the key to its lock rested on the desk, directly under a bright lamp.

When Charles appeared he was clear-eyed and calm. He smiled a greeting and went directly to his chair by the desk. Once seated, he took up the key and toyed with it for a long minute. Then he glanced at me questioningly. I nodded assent. Without a word, he opened the box. One by one, smiling, he removed the things I had placed inside instead of the drugs and medicines—a miniature pistol, a knife, a small doll, some coins—anything I could think of that might touch off an associative train.

His amusement was patent as he said, "No; it's none of these."

"Then what is it?" I asked.

He remained silent so long this time that I began to doubt my ability to contain the curiosity that had been piling up within me since the previous night. Finally, he said, "It's awful funny. Last night I could have sworn it was in the box."

"Sworn *what* was in the box?" I asked in what must have been a desperately eager voice loaded with exasperation.

"The ring," he answered.

"What ring?"

"My mother's wedding ring."

. . . On a visit to his mother shortly after he had turned thirteen, Charles discovered the trunk and the ring. The details of this discovery and its consequences were severely repressed since his crime and would possibly have been lost to us in the analysis had not the incident with the drug box occurred. Now, however, he was able to tell me about it and to examine its dynamic significance.

Without effort he recalled the morning after his return

53

home for the birthday visit when, his mother gone and his small morning tasks completed, he became bored with his comic book and decided on a walk. When he opened the door of the hall closet to get his coat, the mirror inside reflected the cushion-piled trunk in the bedroom. Suddenly it seemed mysterious and full of secrets, and it crossed his mind that he had always wanted to investigate its contents. Letting his coat fall to the floor, he went over to the trunk and knelt before it. Impatiently, but with a feeling that he was about to violate some secret agreement he had made with himself, he swept away the cushions and undid the brass hinges. He fumbled with the lock but it refused to open. Rising, he went to the kitchen and took a hammer and a knife from a drawer. As he did, he noticed how his hands were trembling and he felt again that curious turning of his insides.

Kneeling before the trunk, Charles hammered and pried at the bolt until the hinge finally fell back. With both hands he raised the creaking lid. A wave of scent compounded of fading perfumes, camphor, and old things laid away rose to his nostrils, and a moment of dizziness forced him to close his eyes. When he opened them, he saw that the inside of the trunk was divided into two layers. The top layer was made of boxes, each with its own lid and the whole covered with blue cloth on which small bunches of red and white flowers had been printed. One after the other he raised the lids of the boxes. Inside of one there were papers and envelopes, a packet of letters held by a thick but withered rubber band, and some faded pictures of people Charles never knew. Another drawer, larger than the rest, contained folded linens and lengths of gauzy stuff. In a third there was a metal box. Intrigued by a jingling sound as he lifted it, Charles set this on the floor beside him. A hasty rummaging through the bottom layer of the trunk revealed only clothing, blankets and shoes.

Charles now turned his attention to the metal box. There was no visible catch and his impatience rose as he pressed and poked all over the surface. He had almost decided to assault the box with his tools when he noticed a place along the bottom where the corners were unjoined. Cautiously, he removed the panel, disclosing the true bottom of the box. In a depression he found the key to the lock. Hastily he inserted the key and opened the box. Inside was a sheaf of bills and a pile of coins, and among them glistened a few jeweled pins, a string of pearls, a brooch of heavy gold, and a wedding ring studded with small diamonds. Hurriedly, feeling as if watched, Charles took a ten-dollar bill and put it in his pocket. Then he closed and locked the box. Replacing it carefully, he pulled down the lid of the trunk and rearranged the cushions. He spent that afternoon at the movies.

Each day until he returned to the Protectorate, Charles probed further into the secrets of the trunk. He studied the photographs until he knew them by heart, assigning names to the faces and inventing biographies for each. The contents of the letters, which he read with difficulty, puzzled him; they were hard to understand and the names in them without meaning for him. But, finally, from them he learned a shocking truth: his father was not dead—as his mother had told Charles and his brother; instead, the unremembered man had gone away, had remarried, and now, in another city, lived with a family by his second marriage. Slowly Charles pieced together the story. The marriage of his mother to this forgotten man had been unhappy from the start. Because of religious differences a divorce had been easy to obtain. His mother had then, apparently, followed the advice Charles read in one of the letters: "You should live as if he is dead because he's really dead as far as you and the children are concerned. . . ."

Always before closing the trunk for the day, Charles returned to the metal box, which he saved for last in the ritual of his investigations. Somehow it seemed to him to represent the living heart of this room. Never could he even touch it without sensing his quickening pulses and the uneasy beginnings of that familiar sick feeling. It was even worse with the wedding ring. When he first held it in his hand it seemed to burn his flesh, while beneath him it was as if the floor moved, and in his ears there was the sound of waves breaking. On the last day of his visit he carried it in his pockets, secure in a sweating hand, until it was time to call for his mother so that she could take him back to the Protectorate. Replacing it, he took in its stead another ten-dollar bill.

Between his thirteenth birthday and the summer of that year, Charles's mother was called to the orphanage and told he would have to go elsewhere. He could no longer, they said, be managed, and it was feared that his presence was harmful to "the moral and spiritual welfare" of the other boys. Perhaps he would do better, they said, on a farm. It would take a few days to make the necessary arrangements; meanwhile his mother must take him, for the Protectorate had reached the limits of its patience.

The taxi stopped to let Charles and his suitcase off at his mother's place. She had to return to her job and would be home later.

The trunk was waiting for him. Hastily, Charles began to live the dream that had nourished intervening nights and days. Without pausing to notice that the metal box no longer contained money, he reached for the wedding band.

56

Holding it, he rose, walked over to the dressing table, and laid it carefully on the mirrored top. Then he undressed. Nervously, he tore at the buttons of his shirt, at the snaps of his underclothes, at the laces of his shoes. Now he stood naked. The thing within him turned swiftly and in his head a thick liquid boiled. He took the ring in his hands. Into it, one after another, he thrust each finger. Then he put the ring in his mouth, sliding his tongue into its circle. At last he held it against his quivering, awakened sex . . .

During the almost two years Charles spent on the farm his thoughts turned often to the ring and the trunk. The image of the gold circlet haunted work-ridden days and the nights when heavy reverie preceded sleep. It invaded his dreams: it was the visual obbligato to all he did: it was the beckoning vision that day when he wandered, like a sleepwalker, across the meadow to the road and quit the farm forever. His first act on the morning after his arrival at home was to repeat the experience his memory had stored, the experience that by now had become nuclear in his life; and each day, at least once and often many times, he repeated the ceremony until it was fixed as a ritual.

How potent the secret rite of the ring became for Charles he did not know until the day when he put into action a plan devised during the aimless hours of his first week at home from the farm. For the seven or so days after his home-coming he prepared for this adventure by stealing small sums from his mother's purse. When he had accumulated about five dollars, he left the house shortly after noon one day and made for a section of the city known as "The Block." Here, on both sides of the street, for a quarter of a mile, the gin mills and honky-tonks even at this early hour literally shook with activity. Neon signs competed for attention, and in the dark, cool recesses of shabby bars the human debris of a great city gathered to prepare its illusions against the inevitable night.

Into one of these bars, the name and location of which he recalled from a boast an older boy had made, Charles strode. Assuming a confidence he did not feel despite his careful selection of clothing to make himself look older than his fifteen years, he seated himself at a bar and ordered a beer. The bartender glanced at him only casually—either the fact of Charles's youth did not register with the man or the place was not particularly concerned with the law—and served the request. That he was not ordered out because of his age heartened Charles and, after sipping his beer, he turned on his stool to survey the premises. In a booth toward the rear he saw a lone woman. She was hatless, and over her shoulders draped a short coat of fur. Her fingers toyed with an empty shot glass on which her eyes seemed to be fixed hypnotically. Charles stared at her until her head came up and she returned his gaze. Soon she smiled and beckoned him with a finger. Inwardly quaking, but carefully controlled, Charles carried his glass to where she sat.

"Sit down, Sonny," she said.

Charles sat.

"Buy me a drink," she commanded.

Charles waved at a waitress, gulped his beer, and pushed the two glasses to the edge of the table.

While they waited for their drinks Charles and the woman regarded each other closely.

After a moment, "Relax," she said. "There's nothing to be nervous about."

"I'm not nervous," Charles said, surreptitiously wiping his sweating palms on his trousers.

"How much money you got?" the woman asked.

58

"About five dollars," he answered.

"Count it," she ordered.

Charles put his money on the table. There were five crumpled bills and then some change. The woman took the bills and put them in her purse while the waitress set their drinks before them and counted the price from the silver on the table.

"Cheerio," the woman said, and drained the whisky from her glass. Then, "Come on," she said.

Charles followed her out into the street. Without once turning around to see if he was behind her, she walked swiftly the two blocks to a rooming house on an alley paralleling "The Block." She climbed two flights of stairs, turned down a dim hallway, and opened a door. Only then did she stop and wait for him.

Inside the room the woman threw her coat on a chair, kicked off her shoes, lit a cigarette, and sat on the edge of an unmade bed. Her eyes moved over the boy's slim figure as he stood diffidently by the only chair in the room. When, after some minutes of silence, she understood that he would very likely remain mute and transfixed unless she took the lead, she smiled.

"This is your first time, ain't it, Sonny?" she said.

Charles nodded.

"Well," she said. "It's a good thing you got me and not just any old bag. Come here."

Charles went over to the bed, slowly, nervously, and stood by her, his hands hanging limply at his sides. As he did so, she stood up and, with a quick movement, pulled her dress over her head. Underneath it, she was completely naked.

It was the first time Charles had seen a naked woman.

59

Slowly his eyes roved over her form while his pulses pounded and the pores of his skin opened, flooding his body with sweat.

"Touch me," she said—but he stood immobilized. "Come on," she said, taking his wet hands and guiding them over her breasts. "Like that. . . . Go on. . . . Don't be afraid." Then, abruptly, she fell back on the bed. "Now take your clothes off," she said.

Hastily the boy undressed. Nude, trembling, and sick, he let himself down beside her. Her eyes swept over him professionally while she clucked her tongue in amusement at his helpless distress. "You're really going to make me work for my dough, aren't you, Sonny?" she said as her hands reached toward him.

After a quarter of an hour the woman sighed and sat up. "To hell with it," she said. "You're too scared." She lit a cigarette and reached for her dress where she had thrown it over the bed. "You come back another time. . . ."

"Wait," Charles cried. "Please. . . . Not yet. . . ." He sprang from the bed and searched through his clothing. Finally he found what he was looking for. With one hand he swept the dress out of her grasp, while with the other he pushed her back on the bed.

"Put this on," he said, his voice desperate with need as he pressed the ring into her hand.

"Sure," she said, "but why . . . ?"

"Please . . ." he begged.

The woman, puzzled, slid the ring over a finger and held it up to where light from the window was caught by the small gems. She looked at it briefly, then her eyes turned on Charles.

"Well, I'll be goddamned!" she said. . . .

With the recovery of the entire story of the ring, the last barriers of repression were removed. It became possible now to reconstruct the terrible crime Charles had committed, to understand its inexorable unconscious logic, and to comprehend its hidden motivation. From the point of view of Charles's therapy we were at last in possession of all the "facts" in his history and had explored his personality to its deepest levels.

This orphaned, rejected, deprived boy represented a clear instance of utter personal distortion consequent upon denial to a child of all it requires for psychological growth. The total frustration of his deepest affectional needs produced an emotionally starved individual. Those dreadful events of life in homes and orphanages, acting upon the original twist given his personality, compounded the basic deformation of character; and upon this rotten foundation had been added layer after layer of further distortion—until he became, at adolescence, a veritable monster who could obtain satisfaction for his instincts and needs only through violence, perversion and destruction.

So far as the crime itself was concerned, it was obvious that the intended (psychologically, the real) victim of murder was not the unhappy girl Charles killed. She was but the substitute, the unfortunate innocent bystander in a drama of incest and matricide whose origins were removed almost two decades from the time the last scene was played.

If we needed further evidence that in killing and raping the girl Charles was symbolically destroying and possessing his mother, such evidence is supplied by the events immediately preceding the crime. On that morning Charles had awakened late. He felt, he said, "kind of fuzzy and heavy." Three days before this he had lost his Western

61

Union job and by now he was broke. Before going to sleep the previous night he had tried to devise a plan to obtain money for a visit to a prostitute. But each scheme involved pawning the precious ring. This, in the light of previous experience, was not a good solution. Without the ring he would very likely be impotent. But what other source of funds was there? The dilemma tormented him until he fell into a restless, dream-tormented sleep.

On arising that fateful forenoon Charles tried to open the trunk almost before he was fully awake. For some unaccountable reason the lock had jammed. He tore at it until his fingers were sore. Dressing hastily, he went to the basement to borrow a hammer and an ice-pick from the janitor. These he placed on the refrigerator in the kitchen, thinking to use them after completing his toilet and breakfast. The doorbell rang when he emerged from the bathroom. From this moment on it was as if a dark, swirling cloud enveloped his senses, a cloud pierced by a voice that commanded him to Kill! Kill! Kill!

I was never able to identify the voice that urged Charles to murder, although I made its personal acquaintance soon after the incident of the drug box. . . .

The time was half past twelve noon of a bright September day. Together with other members of the medical staff I was lunching in the Officers' Mess when an urgent call from the hospital interrupted my meal. The attendant on the desk told me that Charles had just reported in, asking my whereabouts, and demanding to see me immediately. The boy looked, so the attendant said, "like something was terribly wrong, so I sent him up to your office and told him to wait for you."

On the way over to the hospital I speculated on what could be wrong with my patient. I had seen him earlier that day and recalled nothing unusual about our session. As a matter of fact, we had been working through some rather innocuous material, and all I had registered about it was a certain amount of disappointment that our recent meetings had been relatively unproductive. Since the dramatic and important disclosures of the previous weeks, Charles had been somewhat apathetic about things. I was inclined to interpret this dull interval as due to a natural, even expected, lull. A period of quiescence and recovery necessarily follows each high point in therapy. This permits the personality to assimilate its new insights and to reorient itself accordingly, and I felt that Charles was now in such an interim phase. Indeed (I thought as I hurried to the hospital), I had even exploited this period to strengthen the transference bonds between the boy and myself. Because I knew that the hurt of his past had to be undone, that he needed to feel wanted, appreciated, even loved before he could recover a sense of identity basic to the remaking of his personality, I had been more than usually permissive with him. I had increased the responsibilities of his job, allowed him free access to the cabinet where the materials of his treatment were kept, and generally relaxed the entire atmosphere in which he lived and worked. What had arisen to disturb his calm, I could not imagine.

As I passed the desk at the entrance to the hospital I noticed that the attendant there had left his post. The custodial officer, the only man on duty in the entire building at this hour, was dozing comfortably in a corner, his legs propped up on a table and his mouth wide open. As I ascended the stairs to my office on the second floor I remember thinking fleetingly about the quiet of the hospital, sunk as it was in a postprandial lethargy that would last for at least another half hour. There was no sound except the remote clatter of a typewriter and the distant murmur of voices from the horde of men at their noonday meal in the gigantic mess hall in the main building.

At the door to my office I paused and looked in. There, sitting on the edge of the cot, was Charles. I will never forget the spectacle he presented. His hands were gripping the black leather mattress as if holding on for dear life. His eyes were closed tightly while tears streamed from between his lids. His mouth was set over clenched teeth through which incomprehensible noises and moans issued. His face was twisted with agony and flushed a beet-red. His denim shirt was stained with sweat in great dark patches. His legs and feet were twitching, and his whole body seemed to be trembling.

I went over to him and stood in the small space between the cot and my desk. Softly, I called his name. There was no response. He seemed to be struggling with himself, to be fighting some internal battle. I bent closer to hear, if I could, the sounds he was making: between animal-like moans and huge sobs I made out the words, "No! No!" and "Don't! Don't!"

I listened for a moment, then put my hand on his shoulder. "Charles," I called, "Charles—what's wrong?" There was no answer, no sign that he even heard me. I came closer, bending down until my face was level with his.

I tried again: "Charles . . . Charles."

Suddenly the telephone on my desk rang. As if electrified by the sound, Charles's eyes opened and his body stiffened. Then, with a leap that sent me sprawling back across the desk, he was on me. I felt his hands go around my throat, and saw as if in a crazy nightmare his blazing eyes and his red, open mouth—and in my ears I heard his chilling shrieks,

"Kill!—Kill!—Kill!", drowning out the frantic ringing of the telephone.

The universe whirled as I tried to pull his hands from my throat. White pain stabbed through my lungs and things exploded in my head. Then—I passed out. . . .

I awakened a few minutes later. I was on the floor and someone was holding my head in his lap while he tried to force an aromatic liquid through my swollen lips. The room was full of people—doctors, attendants, guards, patients from the ward. Seated on a chair, two burly inmate nurses guarding him, a sheet twisted around his torso and his arms pinioned behind him, was Charles. He was smiling—apologetically.

It was a week before I could speak in a voice above a whisper. During that time I had many conversations with Charles. I also learned what had happened after I fainted and before I came to. It seems that the attendant at the desk downstairs, when he returned to his post after leaving it on some vague errand, was suddenly reminded that he had sent for me to see Charles. He called the mess hall and learned I had left there. Fearing to be reported for a dereliction of duty, he then called my office. When the phone remained unanswered, sensing something wrong, he awakened the dozing guard and together they rushed upstairs. Charles's shrieks were audible from the hall. Both of them said they could hardly detach his hands from my throat.

As for Charles, he acted as if nothing had happened. When I went to see him in the strip-cell where he was now kept, he talked freely and frankly about the incident. With only the vaguest hint of regret or apology in his voice he related how the "fit" (as he called it) had come over him. Casually, he told how he had been sitting in the mess hall among his fellows when a great, inward agitation seized his body. All noises and movements seemed to slow down, and he felt as if some force were isolating him from the surrounding world. With this feeling came a surge of horror, a kind of interior shriveling of his organs, as in a flash he recognized this complex of sensation to be similar to that he had experienced prior to committing his crime. Almost blinded by the emotions that now engulfed him, he rushed from the dining place, some remnant of the self-preservative instinct urging him to seek me out in hope of stemming the forces that were becoming more tumultuous as the seconds passed. He became more distant while he stumbled toward the hospital, literally feeling the ties that connected him with reality straining to the snapping point. By the time he reached the office and seated himself on the cot he was completely separated from the world, split off from his surroundings and unaware of everything except a voice in his head that crescendoed its hateful command.

Charles was not aware of me until the telephone rang. Momentarily, this broke the spell; but then. . . .

"I think my hand touched your shoulder. It felt like a woman's breast. I got excited. Then the voice took over. All I wanted to do was get my hands around a throat. I couldn't hold it back. . . . That's all I remember."

—I lost Charles as a patient a few weeks after the episode in my office. The authorities insisted on his transfer to a government mental hospital as an extremely dangerous person in need of continuous custodial and psychiatric supervision. I have since heard that Charles has been moved from one place to another in the last twelve years. He is still without a home, still unwanted anywhere, still a stranger everywhere.

I remember his slow smile and the puzzled look in his soft eyes. . . .

come over, red rover

MAC

> " 'A calming influence on the nervous system,' they say, 'can be obtained from travel on the Volga.' "
>
> —Gurevich, M. O., and Sereiskii, M. Ia., *Uchebnik Psikhiatrii*, as quoted by J. Wortis, *Soviet Psychiatry*.

My first encounter with Mac was somewhat dramatic; moreover, it had a public character. We met, not across a desk, but over the heads of an audience at a meeting.

For many years I have been active politically in a small way out of a conviction that the psychoanalyst belongs in the world, among men, and should participate in the life of his community. I have felt that he has a public responsibility which cannot be discharged by living the anchorite existence most analysts live, limiting their purview to the dim caves in which they practice their art like oracular recluses surrounded by the esoteric symbols of a mystic craft. Because of this belief I have, from time to time, joined movements and societies of a progressive cast, and have loaned my name—for whatever its value—to causes I've considered worthy. Sometimes these movements and causes have been called radical, and often I have known, not directly, but in the way such things are known, that their active membership included Communists. But this has not concerned me much, since my position has been that I would work for and lend whatever talents I possess toward the realization of the things in which I believe. If, incidentally, a Communist happens to want what I want, and works for it with ethical means, that does not in any way reflect discredit on the aim or end of the action. I have always regarded throwing out babies with bath water as the height of stupidity.

For example, take segregation. I am unalterably and unconditionally opposed to it in any form, to any extent, and for whatever reason. If the Communists oppose segregation, I will struggle with them against such injustice. I would not tolerate segregation just because it is opposed by Communists. Nor do I care *why* Communists oppose segregation, or what part their opposition to it plays in their grander revolutionary schemes. What matters solely to me is that segregation is an evil. As a psychoanalyst I know what it does both to its victims and their tormentors: as a human being the idea is revolting to me: as a responsible citizen I know that the less there is of segregation the less there will be of Communism. Now I am well aware that Communists use the issue of segregation for their own purposes, and that the sheer immorality and inhumanity of it is the least of their concerns. I know that could their purposes be served better by promoting segregation, they probably would not hesitate to do so. On the individual level a striking example of this kind of hypocrisy was presented to me recently. While this is being written, I am analyzing another Communist. A few days ago, during his hour, he complained that his vacation plans had been disrupted: a Party directive had been issued forbidding members to vacation in places where segregation is practiced, and now my patient would have to change his plans because the resort at which he had made a reservation was restricted to white Gentiles only. He was greatly disturbed and resentful about this. I pointed out to him that until he was ordered to do otherwise, and despite the general position of the Party on the issue, he had personally been willing to support this institution. In his defense he argued that until the Party stated otherwise, he considered himself free to do what he liked. For my part I rejoined that many people would naturally and effortlessly reject the entire idea of segregation, and would never in the first place have considered attending a resort of the kind he had "freely" chosen. I remarked, further, that with him, as with so many like him, it took a Party directive to make him into a decent human being. He did not take kindly to this remark.

All of this is by way of explaining my presence at a public meeting where the audience included a number of Communists, among whom was Mac. And it is not strange that I should illustrate my digression by writing of segregation, for this is the issue on which we clashed at our first meeting. At that time a debate on socialized medicine was being planned by the organization of which I was nominally the chairman, and the topic we were considering related to the choice of members for a panel which would discuss the points raised by the debaters when they had finished their presentations. I remember that, as I was reading aloud a list of the names that had been proposed for this panel, an angry voice from the rear of the room interrupted me. Someone called, "Are there any Negroes on that list?"

I replied that I didn't know, and asked the secretary, who shook his head in negation. As I turned again to face the audience, the same voice cried out, "I demand to know why Negroes have been deliberately excluded from that panel!"

71

I answered that I was sure the exclusion had not been deliberate, the list had been composed from names submitted to the committee, the final selection made on the basis of an individual's qualifications to discuss such an issue and on nothing else. Then, believing this answer would satisfy whomever it was had interrupted, I proceeded with the business at hand. But I had no sooner begun than the voice called out again.

"We're not satisfied with that answer," it shouted. "We demand that the Negro people be represented on that panel!"

The belligerence of the voice and the presumption of the "we" were challenging. I asked the speaker to stand up and identify himself. There was a stir at the rear of the room, and then a tall figure detached itself from the group and rose. It was Mac: six feet and three inches, pock-marked face, crown of sandy hair, sport coat, turtle-neck sweater and G.I. fatigue pants.

"My name has nothing to do with it," he said in a quieter voice in which a small quaver indicated that he was less sure on his feet and alone than seated in a crowd. "The point is that there should be a Negro on that panel."

"The committee will be glad to consider any names you care to submit to it," I said. "If you want to suggest someone qualified to be a member of the panel, no one's going to ask the color of his skin."

Mac stirred uncomfortably. Gruffly, he said, "That's not enough. That panel has to have a Negro on it."

"Why?" I asked.

"Because there should be a Negro on the platform of every public meeting sponsored by a democratic organization, which this is supposed to be."

"Why?" I asked again.

"To represent the interests of the Negro people of this community," he answered.

"Don't you trust the other members of the panel to represent those interests?"

"That's not the point, whether I trust them or not. A Negro should be up there, that's all!"

"But suppose we can't find anyone qualified to participate on the panel? Isn't it better to have the interests of all the people well represented than to have any particular group poorly represented?" I asked.

"I'm not arguing that point," he said. "All I think is that a Negro should sit on that platform."

"Just as an exhibit?" I asked.

Now Mac was angry. "Even if he just sits there and don't open his mouth, it will still show how we stand on the Negro question," he said.

"It seems to me," I said, "that if you put anyone on that platform merely to exhibit him and not because he's qualified to take part in the discussion, you're exposing him to ridicule. Frankly, I question your motives."

Spurred by whispered encouragement from his neighbors, Mac shook his head. "You can question all you like," he said. "Anyhow, you're not the only member of this organization. I put my question in the form of a motion instructing the committee to place a Negro on the panel." He sat down amid cries of "Second!" from various parts of the room. There was some brief discussion, the question was called, a vote taken and the motion carried.

Coffee was served when the meeting had ended and the crowd broke up into small groups. Later, when I went up for a second cup, I found myself standing in line behind Mac. He waited for me after he'd been served and we took our drinks to a quiet corner of the room. For a few minutes we drank in silence. I could feel his eyes on me and, slipping into the clinical attitude of relative detachment which my years of psychoanalytic practice have taught me is a necessary protection against the personal discomfort of having yourself scrutinized for your weaknesses, I allowed him enough time for his examination. When he had finished, I offered him a cigarette. He lit his with a Zippo on the surface of which was scratched a legend, partly obscured by his large hand.

"So," I said, "you're a seaman, an ex-G.I., you were in the landing at Salerno, and you're married and you're a Party member. What's your name?"

"Name's Mac," he said, "but you're wrong almost all across the board. I was in the Merchant Marines, I work in a canning factory, I got the lighter from a buddy who was at Salerno, I used to wear a wedding ring but my wife is divorcing me."

"And the C.P.?" I asked.

"That's where you're right, Mr. Holmes," he said.

We laughed, and then I could feel his eyes searchingly on me again.

"That must be quite a racket you're in," he said. "I bet that suit cost a hundred bucks."

"It's a living," I said, "and the suit cost eighty-five."

"What'd you mean by what you said before about questioning my motives?" he asked. I was puzzled. "On the Negro question," he explained.

"Oh, that," I answered. "You see, I just don't believe you Party people are honest about Negroes. I think your actions regarding them are what we call in psychoanalysis 'reaction-formations.' For example, like tonight, I know you came here with instructions to see that a Negro was seated on that panel. It doesn't matter to you that your Negro may

74

not be qualified, may not be able to hold his end up in a discussion because he just lacks qualification. You're willing to have him sit up there even if he says nothing or makes a fool of himself. You don't realize—but I think you do, unconsciously—that if you're using him as a symbol, what he does up there in front of the audience will be symbolic of the Negro community and not of that individual Negro himself. I think you people do this with an unconscious purpose; that you bend way over this way because you really want to bend the other way."

"I think that's a lot of crap," Mac said. "But anyway, what makes you so damned sure there are no Negroes qualified to discuss this point?"

"I'm not sure," I said. "I have to take the committee's word for it that they've done the job they were supposed to do—find qualified people to serve on that panel. Anyhow, you had a man on the committee."

Mac seemed startled. "How do you know?" he asked.

"I appointed him," I replied. "I'm a democrat."

Soon after this the evening ended. I forgot all about Mac—although we nodded a greeting to each other the night of the debate—until a few months later when a man called to make an appointment with me to discuss an analysis. I explained that my schedule was full and I could take on no more patients, but offered to give him a list of names of other psychoanalysts in town who might be able to see him. However, he said this was an emergency matter and that he could talk only to me. When I reminded my caller that in an emergency one uses the nearest exit, he replied that I would understand better when I saw him why I was the only analyst in Baltimore to whom he could talk. I was naturally intrigued to learn the reason for this and departed from my usual custom to set aside an hour for him

75

in my study at home on the following Sunday. Accordingly, on that day and at the appointed hour, Mac appeared.

I at once confessed to him that I had forgotten his name—possibly in retaliation for my defeat in the balloting that night at the meeting—and therefore hadn't recognized him over the telephone. He acknowledged the apology with a wave of his hand and sank into the chair near my desk, his big frame collapsing as if it were falling apart at all its joints. He closed his eyes in weariness for a moment, then opened them and looked around—at the books, the couch, the framed etching of Freud at his desk, the African and New Guinea sculpture in the room.

"This is a nice place," he said. "Quiet. Away from the world."

He reached for the cigarettes on the desk, lit one, filled his lungs and then fixated the glowing end as he spoke.

"A big guy like me. I've been all over, done everything. Now I gotta come here and lie on a couch and cry off to you." He shook his head with a grimace of disgust. "But I can't do it any more by myself. The harder I try the worse it gets.

"If the Party knew I was here, I'd be in for a rough time," he continued. "They don't like psychoanalysis—or psychoanalysts. Especially guys like you. They call you a Social Democrat. . . . D'you know that?" For the first time he looked directly at me.

"I know it," I said. "Psychoanalysis is a bourgeois science: psychoanalysts are the lackeys of the capitalist class. I'm an unstable Social Democrat. So what are you doing here?"

"The Party's position on psychoanalysis——" Mac began. But I interrupted him. "I know the lecture," I said. "That's not why you came to see me."

76

Mac stamped out his cigarette with a stained thumb. "No it isn't," he said: then he smiled, "I'm just trying to put it off a little."

"Everyone does," I said. "What's it all about?"

"It's me," Mac said. "It must be. Everything's shot to hell. I've got no feeling for anything. I feel like what's happening to me somehow isn't happening—like I'm an observer. Sometimes I even think of myself as if I'm a scientist or something, looking down on a bug struggling on a slide under a microscope. You poke it with something: it moves. You put some acid on it: it wriggles. That bug's me, and so's the scientist.

"My wife left me three months ago," he continued. "She threatened before but she never did it. Now she's gone and done it. She's suing for a divorce and I don't even care. It's just a thing that's happened. Once, if anything like this happened I'd have been ripped open inside. Now she's away somewhere with the two kids and it's like I don't even give a damn. . . . And it's the same everywhere. In the Party I once thought I could be something. I cared what was happening. I was a good worker. Now it's a sort of dream. It goes on, like everything else. But it's not important. I go to meetings, distribute literature, do what I'm told—like a machine, because it's the only thing I know how to do."

"But you care enough to come to see me," I said, "and you're certainly not very calm or detached now."

"Now's different," Mac answered. "But usually I'm dead, rotten inside, decaying, shriveling up like a piece of fruit you leave on the shelf."

"Tell me more about your wife leaving you," I asked. "Why was that?"

"This is the part that hurts," Mac replied as he reached for the cigarettes again. "I'm no good to her, haven't been for a long time. You know what I mean. Even my pecker hangs dead." He bent to the light I held and drew deeply. "I haven't been a man in maybe two years. She's tried everything and so have I. Even other women. But it's no good. Sometimes I get a little feeling in me like it's going to be all right. Once, about two months ago, I was on a party and there was a dame there made passes at me. I grabbed her off as quick as I could and took her to a hotel. . . ." Here Mac caricatured a laugh.

"It even sounds funny to me," he continued, "but it was a hell of a night. I tried until I thought my guts would drain out. Just with trying it would get half erect and we'd hurry to make a score; but it was no soap.

"And yet," he went on after a brief pause, "there's something queer about that too. Because I have a discharge every time."

"You mean you ejaculate without an erection?" I asked.

"Yeah. I don't get excited, you understand, and I don't feel anything; but the semen just comes out at a certain time as if it was the real thing."

Anticipating my question, he continued, "After this happened a few times I went to a doctor and he sent me to a urologist. The urologist couldn't find anything wrong. He said it was psychic and I should see a psychiatrist."

"And did you?" I asked.

Mac shook his head. "No," he said. "I knew that this was only a little bit of the problem and I didn't want anyone probing around in my head."

"And yet you came to see me."

"I came to see you for two reasons," Mac said as he ground out the butt. "The first is that it's gotten so bad now I gotta have help. The second is you're the only one in this town I can trust."

"Does ——— know you came to see me?" I asked, mentioning the name of the local chief Party functionary.

"Hell, no!" Mac almost shouted. "He'd have ten fits if he found out. Whenever he hears your name he breathes hard anyhow. Plus the fact that there's a kind of unwritten Party ban on going to a psychoanalyst."

"It can't be a very effective one," I said. "I've already analyzed two people from your 'cell' and a couple more from outside of Baltimore."

"I know that," Mac said. "One of the guys you analyzed quit the Party and the other isn't going to last too long I'd say. That's one of the main gripes against you guys, you know. People who get analyzed don't seem to stay with the Party. Or if they do, they can't be counted on."

"Counted on for what?" I asked.

"Counted on to follow Party discipline," Mac answered. "And that's important—to me at least."

"Why?"

"Because no matter what happens," Mac said deliberately and with emphasis, "I want to stay in the Party. I've got to!"

"Why?"

"Because the Party is my life," Mac answered. "Because the Party is right. Because the Party is the only way to build a new world."

"You're sure of that?"

"I am. It's the one thing I *am* sure of," Mac said. "Look. I've been all over the world, Doc. I've seen the kind of misery no one would believe. The Party's got the only answer for the way out. I've been a Communist for years. I read all the literature before I became one, too. With me it's not like I hear you guys say—because I hated my old man or got pushed around by my sister or something fancy like that. I'm a Communist out of conviction, real convic-

79

tion, from the neck up, even though I feel it in my intestines."

"*There's* something you feel," I observed.

"I can still get hot by what I see all around me and what's happening," Mac said. "It's not the same kind of hot like it used to be, because then I'd be in there pitching for what I believe. Now all I do is——"

I interrupted Mac here. "So what does this mean?" I asked.

"It means," Mac said, "that if getting analyzed means I have to quit the Party, it's not for me."

"You'd rather go on being detached, impotent, miserable and (I gather) ineffective in everything you do?" I asked.

"If I have to," Mac said, "yes. I'm in the Party to stay. Look." Mac held out his hands. "If I thought it would bring Socialism a minute faster than it's coming I'd nail these hands to the cross myself!"

"Interesting you should use just that figure of speech," I observed. "But isn't it true that your even coming to see me is a breach of Party discipline?"

"I'd have my ass eaten out but good if anyone knew about it," Mac agreed. "But I'm doing it because I think that if I can get straight on my personal problems, I'll be a better Communist."

"Why pick on me to do it?"

"Because I think I can trust you not to try to influence me against the Party. Is that true?"

I shrugged. "A psychoanalyst doesn't *influence* for or against anything," I said. "But a patient, an analysand, has to be willing to subject all of his beliefs and opinions to the analysis. Are you?"

"I think I am," Mac said. "I want to shake this thing. I

want to feel human again." Now there was a note of pleading in his speech.

"But not at the expense of the Party."

"That's right." The edge was back in his voice. "Not if it means giving up the Party. But does it have to? That's what I want to know."

"I can't answer that," I said. "I'd be lying to you if I told you one way or the other. I know analysts who would tell you you'd be a better Catholic or Jehovah's Witness or Communist or whatever after an analysis. But I just don't know. I've analyzed Communists before and, as you said, some stay with the Party, some leave it. What'll happen to you is something I can't predict."

Mac thought awhile. Then, as if he had come to a decision, he said, "I feel sure enough of my convictions as far as the Party goes not to have to worry about that. I think my beliefs will stand up under any kind of questioning."

"It's a gamble," I commented.

"Not with me it isn't," Mac countered quickly. Then, "What d'you say? Will you take me on?"

I thought rapidly. My schedule was overful already. I had promised myself to cut down rather than increase my hours. If I took Mac as a patient, it would be for a long and stubborn analysis. Not only were his symptoms among the most difficult to treat—as I had learned from bitter experience before with impotence and depersonalization—but he showed a rigidity of personality, an uncompromising mental structure, that would stand in the way of my best efforts and his best intentions. And as for his being a Communist, here too I knew what could be expected: the moment any of his cherished formulas were questioned there would be hell to pay: his analysis would be hung up for

81

many hours while he did battle with his Marxist conscience: factors that would ordinarily have little or no place in an analysis would be introduced: there would be delays and canceled appointments. Finally, without his having to tell me, I knew that Mac could not afford my fees, and already half my patients were paying reduced fees while I placated myself with the rationalization that I was treating them because they were "interesting" cases.

But the chance to analyze yet another Communist! The chance to test once more my ideas about the breed of men who become militant socialists! I had already, while stationed in a Federal prison, analyzed a high official of the Party and an officer of a trade union who was also a Communist. Then I had treated a social worker, an engineer, a student and a teacher who were all card-holders in the Party. Mac would be the first worker-Communist on my growing list, my first real "proletarian." The temptation was not to be resisted. I found myself already manipulating my schedule and framing excuse-arguments to give my wife when I told her I would be taking another patient for three or four hours a week at a small fee.

"Will you tell them at Party headquarters that you're coming to me?" I asked.

"I don't think so," Mac said. "I'll have to give it a little more thought. A thing like this could be handled in two ways. If I told them and they didn't object, I could probably get a furlough from Party activity for a while. I guess they'd insist on that so I won't be giving away any Party confidences. . . . Or else I could just go ahead without consulting them at all."

"And if they should find out somehow?"

Mac looked directly at me. "Then I'd have to quit," he said.

"The Party or the analysis?" I asked.

"The analysis, of course," Mac answered.

I have seldom had a more enthusiastic patient than Mac was during the first month of his analysis. He seemed to have a flair for the work, and by the end of the first half-dozen hours had mastered the technique of free association. The resistances we encountered during this first month were the usual ones; the kind that result from the ordinary inhibitions of speech due to embarrassment; the unaccustomed disclosure of small personal secrets; the need every analysand has to insure the continued good opinion of the analyst. These minor blocks were quickly dispelled, and I was soon in possession of the bare outlines of my patient's history.

Mac had been born thirty-four years before we met. The place of his birth was a farm in western Ohio where his parents lived with his father's people. The model of a Conestoga wagon on a shelf in my study reminded him of his family origins. Stolid, imperturbable and determined Dutch settlers, they had pushed their way westward in one of the first migrations from the East Coast, coming to rest, characteristically, in a place that reminded them of the home they had left in Europe. Mac's grandfather, who was a very old man when Mac was born, had staked out a large tract of land. As his three sons came of age he parceled it among them, reserving for himself and his second, much younger wife a few acres in the exact middle of the family holdings. White-bearded and with clear blue eyes that remained undimmed to the hour of his death, tall and as strong as one of his work horses, this paternal grandfather was destined to play a major role in the formation of Mac's personality. So was the patriarch's wife, a half-breed illegitimate girl who had been maid of all work on the farm until her mistress died and she was taken to wife as a matter of course.

The youngest of the three sons was Mac's father. He was the old man's favorite, alike to his father in features as an image in a mirror. A vast silence surrounded him. Indeed, Mac recalled no word his father had ever spoken. But his manner was kind and his uncommunicativeness more than made up for by a soothing, peaceful presence. His wife, Mac's mother, died in the moment Mac was born. A faded daguerreotype, its cracked pieces glued to a strip of cardboard, was all that Mac ever knew of her. In her place was a conglomerate fiction composed by the boy over the years from his grandfather's reminiscences and the memory of two brief visits paid the half-orphan by his mother's parents. They were, he remembers, big people with heavy hands and huge feet. As they sat in the kitchen and spoke of their daughter's death, they filled the room with the smell of earth, and their low, hoarse voices blended with the snapping of wood in the fire and the simmering bubble of the water kettle to become fixed for a lifetime as the sense-scenery of Mac's dreams.

A wet-nurse tended Mac the first three years of his life. Actually, she ministered to him only part time, and for the remainder deputized the oldest daughter of her large brood to act as cook, housekeeper and milkmaid for Mac's father and the distant cousin who worked as hired man. The ample-bosomed nurse was like a general who regularly visits the front. Every morning, while it was still dark, she drove up in a rickety buckboard. It was she who would take Mac from his bed, suckle him, clean and dress him, then turn him over to her daughter with a list of instructions for his day's welfare and activity. A wet smack on his cheek and she was off, to return again after supper with a milk-full breast, a sponging, and a final kiss administered while she folded the warm quilt around him. Between the dawn and dusk of her brisk visits there was the sugar-tit, prepared by this natural pediatrician from a lump of honey knotted in a rag and moistened with milk. It was in his mouth all day and most of the night and its taste, recaptured during the early part of his psychoanalysis more than thirty years later, was an assurance of peace and an allayer of fears.

Soon after Mac had turned three he was taken to live in his grandfather's house. Now he came under the dominion of his dour step-grandmother, whom he learned to call "Ma," and the idyll of perfect freedom in which he had lived heretofore was shattered. Ma was a soured woman, intolerant of small boys and dirt, embittered for life by her illegitimacy, and fierce in all her compensations for early experiences as the offspring of an Indian woman and a west-bound hunter hungry for the feel of human flesh. In contrast with the large affections of the wet-nurse who stood in his mother's place, Ma was as sterile in her feelings as in her womb. In her scheme there was no place for this two-legged animal with its wants, its needs, its stinks, its inability to comprehend what was expected of it. The first thing to go was the sugar-tit, and the next a rough wooden horse carved by his father, now smooth and sticky with the love of small, hot hands. From Ma, for the first time, Mac heard the words "bad" and "naughty." They applied to everything he did; but mainly to the contents of his pants and to the twig of flesh that hung between his legs and made his belly turn over with vibrations of secret pleasure when he touched it, when he rubbed the flank of a cow a certain way, or when thunder broke from the sky.

Pa—Grandpa—was different. He was as big as a giant

85

and when he stepped on to the porch the house shook. It almost scared you even to look at him, but beneath his brusque and boom there was a tenderness, and when his huge hand held yours you could feel as safe as if you were held by God. Grandpa looked like God, too, whose picture was on the front of the Bible from which the old man read every night. And Grandpa acted like God, too, dispensing a swift justice to the animals on his farm, to his sons, his hands, his wife and Mac. From Grandpa, Mac learned anger and the indignation that were later to make him want the kind of world where Grandpa's justice would be a matter of course, a society founded on the fairness that was Grandpa's rule of life. For Grandpa saw things directly and simply, black and white, and his fundamentalist faith could as little be shaken as the hills that ringed the horizons of the land where Mac spent his childhood.

The first of the World Wars claimed the life of Mac's father. He was crushed by the carriage of a big gun that fell on him in an accident in training camp. At the time his death meant little to Mac; only as the years piled on each other did the space left by the quiet one's going get bigger and come to matter. Meanwhile, there were the farm chores, the animals, the few brief months of school each year, the river that coiled through bottom land, the woods. There were hunting with the uncles, fishing with Pa, preserving with Ma, and all else that makes life in the country busy. At twelve there were more intimate and secret delights whose forbiddenness came home to him with stabbings of guilt in the evenings when, with the sick fascination of fears of discovery, Mac watched the slow movement across the page of Pa's great forefinger and heard the glottal sonorities of the old man's voice as he read of the wages of sin from the Book. And always there was Ma, fussing behind him, nagging, critical, sharp in her words and tone, forever un-satisfied and bitter-resentful.

When Mac was fourteen, the old man fell on the ice and broke his hip. He was then almost ninety, and with his fall his spirits also fell. When he took to his bed he seemed to shrivel and dry as if his juices were draining through a hidden tap on his body. For six months he lay on his bed, dying a little every day. During this time, Mac was with him constantly. Out of an urge to talk, perhaps to make a pattern of his life, he told his grandson the tales that made up his history. In snatches, and in a sequence that was the old man's alone, dictated by a curious internal logic, there emerged stories of poverty and persecution, the sea voyage to new lands, the heartbreak in the port city and the scroung-ing for silver to buy the gear for the westward march; the yard by yard struggle across the hills and rivers, the fighting with outraged men and angry Nature to clear and hold the land, the tearing down and the building; the great joys and the great sorrows of ninety victorious years. In Mac it made a brew of memories, both bitter and sweet; and when the old man at last closed his eyes, unknowingly Mac had distilled from these six months the essence of Pa, and drunk of it so deeply that it was to flow forever with his own blood.

The old man's death changed the world for Mac. The restlessness that had always been in him, but anchored first by his wet-nurse and then by Pa, broke free. He could not abide Ma and her ways, and the war the two had been waging since the day Mac was moved into her house now flared into open combat. So on a certain night, in traditional fashion with a bundle over his shoulder, Mac left.

He went to Chicago and there began the Odyssey that terminated on the couch in my study. The list of jobs he held is a long one. Always he worked with his hands and earned his money in sweat. Never did any one job last very long, chiefly because of the nature of the times, but also because of his restlessness, his querulousness and his inability to take orders. He knew poverty, not only of the slow kind on the margin of existing, but of the absolute kind, with the threat of starvation and death, the shame of beggary, the humiliation of picking over the contents of waste cans and garbage dumps like an animal, loathing one-self and disgusted but sharp in the eye for a bit of molding bread. And he knew idleness; not the leisurely kind, but the sort that fouls the mind and drugs the spirit; the listless, dragging, debilitating kind that shuffles in long lines at soup kitchens, huddles against the night-cold in musty mis-sion rooms behind windows where JESUS

A
V
E
S

in harsh electric light glares against the sky.

Then one day, with the farm now many years behind him, Mac stumbled upon his destiny. He had been out of work for weeks, living in a Hooverville among other castoffs. A car drove up to the ramshackle picket fence someone had made around the encampment to caricature the community of the undamned, and from it stepped a man with a well-fed look on his face. He asked who wanted work. Some of the older hands apparently knew him and turned their backs. But Mac had hunger in his belly and an itch in his muscles, so with a few others he piled into the truck that followed the man's car. They were driven to a big shed by the docks, where a hot stew and coffee were served. Then the man gave each one a rough club and told them to line up and follow one of his assistants.

88

They walked to a pier by which strikers were parading in a thin picket line. When the strikers saw them coming, the shout of "Scabs!" went up as they closed their ranks to make room for others who came running from behind a shed. At a command, the crew Mac was with charged. After a brief battle, most of them broke through and reached the end of the pier where a freighter was moored beside huge crates of machinery and piles of scrap iron. These they began to load into the hold of the ship. Mac worked eagerly, glad to be feeling the blood flow again through his arms and legs. That night the strikebreakers were fed from the ship's galley and bedded on blankets below deck. From outside, restrained from attacking the scabs by a detachment of police, the strikers taunted and cursed at them, but with little effect, for these were work- and food-starved men.

On the third day the job was done, the scabs were paid off, and a truck came to carry them back to Hooverville. Mac and a buddy left the truck as it passed the railroad yards. They caught a southbound freight. As the train highballed out of the city, through the slats of the cattle car they saw the ship they had just loaded swinging into the current.

"That was a stinkin', lousy thing to do," said Mac's buddy, "and I wouldn'a done it but for hunger."

"What was so stinkin' about it?" Mac asked.

His buddy told him; and out of the telling came hours in libraries with fat books and a dime dictionary, came listening and talking, came hearing with new ears and speaking with a new tongue, came sitting on cane-bottomed chairs in union halls and weary marching round and round on picket lines, came *Solidarity Forever* and *Joe Hill*, came the Party's little booklet with a place for stamps, came new words, new thoughts, new deeds. And in the late 'thirties, came a visit one night to a doctor's office in New York, a job on a tramp for Marseilles; then a long, cold night of walking, running, lying breathless in the snow of a Pyrenees' pass, and in the morning a ride on a truck, and in the evening a dole of dungarees and cap; then marching and a wooden gun and *Link, Zwei, Drei, Vier;* then, at last, the trenches and the splintering brick walls of the University outside Madrid, a real gun and the red blood of a Moor on his bayonet and the sweet smell of rotting fascist corpses pasted for always to the inside of his nostrils.

When the war in Spain ended, Mac returned to the States. He joined the Merchant Marine and was assigned by the Party to union activity. He roved the world during the next years, carrying out Party tasks with efficiency and will. This work took him to strange places, and he did strange things for a farmer boy from the western reaches of Ohio. The internal politics of the Party never interested him, and despite its changes of course, its upsets and veerings, he hewed strongly to the line. When war was declared against Germany and Japan, he wanted to enlist but was told that because of his record as a fighter in Spain he would be marked in the United States Army and hence of little value to the Party. Disappointed but ungrudging, he remained a merchant seaman; but when the Soviet Union joined the Allies and the underground everywhere came alive as if touched by a magician's wand, Mac found his place as a courier and contact man among resistance groups and between national Party units. The work was exciting, dangerous, and the pitch of his life was passionate.

In the last year of the war Mac married a comrade from New York whom he had made pregnant. This was no shabby affair: it had nothing to do with the malicious fictions of the press and the yellow journals about free love among the Reds. The girl was Jewish, of strong moral character, and a virgin when Mac met her. They had been in love for more than a year but had postponed marriage because of the death of the girl's brother in the air over Germany and her respect for the tradition of her people. But in the seventh month of their love, and on the first night of sexual intercourse, there was an accident of contraception. As soon as her year of mourning was over, they were married. The twins were born in the summer of 1945 when the war ended.

With the coming of peace Mac was no longer important to the Party in the Merchant Marine. He was transferred to heavy industry, where he was assigned to organize certain craft workers. At this task he failed miserably, whereupon he was tried in a succession of assignments in New Jersey and Pennsylvania. Finally, he was instructed to move with his family to a place near Baltimore and to place himself at the disposal of the Party officials there. They reviewed his record and ordered him to work in a canning factory where the cleaners and packers were unorganized. On Sundays he had a delivery route for the *Sunday Worker*. This is what Mac was doing when he came to psychoanalysis. . . .

While the analysis was concerned, in its opening stages, with a recounting of the superficial history that has been sketched, it was a veritable honeymoon for both Mac and myself. Long-forgotten experiences and incidents were recovered, and a rough pattern of Mac's basic personality was worked out. He recognized, very soon after he began, that he had romanticized his family origins; that he had

91

stood in awed admiration of his grandfather even though the old man, because of his great size and imposing personality, had terrorized him; that he had hated violently his step-grandmother but—according to a well-tested analytic dictum that a child identifies with the frustrating parent on the principle of the defensive, "if you can't lick 'em, join 'em"—that he had acquired and absorbed many of her traits. He realized, too, that he had been made exceptionally dependent by his wet-nurse, and that the greater part of his restlessness throughout his life came from an inner compulsion to seek situations that could be equated in his unconscious with that happy condition of total surrender to someone or something in utter faith. He achieved, also, some striking insights about his sexual life: for example, that his grandmother's curt disposal of the sugar-tit which was in his mouth constantly was a symbolic castration (the honeyed lump representing to him, by upward transposition, his penis), and that in sexual activities during adult life he was always made anxious by a remote but heretofore never comprehended fear of trusting his sexual organ to a woman. Thus he would never allow his wife, or other women he had been with, to handle or fondle his genitals and, despite the pleasure he had in intercourse, was always somewhat relieved when he was able to withdraw. In this connection he recognized that a habit to which he had never given a passing thought—that of going to the bathroom and urinating the moment intercourse had been accomplished—was in reality a practice he had established in order to permit an examination of his organ to obtain assurance that it was still there, intact and unharmed. And the reverse of this was also an unconscious fact with Mac: that the penis could not only be harmed but was in itself an instrument of harm. He recalled how his step-grandmother had regarded it as something foul, dirty, and an object of shame to be loathed. In his innermost thought he, too, had such an opinion of it; but he also used it to punish his step-grandmother, and his chronic condition of dampness well beyond his eighth year was due not only to the indulgence of his wet-nurse, the laxity of the daughter who substituted for her and an inarticulate expression of the child's wish for attention, but also as a challenge to and aggression against the woman he had to call Ma.

The recovery of so many memories and the working through of them in the weeks that followed enabled Mac, with my assistance, to arrive at a better understanding of himself and his motives. He began, then, to see himself in a new light. The masks he had been wearing for his own and the world's benefit one by one fell away from him. Beneath all the poses he had assumed to hide his true face there emerged the portrait of an adult with the psychology of a child, of a man equipped for manhood but starving for the diet of an infant. And as he recognized his dependent core and the aggression beneath the skin, the dam of his internal rage broke, and for the first time in years he began to feel again.

Mac began to feel, acutely and deeply. In the first flush of the return of feeling he became as one who has been blind many years and who, by a miracle, recovers his sight. He looked about him and everywhere there were only bright colors. His senses responded to life. At night he walked the streets of the city, smelling its odors, gazing into its lights and rejoicing at its sounds. At his work he became lively, full of verve. In the analysis, day after day, he vented what he had so long repressed. On the heads of those who were long dead or until now forgotten, he poured a vitriol of passion, ventilating much of his vagrant

93

but unexpressed fury. In the permissive privacy of my study he relieved himself of the top layers of his hatred for everyone who had ever given him slight or insult or hurt, from his step-grandmother through his employers to the Communist stereotypes Party propaganda provided for him. Meanwhile, he observed himself carefully and with a new vision in his daily life. He saw the little evidences of his yearning for dependency, how he forced people to put him into a dependent relation with them, how he was avid for the infant-security he got when, in the smallest affairs, he could surrender himself to the care of another.

Only in his sexual life did Mac, at this period, remain frustrated and disturbed. At the height of his enthusiasm with the results of the analysis so far, he twice attempted intercourse with girl friends. On the first occasion he reported sexual stirrings, but on neither venture did he experience even the semblance of potency: both episodes were total failures. But were it not for this, Mac would have been satisfied with his progress and have brought his therapy to a premature ending. I, of course, understood what was happening as a "transference-cure," and awaited the day when the flimsy structure he was building would collapse. I knew that he had only scratched at the surface of his neurosis; that what had until now been accomplished was the effect of relieving pressure through ventilation, minute and superficial insight, and the shifting of all of the burdens he bore onto me and the process of analysis. In me he found a new receptacle into which he could pour, and onto whom he could project, the stuff and substance of his life. During this period our relations were more than cordial—at least so far as Mac was concerned; but I, having been through this process many times before, could detect what was hidden in it, and the internal barometer of my previous experience with many patients warned me of a storm over the horizon.

It came; and when it struck, it was with fury.

One day, in the course of a session, Mac mentioned that he had had a dream that he considered foolish and not worth recounting. He had had dreams before, and they had been minimally productive, for the most part, although they had provided valuable clues to his motivations and strivings and had served him well as starting points for associative trains. In the initial phase of psychoanalysis, however, I do not usually insist on deep dream work for fear of stirring unconscious material that my patients are perhaps not yet prepared to handle. I had not, therefore, been insistent with Mac regarding dreams. But when a patient, as Mac did on this day, depreciates a dream, I have found that it usually means his dream is particularly important at the time and not to be disregarded; that he is aware of its significance but fears it, and hopes by his offhandedness to divert the analyst's attention. Moreover, I have found that such an attitude invariably means that the dream in question relates especially to the transference, *i.e.* the relationship between analyst and analysand, and that the chief reasons why the patient seeks to withhold it are that he either fears to disturb the outward tranquillity of the relationship or that he is unwilling thus to surrender a potential weapon the dream has given him against the analyst. Accordingly, I asked Mac to tell me the dream. After some hesitation, then, and protesting that it would be a waste of time, he related the following:

"I am walking along Charles Street (in Baltimore) toward Mount Vernon Place. There is no traffic on the street and I seem to be alone. There is no one behind me but I hear footsteps. This scares me and I open my mouth to

95

scream, but when I do my tongue falls out on the ground. This doesn't surprise me: I just pick it up and put it in my pocket and go on walking.

"Ahead of me I see the monument (The George Washington Monument at Mount Vernon Place in Baltimore). Now I notice that the side of the street I'm on is in very bright sunlight, but the other side is dark, pitch-black almost. Then I see the man who is behind me, but he's on the other side of the street, the black side. He seems to be paying no attention to me but I somehow feel that he is really watching me very carefully. I walk on a little way —begin to feel very tired. It gets so I can hardly lift my legs and Mount Vernon Place seems miles away. I become worried that I'll never make it to the monument, I'm so tired. I try to call the man to help me, but I have no tongue and can't make a sound. I reach into my pocket to get it but it's gone. I search for it frantically and awake in terror with the blankets all tangled up."

When he had finished relating this dream Mac disparaged it as foolish and asked me if I really thought it worth taking time to analyze. I remained silent, and for a few minutes Mac stirred uncomfortably on the couch. Then, gruffly, he said the dream meant nothing to him; it was nonsense and he had no associations to it. I suggested that at least a part of the symbolism in the dream was quite obvious, that he might do well to consider its significance for the analysis. Mac countered with a curse and said he was a fool ever to have gone in for this stupid business. All right! So losing his tongue in the dream meant he wasn't talking. . . . So what? It was all a lot of crap anyhow. What good was it doing him? No wonder the Party had proscribed psychoanalysis! In any case, how could anyone ever get well just by talking? He had been talking, talking, talking for months and he was still as far from his goal as ever; and he was tired of it, sick and tired of the whole thing! At this, I pointed out that he was now actually paraphrasing a part of the dream, that part where he was growing weary and hopeless about attaining his destination. He answered that the monument certainly was an apt representation of his analytic goal: it is shaped like an erect phallus; in Baltimore, perhaps because of this, the park at its base has become a hangout for homosexuals and prostitutes. He passes it everytime he has to go to Party Headquarters, about two or three times each week.

"Obviously, then," I said, "in order to get to the erect phallus, or potency, you have to talk."

"Don't be so smug," Mac answered. "I knew that before I told you the dream. But there's more to talking than you think."

"In the dream," I said, "you lost your tongue when you thought you were being followed. Who was following you?

"You, of course," Mac snorted. "You follow every word I say."

"But you weren't surprised when your tongue fell out."

"No, I wasn't." Mac sighed. "I've known all along that I'd have to clam up at some point in this analysis—when it became necessary to talk about the Party."

"So you choose silence, and therefore impotence, rather than talk about the Party," I commented. "But why did you search so frantically for your tongue in the second part of the dream?"

Mac's agitation became obvious. He lit a cigarette with trembling hands; sweat glistened on his forehead. Slowly, he said, "The dream shows that my sickness and the Party are mixed up together. I guess I've known it all along and

97

I've been afraid of it. From what you say I gather that the tongue falling out business means more than just being unwilling to talk: it means castrating myself."

I interrupted him here. "The first day I spoke with you," I said, "you told me you'd be willing to crucify yourself if it would bring socialism a minute nearer. What you're saying now is that you'd castrate yourself for the same reason."

"I would."

"You are."

Mac turned on the couch and looked at me. I could see the pain and torment in his eyes. "You're a hard guy," he said. He turned away and continued, "But I guess you have to be." He was calmer now as he summed the dream to this point. "Let's see. The Party and potency are tied up in my mind . . . how I don't know. But I gather that in order to solve the potency problem I have to talk about the Party. By not talking about the Party I'm castrating myself—or deliberately choosing castration, as you say. All right, now where do we go from here?"

"To the monument," I answered.

"It would be a lot easier to get there," he said, "if you were a Communist. I could talk to you then."

"You mean if I came over to your side?" I asked.

Now the entire dream fell into place and a flood of associations followed. I (the analyst, man in the dream) am walking in darkness. A not-so-unconscious purpose of Mac's analysis is to get me to come over on his side, *i.e.* to join the Party. This would not only benefit me; it would help him. He needs help in reaching the monument (potency) but fears that to obtain this help he will have to analyze his relationship to the Party and to disclose Party secrets. If the analyst would only see the light and come over to his side, he (Mac) could talk freely and be assisted toward potency. The prospect of continued impotence is a frightening one, but even if he wants to, he can't tell everything that is on his mind. There are secrets, confidences no one outside of the Party can be trusted with. These are perilous times for the Party. Often, while on the couch, he has to suppress a thought, a street address, a name, or something else that crosses his mind. When he does this, the associative chains break; so he will never get well. He is a fool ever to have attempted this business. Maybe he should just go and have his penis amputated, have done with the whole mess; or maybe he should quit the analysis, forget about being impotent. As things stand, he is always afraid of a leak, afraid that something he has been entrusted with will slip out. I (the analyst) am too clever. He has been warned against me. I know how to put two and two together. I'm not to be trusted. How did he know?—maybe I'm an undercover agent for the F.B.I. He knows I worked in a prison once, a federal prison, too. There's rumor going around that in Los Angeles and New York, federal agents are posing as psychoanalysts and abstracting political secrets from people. And he knows, also, that I practice hypnosis. What if I hypnotized him someday and got him to spill all the stuff he had to suppress in the interests of the Party?

Following the analysis of this significant dream, Mac became intensely resistive. The negative transference, latent until now, betrayed itself by his silence, his curt manner with me, and his rudeness. Hour after hour sped by while Mac fought an eternal tug of war over whether he could trust me sufficiently to do the thing he knew he had to do: associate freely without regard to content. Interpretation availed little. When I established the connection between his present attitude toward me and his former attitude toward his step-grandmother about the secrets of his masturbation and sex play with the farm animals, he merely shrugged. When I related his present silence to the silence his father practiced in his brief life, and showed how it was tied to a sense of having sinned against his grandfather, he accused me of being fanciful.

Then his resistance took a new turn. Instead of remaining silent, he began to talk. To an untrained observer, his production now would have seemed like free association. It had every semblance of an unimpeded flow of ideas, thoughts and experiences. He related incidents from his glamorous career as a courier in the underground, described the personalities he had encountered and some of his lurid sexual adventures. Along with this, he began to make me presents of Communist literature. At each visit he brought me a gift of a book or pamphlet, and he would begin his hours by discussing a point raised in some brochure or article he had given me the hour before.

Both of us knew that Mac, during this phase, was using every device possible to avoid the issue. His counterfeiting of the process of free association was designed as a fence-straddling procedure to satisfy his desire to solve his problems without tackling their core. His gifts were aimed to convert me to militant socialism, and at the same time to bribe me. His attempts to convert his hours to a forum for the discussion of Marxism were really intended to convince himself of his own sincerity as much as they were planned for my benefit. But, at last, an hour came when Mac could no longer fool himself, and realized he hadn't at all fooled me.

I remember that a snowstorm was raging outside on the evening Mac's analysis reached a climactic point. He appeared very weary as he stretched out on the couch, lit a cigarette, and began in a monotone that I sensed he was using to disguise an inner excitement.

"They're giving me the business again," he began. "I just came from Party headquarters. From the way they talk it's just a matter of time until they replace me at the cannery. They say they're looking around for a spot where I'll fit in better, be more effective."

"Have you really failed?" I asked.

Mac shrugged. "I guess so. What with the analysis and everything I guess I haven't given the job what it needs. But, Christ! I hate to be pushed around like this. If I had my way I'd . . ."

"You'd what?" I encouraged him.

Mac ground out his cigarette. "Nothing," he said. Then, after a moment of silence, "Look, Doc. This analysis is a frost, isn't it?"

"Why do you ask?"

"Because I'm thinking of chucking it and moving on. I guess I can peddle pamphlets somewhere else; it doesn't have to be Baltimore."

"Why do you think the analysis is a frost?" I asked.

"Because I'm not getting anywhere," he replied. "Look. I had a girl out last night and all I did was dribble all over her. And now they tell me I'm even a failure in my work. And I know I've been a failure here. What more proof d'you want?" He held up his hand. "Wait," he said. "I know what you're going to say. But I can't do it, that's all. I just can't do free association and I know that's the only way out."

"And why can't you?" I asked.

"Because I'm afraid of a leak, that's why. Because if I ever let out what's in my head I'd be punished, that's why. Because as much as I trust you, I don't trust you enough. I've got dynamite in me: Party secrets, names, addresses. These keep crossing my mind. If I open my mouth once I'll spill all over the place. I can't do it, that's all. . . . I just can't do it!"

Now I asked Mac to associate to the word "leak," which had appeared more frequently than any other in discussions we had had about his resistance to the analysis and in connection with the Party. He did: the word was idiomatic and vulgar for urination; urination is a function of the penis; the other function of the penis is to transport semen——. At this Mac jumped from the couch and turned to me in bewilderment and consternation.

"Holy Christ!" he exclaimed. "You don't mean to say . . . ?"

"You've been unconsciously giving away Party secrets all the time," I finished for him.

He began to pace the room, more agitated than I had ever seen him, muttering to himself, over and over, words which I took to be "semen, Party secrets, leak, dribble . . ." Then he stopped before my chair and looked piercingly at me, while I did my best to appear calm despite my exhilaration over the knowledge that this hour would see the analysis brought to a head.

"Let me get this straight," he said. "Somehow it seems I've got semen and secrets mixed up in my head. So when I try to lay a girl and dribble out semen, it means I'm unconsciously giving away Party secrets." I opened my mouth to interrupt, but he held out one restraining hand and covered his eyes with the other.

"Wait! Wait!" he commanded. "It's beginning to fall into place. I really want to give away these secrets but can't do it with my mouth. So I let them dribble out through my penis. Why my penis? Because somewhere that's tied

102

up with the Party like semen's tied up with secrets. Now if I could tell these secrets, with my mouth, I mean, maybe I could have a real ejaculation!" He paused, and his perplexity was plain. "But why should I want to give away Party secrets? Because they're too much of a burden to me? How is that? There're plenty of guys who know a lot more than I do. Why should it affect *me* this way?"

This time it was obvious that he was asking for an answer.

"To find out the answer to that," I said, "we'll probably have to go deeper into your early sex life. But offhand I would guess that your desire to disclose Party secrets means that you have an aggression against the Party, and maybe this has to do with the equation of Party with Grandmother."

Mac returned to the couch and threw himself down on it. "A few months ago," he mused, "I would have laughed in your face if you said that. Now I'm not so sure." And for the remainder of that hour he did little more than express his amazement at what had gone before. When he left that evening, he was in a very different mood.

At his appointment two days later, Mac reported the first successful sexual experience he had had in many years. He had achieved and maintained a strong erection, and the experience of ejaculation had been intensely pleasurable. His enthusiasm knew no bounds. He was going to send for his wife, they would resume their former life, they would . . . Here I checked him.

"Do you think," I asked, "that your problems are solved?"

This sobered him. He sighed. "I guess not," he answered. "But is it really necessary to go on with this? After all, I *know* what's behind it now."

"But do you really?" I said. "It seems to me you have little more than a formula, a series of equations founded

103

on a few good guesses. I'd say there's still a long way to go." So Mac went on.

At this hour, and for some weeks thereafter, the truth of my last statement was brought home to Mac. For there now opened before us the vast panorama of his childhood sexuality and the intensity of his early feelings against his grandmother. Between these and the manner in which both related to the Party, the analysis wove like a shuttle on a loom, back and forth, back and forth. From him poured a seemingly endless series of memories, told with much of their original passion, of a child who was blocked in his expression at every turn, whose every action was called "bad"; of a longing for love and acceptance, the security of a kind word or gesture, and of the hot hatred that eventually came to take their place. Then, in a rush of memories, came what had been hidden, even from Mac, of the first ripples of that sexual tide that was to sweep him later to the edge of destruction. At first, what he had to relate was no more than the usual history of the vicissitudes of the developing sex urge; but with Mac, after his removal to this grandfather's farm, a pathological twist was given to it. From being an instrument for the reception and communication of pleasure as well as the prime organ for reproduction, his penis took on a new significance as the child he was saw how it and its behavior affected Ma. In short, it became a weapon, a tool for revenge; and in the life he lived in fantasy he regarded it—all unknowingly, of course—as a veritable arsenal of destruction; and with it, upon his grandmother—and, later, upon everyone who stood in his way—he wreaked a vengeance in imagination which hardly ever, until the microscope of analysis was trained upon it, reached the level of awareness. And this had a curious result: Mac became afraid of his penis, of the

104

destructive possibilities which he and he alone had given it; and, hence, when his neurosis in adult life formed a tidal crest, he had to inhibit it, to curb its fancied noxious potential.

But where, in all of this, did the Communist Party fit? Another dream supplied the missing links.

> "I am early for my appointment and when I enter your study you're not there. Thinking to occupy myself until you arrive, I go to the bookcase and select a volume from the shelves on the left side of the window. I start to read. Just then I hear you enter. I become confused. For some reason I don't want you to know I've been reading your books. I try to hide the book on me but it won't go into any of my pockets. Suddenly I thrust it into my mouth and it seems to go down my throat. But when I say hello to you, the book flies out of my mouth and hits you in the forehead. You fall down and I'm afraid I've killed you."

Mac's immediate association to the book was education. Correctly, he stated that the Party had given him an education he could not otherwise have obtained. As a child he thought his grandpa was God because he knew so much; sometimes he finds himself thinking the same way about me. But on second thought I (the analyst) don't really know so much. My knowledge runs all over the place. Outside of psychoanalysis I have no framework for what I know—no coherent, consistent, logical, correct way to order my thinking. He, Mac, is really a better-educated man than I am. In the days when he was on the bum, in Public Libraries between here and the West Coast he read everything printed in English on socialism and dialectical materialism—Marx, Engels, Lenin, Stalin, even Hegel and Fuerbach. He knows socialist theory better than—or at least as well as—anyone he has ever met in the Party. No; that isn't quite true. There's one fellow, a leader of the

Baltimore faction, who is really hot stuff. He's a Ph.D. He really knows his Marxism, knows it the way I (the analyst) know my Freud. But personally this Party philosopher is a pompous ass, a twisted neurotic if he (Mac) ever saw one. . . . Married to a dame, a former socialite or something, who is just as screwed up. Christ! How he hates them! Hardly a worker in the lot. If it ever comes to the barricades——

Here I interrupted him. "Then the dream doesn't refer to me," I said. "It refers to your Party philosopher. How do you account for this?"

Mac produced the day remnant, the bricks from his extra-analytic life of which the dream was built. On the previous evening he had gone to Party headquarters for a meeting scheduled to be held around the decision to change his assignment. Mac was the first one to arrive. He read from a book on a table until the others came. The next arrival was B, the Party philosopher and local leader. After greeting Mac, he (B) commented knowingly on the volume Mac had in his hands.

"I felt like throwing it at him," Mac said. "The snide bastard's always showing off his education."

"You hate him, you said."

"I do."

"That's why in the dream you killed him."

By now Mac's anger was out in the open; but it was more than anger; it was pure, primitive rage.

"I hate every last one of them," Mac cried. "And what's more, I hate the Party too, and everything it stands for. I've hated it deep down inside of me from the minute I was recruited." His voice rose almost to a scream. "I hate it! I hate it! I hate it! I'd kill the lot of them if I could. I'd shove this goddam Party so far down their throats it'd come outa

106

their asses! I hate it and I hate them and I hate you and I hate me for being such a chicken son-of-a-bitch that I have to lay here telling you about it!"

In a few more moments the rage had spent itself and Mac closed his eyes, exhausted by his furious outburst. Now, more calmly, he said, "So it's out at last. Now that I've said it I've said everything, I guess. I carried that around in me like a stone in my guts for years. I suppose I should be glad I got rid of it after all this time. I guess that's the bottom of the barrel, Doc. What else can there be?"

"I think we have to find out yet why you joined the Party," I answered, "and why, hating it the way you did, you stuck with it all these years. Do you know?"

Mac shook his head wearily. "No," he said. "I don't know."

We spent the next weeks answering the question I posed that night. Briefly, this is that answer:

At sixteen Mac had run away from home, after Grandpa had at last closed his piercing eyes in death. Between the time the old man died and the night he ran away the boy lived in fear of his own aggression. His hostility toward his grandmother was not just an ordinary resentment, it was a living hate that threatened to engulf both of them in tragedy. Unconsciously, Mac knew that if he stayed, he'd kill the woman; and so he ran from her presence to protect them both. But his experiences in the world only increased his hate and aggression, and provided him with new targets, for as an unskilled, untutored farmer lad, he was at the mercy of every economic breeze, unwanted and without a place. His embitterment during the years of wandering knew no bounds. When his destiny, in the shape of a buddy in a cattle car southbound from the scene of a strike caught up with him, he was ripe for the taking.

It is true that the Party made a rational appeal to Mac, that he was attracted to its doctrines intellectually and as a result of his reading and observation of the world. This appeal was enhanced by the fact that it presented answers— in a simple and easily digested form—to questions he had been asking himself and others through his formative years, especially when he was exposed to the paradoxes of American society in the late 'twenties and early 'thirties. Nor can it be denied that the cheap education he received on his way to, and later within, the Party was a major factor in his allegiance. It compensated for the inferiority he felt as an unlearned farmer boy. Indeed, it even permitted him to feel superior to every man—from Einstein to his analyst— who did not possess his ready formulations and the guidance of a simple set of maxims to meet every situation or prob- lem. But beneath all of these, and of such basic importance that it alone really mattered, the Party provided Mac with an adjustment. Within the Party, Mac could give vent to his hatred and aggression—originally directed against Ma and later the world—with almost unlimited freedom. It not only permitted him to express these qualities, but directed them upon a broad segment of society, channelized them toward a plenitude of objects, gave him the words and even the techniques to implement them. More than this, while making his hatred and aggression acceptable, it also served to contain them. Therefore, at one and the same time the Party gave Mac permission to indulge in aggression, yet saw to it that this aggression was sufficiently controlled that he need not fear its getting out of hand as it once almost did with his grandmother. So, in essence, for Mac the Party was a way of adjusting, of compromising, of containing a negative rebellion that might have destroyed him had he not found his way into it. In the Party's ranks he discovered a solution to the problem of how to be hostile without suffering the effects of hostility, of how to gain acceptance for his aggressiveness and to hold on to it without being treated as a mad dog and destroyed for it. The Party, then, *was* Mac's neurosis—a neurotic solution he deliberately chose as a lesser evil than the madness to which his hate was leading him.

But like all such solutions that men under pressure to adjust improvise for their perplexities and conflicts, the Party did not work. It offered no real answer: it could not, because it was nothing more than a symptom of Mac's difficulty, a stopgap "adjustment" doomed to failure from the outset as every "adjustment" has to fail.

The price Mac had to pay for what the Party did for him was in the coin of discipline and at the exorbitant rate of human cipherdom. The discipline demanded by the Communist Party is almost incomprehensible to those who have not met it first-hand. It is absolute, rigorous, uncompromising. It holds every member strictly accountable for his smallest acts, it permits of no slightest deviation or breach. It calls for the continuous criticism of behavior and thought by the self and others and, like Party policy, discipline veers and shifts with the prevailing currents of the time. Its impermanence in all save the proposition that under every circumstance the Party is correct requires an unusual kind of plasticity among those whom it affects. For a time Mac could follow it and be governed by it without strain— so long, that is, as his neurotic needs were being met by the permissive framework the Party provided for his aggression and hostility. He was therefore compliant to the discipline during the years of industrial strife and the war years, but following them—in the halcyon days when for a time there was no one to hate or fight—he began to chafe

109

under it. It became burdensome and nagging, resembling the regime of his grandmother. So in unconscious ways he flaunted and tried to defeat it. Borrowing from childhood, he symbolically betrayed its secrets. In other and smaller ways too numerous to catalogue he also tried to undermine it, and as the analysis progressed Mac was amazed to see how extensively he had been working against this discipline which, on the surface, he had for so many years taken for granted and complied with.

The reduction to cipherdom, to simple cog-ship in the grand wheel of the Party's ambition, was also at first un-protestingly—and, indeed, with relief—accepted by Mac. Recall that he was, underneath all, a wholly dependent type whose primary longing was forever to be a kind of suckling as he once was to his wet-nurse. After the homeless, friend-less years he spent in the world, when the Party bared its bosom to him at recruitment, he nestled to it in gratitude as he did long ago to the breast of the wet-nurse. But he overestimated its ampleness and plenitude, and in a short while he had drained it dry. While policy demanded and gave latitude to his hate, aggression and hostility, even Mac's voracious appetites were satisfied; but, in the middle 'forties, as the weather vane of policy turned, for Mac the bosom he had counted on to replace the one he had lost, the breast he had believed a fountain that would nourish him for all time, shriveled in his mouth. In anger and frustration, then, he turned upon it, prepared to rend it with the teeth of his basic hatred.

So this is the story of the psychoanalysis of Mac. It has told how and why he became a member of the Communist Party in the United States. He joined in an attempt to make an adjustment to the contrasts and conflicts within him that were destroying him, and would likely have destroyed

110

others. He joined, not primarily out of belief or conviction in the aims and goals of the Party, nor as a missionary to mankind, nor even as a rebel against injustice: he joined as one would voluntarily enter a prison in anticipation of crimes, as a preventive against becoming criminal and, because by joining, he could—or felt he could—remain a dependent infant.

In the course of his analysis Mac learned that the Party *was* his neurosis. When he concluded his analysis, it went with his symptoms. About six months after we had terminated, Mac quit the Party. He no longer needed it. . . .

:
solitaire

LAURA

"Sooner murder an infant in its cradle than nurse unacted desires."
    —Wm. Blake, *Marriage of Heaven and Hell.*

Laura had two faces. The one I saw that morning was hideous. Swollen like a balloon at the point of bursting, it was a caricature of a face, the eyes lost in pockets of sallow flesh and shining feverishly with a sick glow, the nose buried between bulging cheeks splattered with blemishes, the chin an oily shadow mocking human contour; and somewhere in this mass of fat a crazy-angled carmined hole was her mouth.

Her appearance astonished and disgusted me. The revulsion I felt could not be hidden. Observing it, she screamed her agonized self-loathing.

"Look at me, you son-of-a-bitch!" she cried. "Look at me and vomit! Yes—it's me—Laura. Don't you recognize me? Now you see, don't you? Now you see what I've been talking about all these weeks—while you've been sitting back there doing nothing, saying nothing. Not even listening when I've begged and begged you for help. Look at me!"

"Lie down, please," I said, "and tell me about it."

A cracked laugh, short and rasping, came from her hidden mouth. The piglike eyes raised to some unseen auditor above, while clenched fists went up in a gesture of wrath.

"Tell him about it! Tell him about it! What the hell do you think I've been telling you about all this time!"

"Laura," I said more firmly, "stop yelling and lie down"— and I turned away from her toward the chair behind the couch. But before I could move she grabbed my arms and swung me around to face her. I felt her nails bite through my coat and dig into the skin beneath. Her grip was like a vise.

She thrust her face toward mine. Close up, it was a huge, rotting wart. Her breath was foul as she expelled it in a hoarse, passionate whisper.

"No," she said. "I'm not going to lie down. I'm going to stand here in front of you and make you look at me— make you look at me as I have to look at myself. You want me to lie down so you won't have to see me. Well, I won't do it. I'm going to stand here forever!" She shook me. "Well," she said. "Say something! Go on, tell me what you're thinking. I'm loathsome, aren't I? Disgusting. Say it! Say it!" Then suddenly her grasp loosened. Collapsing, she fell to the floor. "O, God," she whimpered, "please help me. Please . . . please. . . ."

I had never met anyone like Laura before, nor had I encountered the strange symptoms she presented. In the literature of morbidity occasional reference was made to a disorder called bulimia, or pathological craving for food; and I had of course met with numerous instances of related

116

oral disturbances, such as perverted appetite or addiction to a specific food. As a matter of fact, one of the most amusing incidents of my career concerned a case in this category. It happened at the Federal Penitentiary in Atlanta, where I had been sent on a special assignment during the first years of the war. One day I received a note from an inmate requesting an answer to the engaging question, "Do you think I will get ptomaine poisoning from eating tomatoes on top of razor blades?" I showed this provocative communication to my colleagues in the Clinic who thought, as I did, that someone was pulling my leg. In reply, therefore, I wrote the questioner that the outcome of such a meal depended on whether the razor blades were used or new. Much to my chagrin, a few days later the X-ray technician called me into his office and exhibited two pictures on the stereoscopic viewer, inviting me to look at the "damndest thing you ever saw." I looked. In the area of the stomach I saw a number of clearly defined, oblong shadows. "What the heck are those?" I asked. "What do they look like to you?" he responded. I looked again. "To me," I said "they look like— well, I'll be damned! Razor blades!"

We called the inmate from the hall where he had been sitting hunched over on a bench, moaning with pain. When he saw me, he complained, "I did what you said. I only ate new blades like you told me. . . . Now look what's happened!"

"Musta been the tomatoes, then," was the technician's dry comment.

When the surgeons went to work on this man they discovered him to be a veritable walking hardware store. I was present in the operating room when they opened him up, and my eyes bulged with amazement as they carefully removed piece after piece of the junk he later told us he had

117

been swallowing for many years. Somewhere in my private collection of psychological curiosa, I have a photograph of the debris collected from this man's interior. It shows not only numerous fragments of razor blades, but also two spoons, a coil of wire, some bottle caps, a small screw driver, a few bolts, about five screws, some nails, many bits of colored glass and a couple of twisted metallic objects no one can identify.

Laura's difficulty, however, did not involve the perversion of appetite but something far more distressing psychologically. She was subject to episodes of depression during which she would be seized by an overwhelming compulsion to gorge herself, to eat almost continuously. A victim of forces beyond her ken or control, when this strange urge came upon her she was ravenous—insatiable. Until she reached a stage of utter exhaustion, until her muscles no longer responded, until her distended insides protested with violent pain, until her strained senses succumbed to total intoxication, she would cram herself with every available kind of food and drink.

The torment Laura suffered before, during and after these fits (as she called them) is really beyond description, if not beyond belief. Articulate as she was, I could not appreciate the absolute horror, the degradation, the insensate passion of these wild episodes until, with my own eyes, I saw her in the midst of one. Her own report of the onset and course of these experiences, a report I heard many times, is as follows:

"It seems to come out of nowhere. I've tried to discover what touches it off, what leads up to it, but I can't. Suddenly, it hits me. . . . It seems I can be doing anything at the time—painting, working at the Gallery, cleaning the apartment, reading, or talking to someone. It doesn't matter

118

where I am or what's going on. One minute I'm fine, feeling gay, busy, loving life and people. The next minute I'm on an express highway to hell.

"I think it begins with a feeling of emptiness inside. Something, I don't know what to call it, starts to ache; something right in the center of me feels as if it's opening up, spreading apart maybe. It's like a hole in my vitals appears. Then the emptiness starts to throb—at first softly like a fluttering pulse. For a little while, that's all that happens. But then the pulsing turns into a regular beat; and the beat gets stronger and stronger. The hole gets bigger. Soon I feel as if there's nothing to me but a vast, yawning space surrounded by skin that grabs convulsively at nothingness. The beating gets louder. The sensation changes from an ache to a hurt, a pounding hurt. The feeling of emptiness becomes agony. In a short while there's nothing of me, of Laura, but an immense, drumming vacuum."

I remember asking her, when she reached this point in her description, where the hunger started, at what place in the course of this weird, crescendoing compound of emptiness and pain the compulsion to eat entered.

"It's there from the first," she would say. "The moment I become aware of the hole opening inside I'm terrified. I want to fill it. I have to. So I start to eat. I eat and eat—everything, anything I can find to put in my mouth. It doesn't matter what it is, so long as it's food and can be swallowed. It's as if I'm in a race with the emptiness. As it grows, so does my hunger. But it's not really hunger, you see. It's a frenzy, a fit, something automatic and uncontrollable. I want to stop it, but I can't. If I try to, the hole gets bigger, I become idiot with terror, I feel as if I'm going to *become* nothing, become the emptiness—get swallowed up by it. So I've got to eat."

119

I tried to find out, in the early days of her analysis, if there was any pattern to her eating, any design, any specificity.

"No," Laura told me. "It's just a crazy, formless thing. There's nothing I *want* to eat, nothing in the world that will satisfy me—because, you see, it's the emptiness that has to be filled. So it doesn't matter what I swallow. The main thing, the only thing, is to get it inside of me. So I stuff anything I can find into my mouth, loathing myself while I do it, and swallowing without tasting. I eat. I eat until my jaws get numb with chewing. I eat until my body swells. I swill like an animal—a pig. I get sick with eating and still I eat—fighting the sickness with swallowing, retching, vomiting—but always eating more and more. And if my supply of food runs out, I send for more. Before it comes I go mad with the growing emptiness, I shiver with fear. And when it arrives I fall on it like someone who's been starved for weeks."

I would ask her how the frenzy ended.

"Most of the time I eat myself into unconsciousness. I think I reach a state of drunkenness, or something very like it. Anyhow, I pass out. This is what usually happens. Once or twice I've been stopped by exhaustion. I couldn't open my mouth any more, couldn't lift my arms. And there've been times, too, when my body just revolted, refused to take in any more food.

"But the very worst is the aftermath. No matter how the fit ends, it's followed by a long sleep, sometimes for as much as two whole days and nights. A sleep of sick dreams that go on and on, terrible dreams I can hardly recall on awakening—thank goodness. And when I awaken I have to face myself, the mess I've made of Laura. That's even more horrible than what's gone before. I look at myself and

120

can hardly believe the loathsome thing I see in the mirror is human, let alone me. I'm all swollen, everywhere. My body is out of shape. My face is a nightmare. I have no features. I've become a creature from hell with rottenness oozing from every pore. And I want to destroy this disgusting thing I've become."

Three months of intensive analytic work had passed before the morning Laura confronted me with her tragically distorted body and insisted I look at it. They had been stormy months for both of us, each analytic hour tearful and dramatic as Laura recited the story of her life. In the recounting she could find no relief, as many other patients do, since it was a tale of almost endless sorrow in which one dismal incident was piled upon another. Used as I am to hearing the woeful stories of abuse, neglect and unhappiness that people bring to an analyst, I was nevertheless moved by Laura's narrative and could hardly help expressing my sympathy. By this I do not mean that I verbalized the feelings she aroused in me, for the discipline of these long years of practice and the experience gained through the many errors I have made safeguard against such a gross tactical blunder; but in small ways of which I was largely unaware I communicated my compassion to her. With Laura, this turned out to be a serious mistake. Typically misreading my attitude for one of pity, hardly had the analysis begun than she set out to exploit this quality and to demand more and more of it. Paradoxically, just because I somehow betrayed sympathy for her, she charged me increasingly with a total lack of warmth, and upbraided me almost daily for my "coldness," my "stonelike impassivity," my "heartless indifference" to her suffering. Our meetings, therefore, followed a curious pattern after the first few weeks. They would begin with one of her moving chronicles, to the telling of which she brought a remarkable histrionic talent; then she would wait for some response from me: when this was not forthcoming in the manner she desired, she would attack me viciously.

I recall one such hour quite clearly, not only because of its content but also, perhaps, because it preceded by a few days the episode I described earlier; and the contrast between the way Laura looked on the day I have in mind and her appearance only a short while thereafter remains vivid in my memory. For Laura between seizures was nothing like the piteous wreck she made of herself at those times. Although poor, she always dressed becomingly, with a quiet good taste that never failed to emphasize her best features. The ascetic regime she imposed on herself between bouts of abnormal eating kept her fashionably thin. Her face, set off in a frame of hair so black that it reflected deep, purple lights, was not pretty in the ordinary sense, but striking, compelling attention because of its exotic cast. It conveyed an almost Oriental flavor by the juxtaposition of exceptionally high cheekbones, heavy-lidded brown eyes, a moderately small, thin nose with widely flaring nostrils, and an ovoid mouth. On the day I wish to tell about, one could hardly imagine the ruin that was even then creeping up on her.

She began the hour with her usual complaint of fantastic nightmares populated by grotesque forms whose exact description and activities always eluded her. These dreams occurred every night, she said, and interfered with her rest. She would awaken in terror from one, often aroused by her own frightened screams, only to have another of the same kind as soon as she fell asleep again. They were weird dreams, she claimed, and left her with only vague memories

122

in the morning of surrealistic scenes, faceless figures, and nameless obscenities just beyond the perimeters of recall. Water—endless, slow-moving stretches of it, or torrential cascades that beat upon her with the fury of whips; footsteps—the haunting, inexorable beat of a disembodied pair of shoes mercilessly following her through empty corridors, or the mad staccato of an angry mob of pursuers; and laughter—the echoing hysteria of a lone madwoman's howl of mockery, or the shrieking, derisive chorus of countless lunatics: these three elements were never absent from her nighttime gallery of horrors.

"But you can't remember anything more?" I asked.

"Nothing definite—only water again, and being chased, and the sound of laughter."

"Yet you speak of odd shapes, rooms, landscapes, action of some sort, scenes. . . . Describe them."

"I can't," she said, covering her eyes with her hands. "Please don't keep after me so. I'm telling you everything I remember. Maybe they're so terrible I have to forget them—my dreams, I mean."

"What else could you mean?" I entered quickly.

She shrugged. "I don't know. My memories, I guess."

"Any particular memory?"

"They're all terrible. . . ."

I waited for her to continue, observing meanwhile that her hands were no longer over her eyes but interlocked tightly over her forehead, the knuckles slowly whitening and the fingers flushing as she increased their pressure against each other.

"I'm thinking," she began, "about the night my father left. Have I ever told you about it?"

. . . It was raining outside. The supper dishes had just been cleared away; Laura and her brother were sitting at

123

the dining-room table doing their homework. In the kitchen Freda, the oldest child, was washing up. Their mother had moved her wheel chair into the front bedroom, where she was listening to the radio. The apartment, a railroad flat on the edge of the factory district, was cold and damp. A chill wind from the river penetrated the windows, whistling through newspapers that had been stuffed into cracks around the frames. Laura's hands were stiff with cold. From time to time she would put her pencil down and blow on her fingers or cross her arms, inserting her hands beneath the two sweaters she wore and pressing them into her armpits. Sometimes, just for fun and out of boredom with her sixth-grade geography lesson, she would expel her breath toward the lamp in the middle of the table, pretending the cloud it made was smoke from an invisible cigarette. Across from her Little Mike, intent on forming fat letters according to the copybook models before him, seemed unaware of the cold as he labored. Laura could tell which letter of the alphabet he was practicing from watching his mouth as lips and tongue traced familiar patterns.

When the door opened, Little Mike glanced up at her. Their eyes met in a secret communication of recognition and fear as heavy footsteps came down the hall. Bending again to their lessons, they now only pretended to work. In the kitchen Freda closed the tap so that she, too, could listen.

In a moment, they heard their father's grunting hello and a mumbled reply in kind from their mother. Then there was a creak of the springs as he sat heavily on the bed, followed by the sharp noise of his big shoes falling to the floor when he kicked them off. The bedsprings groaned again as he stood up.

"Peasant," they heard their mother say over the music

124

from the radio, "if you're not going to bed, wear your shoes. It's cold in here."

"Let me alone," he replied. "I'm not cold."

" 'I'm not cold,' " their mother mimicked. "Of course you're not cold. Why should you be? If I had a bellyful of whisky I wouldn't be cold either."

"Don't start that again, Anna," he said. "I'm tired."

"Tired," she mocked. "And from what are you tired?— Not from working, that's for sure."

"Oh, shut up, Anna," he said wearily over his shoulder as he walked through the doorway. Behind him there was the click of the dial as their mother shut off the radio, then the rasping sound of her wheel chair following him into the dining room.

Laura looked up at her father and smiled. He bent to brush his lips against the cheek she offered. The stiff hairs of his thick mustache scraped her skin and the smell of whisky made her slightly dizzy. Straightening, he ruffled Little Mike's hair with one huge hand, while with the other he pulled a chair away from the table.

"Freda!" he called as he sat down.

The older girl came to the door, smoothing her hair with both hands. "Yes, Papa," she answered.

"Get the old man something to eat, huh?" he asked.

Anna wheeled herself into the space between the table and the open kitchen door where Freda stood. "There's nothing here for you," she said. "You want to eat, come home when supper's ready. This ain't a restaurant."

Ignoring her, he spoke over her head to Freda. "Do like I said, get me some supper."

As Freda turned to obey, Anna shouted at her. "Wait! Don't listen to him!" She glared balefully at her husband, her thin face twisted with hate. When she spoke, the veins in her long neck stood out and her whole shrunken body trembled. "Bum! You come home to eat when you've spent all the money on those tramps. You think I don't know. Where've you been since yesterday? Don't you know you've got a family?"

"Anna," he said, "I told you to shut up."

"I'm not shutting up. . . . You don't care what happens to us. You don't care if we're cold or starving or what. All you think about is the lousy whores you give your money to. Your wife and children can rot for all it matters to you."

"Anna," he started to say, "the kids . . ."

"The kids," she screamed. "You think they don't know what kind of a rotten father they've got? You think they don't know where you go when you don't come home?"

He slammed his palm down on the table and stood up.

"Enough!" he yelled. "I don't have to listen to that. Now keep quiet!"

He started for the kitchen. Anticipating him, Anna whirled her chair across the entrance. "Where're you going?" she asked.

"If you won't get me something to eat I'll get it myself."

"No you won't," she said. "There's nothing in there for you."

"Get out of my way, Anna," he said menacingly, "I want to go in the kitchen."

"When you bring home money for food you can go in the kitchen," she said.

His face darkened and his hands clenched into fists.

"Cripple!" he spat. "Move away or I'll——"

Her laugh was short and bitter. "You'll what? Hit me? Go ahead—hit the cripple! What're you waiting for?"

Framed in the doorway they faced each other, frozen in a tableau of mutual hatred. Behind the father Laura and

126

Little Mike sat stiffly, eyes wide and bodies rigid. In the silence that followed Anna's challenge they heard the rain slap against the windows.

Their father's hands relaxed slowly. "If you don't move out of the way," he said evenly, "I'm getting out of this house and I'm never coming back."

"So go," Anna said, leering up at him. "Who wants you here anyway?"

Like a statue, he stood still for a long minute; then he turned and walked swiftly toward the bedroom, followed by their eyes. Now the tense quiet was broken by the noises he made as he moved around the next room, and shadows, cast by his tall figure, crossed and recrossed the threshold.

On Anna's face, when she became aware of what he was doing, the look of triumph gave place to alarm. Her bony fingers clutched the wheels of her chair. Hastily, she propelled herself around the table. In the doorway, she stopped.

"Mike," she said, "what're you doing?"

There was no answer—only the sound of the bedsprings, twice, and the firm stamp of his shoes against the naked floorboards.

"Mike"—her voice was louder this time and tremulous with fright—"where're you going?—Wait!"

The wheel chair raced into the bedroom, beyond sight of the children. They listened, their chests aching with terror.

She clutched at his coat. "Mike. Wait, Mike," she cried. "Please don't go. I didn't mean it. Please. . . . Come back. Come into the kitchen. I was only fooling, Mike. Don't go."

He pulled away from her, lifting her body from the chair. Her hands broke the fall as useless legs collapsed. The outer door slammed. Then there was the slapping sound of rain again between her heavy sobs. . . .

127

"—He meant it," Laura said. "I guess she went too far that time. He never did come back. Once in a while he'd send a few dollars in a plain envelope. On my next birthday I got a box of salt-water taffy from Atlantic City. . . . But we never saw him again."

She fumbled with the catch on her purse and groped inside for a handkerchief. Tears were streaming from the corners of her eyes. Some caught on the lobes of her ears and hung there like brilliant pendants. Idly, I wondered if they tickled.

She dabbed at her eyes, then blew her nose noisily. Her bosom rose and fell unevenly. The room was quiet. I glanced at my watch.

"Well?" she said.

"Well what?" I asked.

"Why don't you say something?"

"What should I say?"

"You might at least express some sympathy."

"For whom?"

"For me, of course!"

"Why only you?" I asked. "What about Freda, or Little Mike, or your mother? Or even your father?"

"But I'm the one who's been hurt most by it," she said petulantly. "You know that. You should feel sorry for me."

"Is that why you told me this story . . . so that I'd feel sorry for you?"

She turned on the couch and looked at me, her face drawn in a grimace of absolute malice.

"You don't give an inch, do you?" she said.

"You don't want an inch, Laura," I responded quietly. "You want it all . . . from me, from everybody."

"What d'you mean?" she asked.

"Well, for example, the story you just told. Of course

it's a dreadful one, and anyone hearing it would be moved, but——"

"—But you're not," she almost spat. "Not you. Because you're not human. You're a stone—a cold stone. You give nothing. You just sit there like a goddam block of wood while I tear my guts out!" Her voice, loaded with odium, rose to a trembling scream. "Look at you!" she cried. "I wish you could see yourself like I see you. You and your lousy objectivity! Objectivity, my eye! Are you a man or a machine? Don't you ever *feel* anything? Do you have blood or ice water in your veins? Answer me! Goddam you, answer me!"

I remained silent.

"You see?" she shouted. "You say nothing. Must I die to get a word out of you? What d'you want from me?"

She stood up. "All right," she said. "Don't say anything. . . . Don't give anything. I'm going. I can see you don't want me here. I'm going—and I'm not coming back." With a swirl of her skirt she rushed from the room.

Curious, I reflected, how well she enacted the story she had just told. I wondered if she knew it too?

Laura came back, of course—four times each week for the next two years. During the first year she made only few—and those very minor—advances so far as her symptoms were concerned, particularly the symptoms of depression and sporadic overeating. These persisted: indeed, for several months following the "honeymoon" period of psychoanalysis—when, as usual, there was a total remission of all symptoms and Laura, like so many patients during this pleasant time, believed herself "cured"—her distress increased. The seizures of abnormal appetite became more frequent, and the acute depressions not only occurred closer to each other in time but were of greater intensity. So, on the surface, it seemed that treatment was not helping my patient very much, even that it might be making her worse. But I knew—and so did Laura—that subtle processes had been initiated by her therapy, and that these were slowly, but secretly, advancing against her neurosis.

This is a commonplace of treatment, known only to those who have undergone the experience of psychoanalysis and those who practice the art. Externally, all appears to be the same as it was before therapy, often rather worse; but in the mental underground, unseen by any observer and inaccessible to the most probing investigation, the substructure of the personality is being affected. Insensibly but deliberately the foundations of neurosis are being weakened while, at the same time, there are being erected new and more durable supports on which, eventually, the altered personality can rest. Were this understood by the critics of psychoanalysis (or better still, by friends and relatives of analysands who understandably complain of the lack of evident progress), many current confusions about the process would disappear, and a more rational discussion of its merits as a form of therapy would be made possible.

For a year, then, Laura seemed to be standing still or losing ground. Chiefly, as in the episode I have already related, she reviewed her past and, in her sessions with me, either immediately or soon after, acted out their crucial or formative aspects. My consulting room became a stage on which she dramatized her life: my person became the target against which she directed the sad effects of her experience. In this manner she sought compensation for past frustrations, utilizing the permissive climate of therapy to obtain benefits she had missed, satisfactions that had been denied, and comforts she had lacked. Since the total effect of this pattern of

130

emotional damming had been to cut her off from the many real satisfactions life offered, and to force her energies and talents into unproductive and even self-destructive channels, I allowed her, for that first year, almost endless opportunity for the "drainage" she required. The idea behind my attitude of complete permissiveness in therapy was to hold up to her a mirror of her behavior and to let her see not only the extravagance of the methods she used to obtain neurotic gratification, but also the essential hollowness, the futility and the infantilism of the desires she had been pursuing by such outlandish methods all of her life. Finally, the procedure was designed to illustrate, in sharpest perspective, the impossibility of securing basic, long-lasting and solid satisfactions from her accustomed modes of behavior. The latter aim, of course, set definite limits on my responsiveness to her conduct: I had to be careful to measure out to her, at the proper time and in correct amounts, the rewards she deserved when these were due her as a consequence of mature behavior toward mature goals.

Yes, this first year with Laura was a trying one, not only for her but for her analyst. I often wished she had chosen someone else to take her troubles to, and could hardly help hoping, on those many occasions when she threatened to break off treatment, that I would never see her again.

One episode from this time haunts me. I set it down here to show the strain she placed me under as much as to illustrate my technique with her and the weird dynamics of her neurosis that were uncovered by this technique.

According to my notes, what I am about to tell took place in the eleventh month of psychoanalysis. By that time the pattern of treatment had stabilized, I was in possession of most of the accessible facts of Laura's life, and the more obvious psychodynamics of her personality disorder were

131

known to us. She, meanwhile, was in a period of relative quiet and contentment. It had been a month or more since her last attack, her job at the Gallery was going well, and she had recently formed a promising relationship with an eligible young man. It was on the theme of this affair that the first of these two crucial hours began, for Laura was deeply concerned about it and wished ardently that it might develop into something more rewarding and more lasting than her many previous romances.

"I don't want to foul this one up," she said, "but I'm afraid I'm going to. I need your help desperately."

"In what way d'you think you might foul it up?" I asked.

"Oh," she replied airily, "by being my usual bitchy self. You know—you ought to since you pointed it out; you know how possessive I get, how demanding I become. But I'd like, just for a change, not to be that way. For once I'd like to have a love affair work out well for me."

"You mean you're thinking of matrimony?" I asked.

She laughed brightly. "Well," she said, "if you must know, I've had a few choice daydreams—fantasies, you'd probably call them—about marrying Ben. But that's not what I've got my heart set on now. What I want is love— I want to give it and I want to get it."

"If that attitude is genuine," I said, "you don't need my help in your affair."

She ground out the cigarette she was smoking against the bottom of the ash tray with short, angry jabs.

"You're horrible," she complained, "just horrible. Here I tell you something that I think shows real progress, and right away you throw cold water on it."

"What d'you think shows progress?"

"Why my recognition of giving, of course. I hope you noticed that I put it first."

"I did."

"And doesn't that mean something to you? Doesn't that show how far I've come?"

"It does," I said, "if it's genuine."

"Goddammit!" she flared. "You call *me* insatiable; *you're* the one who's never satisfied. But I'll show you yet."

She lit another cigarette and for the next few moments smoked in silence. Quite naturally my skepticism had shaken her confidence somewhat, as I had meant it to do, since I knew from experience how much she was given to these pat, semianalytical formulations that were consciously designed to impress as well as mislead me. I was just considering the wisdom of pursuing the topic she had opened and getting her somehow to explore her real goals in this new relationship when she began talking again.

"Anyhow," she said, "that's not what I wanted to talk about today. I had a dream. . . . Shall I tell you about it?"

I have found that when a patient uses this way of presenting a dream—announcing it first, then withholding until the analyst asks for it; actually dangling it like some tantalizing fruit before the analyst's eyes but insisting he reach out for it—the analyst had better listen closely. For this particular mode of dream presentation signifies the special importance of the dream, and it can be anticipated that it holds some extraordinarily meaningful clue to the patient's neurosis. Unconsciously, the patient, too, "knows" this, and by the use of the peculiar formula communicates his inarticulate but nonetheless high estimate of the dream's value. More than this, he is offering the dream, when he invites attention to it this way, as a gift to the analyst, a gift that has implications extending far beyond the dream itself and including the possibility of surrendering an entire area of neurotic functioning. His reservations about giving up a

133

piece of his neurosis and the gratifications he has been receiving from it are betrayed by his use of the "shall I tell you about it?": he wants assurance, in advance, that the sacrifice will be worth while, that the analyst will appreciate (and love him for) it, and that he (the patient) will experience an equal amount of gratification from the newer, healthier processes which will henceforth replace the old. For this reason the analyst must be wary of reaching for the tempting fruit being offered him: to grasp at it would be to rob his patient of the painful but necessary first steps toward responsible self-hood, and to commit himself to bargains and promises he has no right to make.

Therefore, when Laura held out the gift of her dream, although I was most eager to hear it, I responded with the evasive but always handy reminder of the "basic rule": "Your instructions have always been to say what comes to you during your hours here. If you're thinking of a dream, tell it."

"Well," she said, "this is what I dreamed. . . . I was in what appeared to be a ballroom or a dance hall, but I knew it was really a hospital. A man came up to me and told me to undress, take all my clothes off. He was going to give me a gynecological examination. I did as I was told but I was very frightened. While I was undressing, I noticed that he was doing something to a woman at the other end of the room. She was sitting or lying in a funny kind of contraption with all kinds of levers and gears and pulleys attached to it. I knew that I was supposed to be next, that I would have to sit in that thing while he examined me. Suddenly he called my name and I found myself running to him. The chair or table—whatever it was—was now empty, and he told me to get on it. I refused and began to cry. It started to rain—great big drops of rain. He pushed me to the floor and spread my legs for the examination. I turned over on my stomach and began to scream. I woke myself up screaming."

Following the recital Laura lay quietly on the couch, her eyes closed, her arms crossed over her bosom.

"Well," she said after a brief, expectant silence, "what does it mean?"

"Laura," I admonished, "you know better than that. Associate, and we'll find out."

"The first thing I think of is Ben," she began. "He's an interne at University, you know. I guess that's the doctor in the dream—or maybe it was you. Anyhow, whoever it was, I wouldn't let him examine me."

"Why not?"

"I've always been afraid of doctors . . . afraid they might hurt me."

"How will they hurt you?"

"I don't know. By jabbing me with a needle, I guess. That's funny. I never thought of it before. When I go to the dentist I don't mind getting a needle; but with a doctor it's different. . . ." Here I noticed how the fingers of both hands clutched her arms at the elbows while her thumbs nervously smoothed the inner surfaces of the joints. "I shudder when I think of having my veins punctured. I'm always afraid that's what a doctor will do to me."

"Has it ever been done?"

She nodded. "Once, in college, for a blood test. I passed out cold."

"What about gynecological examinations?"

"I've never had one. I can't even bear to think of someone poking around inside me." Again silence; then, "Oh," she said, "I see it now. It's sex I'm afraid of. The doctor in the dream *is* Ben. He wants me to have intercourse, but it scares me and I turn away from him. That's true. . . . The other night after the concert he came to my apartment. I made coffee for us and we sat there talking. It was wonderful—so peaceful, just the two of us. Then he started to make love to me. I loved it—until it came to having intercourse. I stopped him there: I had to; I became terrified. He probably thinks I'm a virgin—or that I don't care for him enough. But it isn't that. I do—and I want him to love me. Oh, Dr. Lindner, that's why I need your help so much now. . . ."

"But other men have made love to you," I reminded her.

"Yes," she said, sobbing now, "but I only let them as a last resort, as a way of holding on to them a little longer. And if you'll remember, I've only had the real thing a few times. Mostly I've made love to the man—satisfied him somehow. I'd do anything to keep them from getting inside me— poking into me . . . like the needle, I guess."

"But why, Laura?"

"I don't know," she cried, "I don't know. Tell me."

"I think the dream tells you," I said.

"The dream I just told you?"

"Yes. . . . There's a part of it you haven't considered. What comes to your mind when you think of the other woman in the dream, the woman the doctor was examining before you?"

"The contraption she was sitting in," Laura exclaimed. "It was like a—like a wheel chair—my mother's wheel chair! Is that right?"

"Very likely," I said.

"But why would he be examining *her?* What would that mean?"

"Well, think of what that kind of examination signifies for you."

"Sex," she said. "Intercourse—that's what it means. So that's what it is—that's what it means! Intercourse put my mother in the wheel chair. It paralyzed her. And I'm afraid that's what it will do to me. So I avoid it—because I'm scared it will do the same thing to me. . . . Where did I ever get such a crazy idea?"

—Like so many such "ideas" all of us have, this one was born in Laura long before the age when she could think for herself. It arose out of sensations of terror when she would awaken during the night, shocked from sleep by the mysterious noises her parents made in their passion, and incapable yet of assembling these sounds into a design purporting the tender uses of love. The heavy climate of hate, the living antagonism between her parents, made this impossible; so the sounds in the night—the "Mike, you're hurting me," the moans and cries, the protestations, even the laughter—impressed upon her the darker side of their sex, the brutish animality of it and the pain. And when the disease struck her mother a natural bridge of associations was formed between the secret drama that played itself out while Laura slept—or sometimes awakened her to fright —and the final horror of the body imprisoned on the chair.

I explained this to Laura, documenting my explanation with material the analysis had already brought out. For her, the interpretation worked a wonder of insight. Obvious as it may seem to us, to Laura, from whom it had been withheld by many resistances and defenses, it came as a complete surprise. Almost immediately, even before she quit the couch at the end of that hour, she felt a vast relief from the pressure of many feelings that had tormented her until that very day. The idea that sexual love was impossible for her, the idea that she was so constructed physically that the joys of love would forever be denied her, feelings of self-dissatisfaction, and numerous other thoughts and emotions

137

collected around the central theme of sex—these vanished as if suddenly atomized.

"I feel free," Laura said as she rose from the couch when time was called. "I think this has been the most important hour of my analysis." At the door she paused and turned to me with moist, shining eyes. "I knew I could count on you," she said. "And I'm very grateful—believe me."

When she left, in the ten-minute interval between patients during which I ordinarily make notes, attend to messages or read, I reviewed the hour just ended. I, too, had a feeling of satisfaction and relief from it. And while I did not consider it to have been her most important hour—for the analyst's standards are markedly different from the patient's—nevertheless I did not underestimate its potential for the eventual solution of Laura's difficulties. I therefore looked forward to her next hour with pleasurable anticipation, thinking that the mood in which she had departed would continue and hoping she would employ it to stabilize her gains.

The session I have just described took place on a Saturday. On Monday, Laura appeared at the appointed time. The moment I saw her in the anteroom I knew something had gone wrong. She sat dejectedly, chin cupped in her hands, a light coat carelessly draped about her shoulders. When I greeted her, she raised her eyes listlessly.

"Ready for me?" she asked in a toneless voice.

I nodded and motioned her into the next room. She stood up wearily, dropping the coat on the chair, and preceded me slowly. As I closed the door behind us, she flopped on the couch sideways, her feet remaining on the floor. In the same moment she raised one arm to her head and covered her brow with the back of her hand. The other arm dangled over the side of the couch.

138

"I don't know why we bother," she said in the same flat voice.

I lit a cigarette and settled back in my chair to listen.

She sighed. "Aren't you going to ask me what's wrong?"

"There's no need to ask," I said. "You'll tell me in due time."

"I guess I will," she said, sighing again.

She lifted her feet from the floor, then squirmed to find a more comfortable position. Her skirt wrinkled under her and for some moments she was busy with the tugging and pulling women usually go through in their first minutes of each session. Under her breath she muttered impatient curses. At last she was settled.

"I don't have to tell you I went to bed with Ben, do I?" she asked.

"If that's what you're thinking of," I said.

"I think you must be a voyeur," she commented acidly after another pause. "That's probably the way you get your kicks."

I said nothing.

"Probably why you're an analyst, too," she continued. "Sublimating . . . isn't that the word? Playing Peeping Tom with your ears. . . ."

"Laura," I asked, "why are you being so aggressive?"

"Because I hate you," she said. "I hate your guts."

"Go on."

She shrugged. "That's all. I've got nothing more to say. I only came here today to tell you how much I despise you. I've said it and I'm finished. . . . Can I go now?" She sat up and reached for her purse.

"If that's what you want to do," I said.

"You don't care?" she asked.

"Care isn't the right word," I said. "Of course I'll be

139

sorry to see you leave. But, as I said, if that's what you want to do . . ."

"More double talk," she sighed. "All right. The hell with it. I'm here and I may as well finish out the hour—after all, I'm paying for it." She fell back on the couch and lapsed into silence again.

"Laura," I said, "you seem very anxious to get me to reject you today. Why?"

"I told you—because I hate you."

"I understand that. But why are you trying to make *me* reject *you?*"

"Do we have to go through that again?" she asked. "Because that's my pattern—according to you. I try to push people to the point where they reject me, then I feel worthless and sorry for myself, and find a good excuse to punish myself. Isn't that it?"

"Approximately. But why are you doing it here today?"

"You must be a glutton for punishment, too," she said. "How many times must I say it?—I hate you, I loathe you, I despise you. Isn't that sufficient?"

"But why?"

"Because of what you made me do over the week end."

"With Ben?"

"Ben!" she said contemptuously. "Of course not. What's that got to do with it? All that happened was that I went to bed with him. We slept together. It was good . . . wonderful. For the first time in my life I felt like a woman."

"Then what . . . ?" I started to say.

"—Keep quiet!" she interrupted. "You wanted to know why I hate you and I'm telling you. It's got nothing to do with Ben or what happened Saturday night. It's about my mother. What we talked about last time . . . that's why I hate you so. She's haunted me all week end. Since Saturday I can't get her out of my mind. I keep thinking about her—the awful life she had. And the way I treated her. Because you forced me to, I remembered things, terrible things I did to her . . . That's why I hate you—for making me remember." She turned on her side and looked at me over her shoulder. "And you," she continued, "you bastard . . . you did it purposely. You fixed it so I'd remember how rotten I was to her. I've spent half my life trying to forget her and that goddam wheel chair. But no; you won't let me. You brought her back from the grave to haunt me. That's why I hate you so!"

This outburst exhausted Laura. Averting her head once more, she lay quietly for some minutes. Then she reached an arm behind her.

"Give me the Kleenex," she commanded.

I gave her the box of tissues from the table by my chair. Removing one, she dabbed at her eyes.

"Let me have a cigarette," she said, reaching behind her again.

I put my cigarettes and a box of matches in her hand. She lit up and smoked.

"It's funny," she said. "Funny how I've clung to everything I could find to keep on hating her. You see, I always blamed her for what happened. I always thought it was her fault my father left us. I made it out that she drove him away with her nagging and complaining. I've tried to hide from myself the fact that he was just no good—a lazy, chicken-chasing, selfish son-of-a-bitch. I excused him for his drinking and his neglect of us all those years. I thought, 'Why not? Why shouldn't he run around, stay out all night, have other women? After all, what good was she to him with those useless legs and dried-up body?' I pushed out of my head the way he was before . . . before she got

141

sick. The truth is he was never any different, always a bum. Even when I was small he was no good, no good to her and no good to us. But I loved him—God! how I loved that man. I could hardly wait for him to come home. Drunk, sober—it didn't matter to me. He made a fuss over me and that's why I loved him. She said I was his favorite: I guess I was. At least he made over me more than the others.

"When I'd hear them fighting, I always blamed her. 'What's she picking on him for?' I'd think. 'Why doesn't she let him alone?' And when he went away, I thought it was her fault. Ever since then, until Saturday, I thought it was her fault. And I made her suffer for it. I did mean things to her, things I never told you about, things I tried to forget—did forget—until this week end. I did them to punish her for kicking him out, for depriving me of his love. His love!

"Would you like to hear one of the things I did? I've thought this one over for two days. . . . Maybe if I tell you I can get rid of it."

. . . Everyday on the way home from school she played the same game with herself. That was the reason she preferred to walk home alone. Because what if it happened when the other kids were around? How would she explain it to them? As far as they were concerned she didn't have a father. Even on the high-school admission blank, where it said: "Father—living or dead—check one," she had marked a big X over "dead." So what would she say if, suddenly, he stepped out of a doorway, or came around a corner, or ran over from across the street—and grabbed her and kissed her like he used to? Could she say, "Girls, this is my father?" Of course not! It was better to walk home alone, like this, pretending he was in that alley near the bottom of the hill, or standing behind the coal truck, or hiding behind the news-

142

stand by the subway entrance . . . or that those footsteps behind her—the ones she kept hearing but there was no one there when she turned around—were his footsteps.

The game was over. It ended in the hallway of the tenement house, the same house they had lived in all of her life. If he wasn't here, in the smelly vestibule, on the sagging stairs, or standing expectantly on the first-floor landing in front of their door, the game had to end. And he wasn't: he never was. . . .

She heard the radio as she climbed the stairs, and her insides contracted in a spasm of disgust. "The same thing," she thought, "the same darned thing. Why can't it be different for once, just for once?" With her shoulder she pushed open the door. It closed behind her with a bang; but Anna, sleeping in her chair as usual, hardly stirred.

Laura put her books down on the dresser, then switched the dial of the radio to "off" with a hard, vicious twist of her fingers. Crossing the room she opened the closet, hung up her coat, and slammed the door hard, thinking, "So what if it wakes her? I hope it does!" But it didn't.

On the way to the rear of the apartment she glanced briefly at her mother. In the wheel chair Anna slumped like an abandoned rag doll. Her peroxided hair, showing gray and brown at the roots where it was parted, fell over her forehead. Her chin was on her breast, and from one corner of her mouth a trickle of spittle trailed to the collar of the shabby brown dress. The green sweater she wore was open; it hung about her thin shoulders in rumpled folds, and from its sleeves her skinny wrists and the fingers tipped with bright red nails protruded like claws of a chicken, clutching the worn arms of the chair. Passing her, Laura repressed an exclamation of contempt.

In the kitchen Laura poured herself a glass of milk and

stood drinking it by the drain. When she had finished, she rinsed the glass under the tap. It fell from her hand and shattered against the floor.

"Is that you, Laura?" Anna called.

"Yeah."

"Come here. I want you to do something for me."

Laura sighed. "O.K. As soon as I clean up this mess."

She dried her hands and walked into the front room. "What is it?" she asked.

Anna motioned with her head. "Over there, on the dresser," she said. "The check from the relief came. I wrote out the store order. You can stop on your way back and give the janitor the rent."

"All right," Laura said wearily. She took her coat from the closet. At the door to the hall she paused and turned to face Anna, who was already fumbling with the radio dial. "Anything else?" she asked, playing out their bi-monthly game.

Anna smiled. "Yes," she said. "I didn't put it on the store list, but if they have some of those chocolate-covered caramels I like . . ."

Laura nodded and closed the door. Music from the radio chased her downstairs.

When she returned, laden with packages, she stopped in the bedroom only momentarily to turn down the volume of the radio. "The least you can do is play it quietly," she muttered. "I could hear it a block away."

In the kitchen, still wearing her coat, she disposed of the groceries.

"Did you get everything, Laura?" Anna called.

"Yeah."

"Pay the rent?"

"Uh-huh."

144

"Did they have any of those caramels?"

This time Laura didn't answer. Somewhere, deep inside, the low-burning flame of hate flickered to a new height.

"Laura!" Anna called.

"What d'you want?" the girl shouted angrily.

"I asked if you got my candy."

About to reply, Laura's gaze fell to the remaining package on the porcelain-topped kitchen table. It seemed to hypnotize her, holding her eyes fast and drawing her hand toward its curled neck. Slowly her fingers untwisted the bag and plunged inside. When they emerged, they carried two squares of candy to her mouth. Without tasting, she chewed and swallowed rapidly.

Behind her Laura heard the shuffle of wheels. She turned to find Anna crossing the threshold of the bedroom. Snatching up the bag, the girl hurried into the dining room and faced her mother across the oval table.

"D'you have the candy?" Anna asked.

Laura nodded and held up the sack.

"Give it here," Anna said, extending her hand.

Laura shook her head and put the hand with the paper bag behind her back. Puzzled, Anna sent her chair around the table toward the girl, who waited until her mother came near, then moved quickly to the opposite side, placing the table between them again.

"What kind of nonsense is this?" Anna asked. In reply, Laura put another piece of candy in her mouth.

"Laura!" Anna demanded. "Give me my candy!" She gripped the wheels of her chair and spun them forward. It raced around the table after the girl, who skipped lightly before it. Three times Anna circled the table, chasing the elusive figure that regarded her with narrowed eyes. Ex-

145

hausted, finally, she stopped. Across from her, Laura stuffed more candy into her mouth and chewed violently.

"Laura," Anna panted, "what's got into you? Why are you doing this?"

Laura took the bag from behind her back and held it temptingly over the table. "If you want it so bad," she said, breathing hard, "come get it." She shook the bag triumphantly. "See," she said, "it's almost all gone. You'd better hurry."

Inside, at the very core of her being, the flame was leaping. A warm glow of exultation swept through her, filling her body with a sense of power and setting her nerves on fire. She felt like laughing, like screaming, like dancing madly. In her mouth the taste of chocolate was intoxicating.

Her mother whimpered. "Give me the candy. . . . Please, Laura."

Laura held the bag high. "Come and get it!" she screamed, and backed away slowly toward the front room.

Anna spun her chair in pursuit. By the time she reached the bedroom, Laura was at the door. She waited until her mother's chair came close, then she whirled and ran through, pulling the door behind her with a loud crash.

Leaning against the banister, Laura listened to the thud of Anna's fists against the wood and her sobs of angry frustration. The wild exhilaration mounted. Hardly conscious of her actions, she crammed the remaining candies into her mouth. Then, from deep in her body, a wave of laughter surged upward. She tried to stop it, but it broke through in a crazy tide of hilarity. The sound of this joyless mirth rebounded from the stair well and echoed from the ceiling of the narrow hallway—as it was to echo, thereafter, along with the sound of footsteps and falling rain, in her dreams. . . .

The weeks following the crucial hours I have just described were very difficult ones for Laura. As she worked through the guilt-laden memories now released from repression, her self-regard, never at any time very high, fell lower and lower. Bitterly, she told the ugly rosary of her pathetic past, not sparing herself (or me) the slightest detail. In a confessional mood, she recited all her faults of behavior—toward her family, her friends, her teachers, her associates—throughout the years. Under the influence of newly acquired but undigested insights the pattern of her sessions with me changed. No longer did she find it necessary to pour out the acid of her hate and contempt, to vilify and condemn me and the world for our lack of love for her. Now she swung the pendulum to the other side: everyone had been too nice to her, too tolerant; she didn't deserve anyone's good opinion, particularly mine.

In keeping with her new mood, Laura also changed the style of her life. She became rigidly ascetic in her dress, adopted a strict diet, gave up smoking, drinking, cosmetics, dancing and all other ordinary amusements. The decision to surrender the novel joys of sex with her lover, Ben, was hard to make, but, tight-lipped and grim with determination, she declared her intention to him and stuck by her word.

For my part, in these weeks of confession and penitential repentance I remained silent and still permissive, revealing nothing of my own thoughts or feelings. I neither commented on the "sins" Laura recounted nor the expiatory measures she employed to discharge them. Instead, as I listened, I tried to reformulate her neurosis in terms of the dynamic information available to us at that point. Naturally, I saw through the recent shift in analytic content and behavior: it was, of course, but a variant of the old design, only implemented by conscious, deliberate techniques.

147

Fundamentally, Laura was still Laura. That she now chose to destroy herself and her relationships in a more circumspect and less obvious fashion; that the weapons she now turned upon herself were regarded—at least by the world outside the analytic chamber—in the highest terms, altered not one whit the basic fact that the core of her neurosis, despite our work, remained intact. Laura, in short, was still profoundly disturbed, still a martyr to secret desires that had not been plumbed.

She did not think so—nor did her friends. As a matter of fact, they were astonished at what they called her "progress," and word reached me that my reputation in Baltimore —an intimate city where who is going to which analyst is always a lively topic at parties—had soared to new heights. And, indeed, to the casual observer Laura seemed improved. In the curious jargon of the analytic sophisticate, she was "making an adjustment." Her rigorous diet, her severity of manner and dress, her renunciation of all fleshly joys and amusements, her sobriety and devotion to "serious" pursuits, above all her maintenance of a "good" relationship with the eligible Ben (*without sex*, it was whispered)—these were taken as tokens of far-reaching and permanent alterations in personality due to the "miracle" of psychoanalysis. Those with whom she came in contact during this time of course never bothered to peer beneath the mask of public personality she wore. They were content to take her at face value. Because she no longer disrupted their gatherings with demonstrations of her well-known "bitchiness," because she no longer thrust her problems on them or called for their help in times of distress, they felt relieved in their consciences about her. In brief, without laboring the point, so long as Laura disturbed no one else and kept her misery to herself; and so long as she represented to her associates the passive

148

surrender to the mass ideal each one of them so desperately but fruitlessly sought, just so long were they impressed by the "new look" that Laura wore.

But we knew, Laura and I, that the battle had yet to be joined, for only we knew what went on behind the closed doors of 907 in the Latrobe Building. In this room the masks fell away: either they were discarded because here they could not hide the truth, or they were taken from her by the soft persuasion of continuous self-examination with insight. The first to go was the last she had assumed: the defensive mask of self-abnegation.

The time came when I found it necessary to call a halt to Laura's daily *mea culpas*, to put a stop to the marathon of confession she had entered at the beginning of her second year with me. Three factors influenced my decision to force her, at last, off the new course her analysis had taken. The first and most important of these was my perception of the danger implicit in this program of never-ending self-denunciation. As she searched her memory for fresh evidence of guilt, I could see how overwhelmed she was becoming by the enormity of her past behavior. Try as she might, I knew she could never salve her conscience by the penitential acts and renunciations she invented, and I feared the outcome of a prolonged contest between contrition and atonement: it could only lead to the further debility of her ego, to a progressive lowering of self-esteem which might wind up at a point I dared not think about.

The second and hardly less important reason why I felt I had to urge Laura away from this attempt to shrive herself in the manner she chose was the simple fact of its unproductiveness for therapy. As I have already said, this psychic gambit of self-abnegation only substituted one set of neurotic symptoms for another and left the basic patho-

149

logical structure untouched. Moreover, it provided precisely the same kind of neurotic satisfaction she had been securing all along by her old techniques. The martyrdom she now suffered by her own hand was equivalent to the self-pity formerly induced by the rejection she had unconsciously arranged to obtain from others. And while it is true that she no longer exercised hate, hostility and aggressive contempt outwardly, it was only the direction in which these negative elements were discharged that had been altered: they remained.

Finally, my decision was also influenced by sheer fatigue and boredom with what I knew to be only an act, a disguise of behavior and attitude adopted to squeeze the last ounce of neurotic gratification from me and the entire world which, by psychic extension from love-withholding parents, she viewed as rejective and denying. To tell the truth, I became tired of the "new" Laura, weary of her pious pretenses, and a trifle nauseated with the holier-than-thou manner she assumed. And while this was the least of my reasons for doing what I did, I hold it chiefly responsible for the almost fatal error in timing I committed when I finally acted on an otherwise carefully weighed decision to eject my patient from the analytic rut in which she was, literally, wallowing.

The session that precipitated the near catastrophe took place on a Thursday afternoon. Laura was the last patient I was to see that day, since I was taking the Congressional Limited to New York where I was scheduled to conduct a seminar that night and give a lecture on Friday. I was looking forward to the trip which, for me, represented a holiday from work and the first break in routine in many months. Something of this mood of impatience to get going and pleasurable anticipation must have been communicated to

Laura, for she began her hour with a hardly disguised criticism of my manner and appearance.

"Somehow," she said after composing herself on the couch, "somehow you seem different today."

"I do?"

"Yes." She turned to look at me. "Maybe it's because of the way you're dressed. . . . That's a new suit, isn't it?"

"No," I said, "I've worn it before."

"I don't remember ever seeing it." She resumed her usual position. "Anyway, you look nice."

"Thank you."

"I like to see people look nice," she continued. "When a person gets all dressed up, it makes them feel better. I think it's because they think other people will judge them on the basis of their outer appearance—and if the outer appearance is pleasing and nice, people will think what's behind is pleasing and nice, too—and being thought of that way makes you feel better. Don't you think so?"

I was lost in the convolutions of this platitude, but its inference was pretty clear.

"What exactly are you getting at?" I asked.

She shrugged. "It's not important," she said. "Just a thought . . ." There was a moment of silence, then, "Oh!" she exclaimed. "I know why you're all dressed up. . . . Today's the day you go to New York, isn't it?"

"That's right," I said.

"That means I won't see you on Saturday, doesn't it?"

"Yes. I won't be back until Monday."

"Is the lecture on Saturday?"

"No, the lecture's tomorrow, Friday."

"—But you're going to stay over until Monday. . . . Well, I think the rest will do you good. You need it. I think

151

everyone needs to kick up his heels once in a while, just get away, have some fun and forget everything—if he can."

The dig at my irresponsibility toward my patients, particularly Laura, and the implication that I was going to New York to participate in some kind of orgy, were not lost on me.

"I hate to miss an hour," Laura continued in the same melancholy tone she had been using since this meeting began. "Especially now. I feel I really need to come here now. There's so much to talk about."

"In that case," I said, "you should take more advantage of the time you're here. For example, you're not using this hour very well, are you?"

"Perhaps not," she said. "It's just that I feel this is the wrong time for you to be going away."

"Now look here, Laura," I said. "You've known about missing the Saturday hour for more than a week. Please don't pretend it's a surprise to you. And, besides, it's only one hour."

"I know," she sighed. "I know. But it feels like you're going away forever. . . . What if I should need you?"

"I don't think you will. . . . But if you should, you can call my home or the office here and they'll put you in touch with me."

I lit a cigarette and waited for her to go on. With the first inhalation, however, I began to cough. Laura again turned around.

"Can I get you something?" she asked. "A glass of water?"

"No, thank you," I answered.

"That cough of yours worries me," she said when the spasm had passed and I was once more quiet. "You should give up smoking. I did, you know. It's been two months since I had a cigarette. And my cough's all gone. I think that's

152

the best of it—no more coughing. I feel fine. You should really try it."

I continued to smoke in silence, wondering where she would take this theme. Before long, I found out.

"It wasn't easy. The first two weeks were agony, but I determined not to give in. After all, I had a reason. . . ."

"To stop coughing?" I suggested, permitting myself the small satisfaction of retaliating for her deliberate provocation of the past half hour.

"Of course not!" she exclaimed. "You know very well I had good reasons for giving up smoking—and other things too."

"What were they?" I asked.

"You of all people should know," she said.

"Tell me."

"Well—it's just that I want to be a better person. If you've been listening to everything I've said these past weeks you know how I used to behave. Now I want to make amends for it, to be different, better. . . ."

"And you think giving up smoking and so on will make you a better person?"

She fell silent. Glancing over at her, I noticed the rigidity of her body. Her hands, until now held loosely on her lap, were clenched into fists. I looked at my watch and cursed myself for a fool. Only ten minutes left and a train to catch! Why had I let myself rise to the bait? Why had I permitted this to come up now, when it couldn't be handled? Was there any way out, any way to avoid the storm I had assisted her to brew? I put my trust in the gods that care for idiots and took a deep breath.

"Well?" I asked.

"Nothing I do is right," she said hollowly. "There's no use trying. I just make it worse."

153

"What are you talking about?"

"Myself," she said. "Myself and the mess I make of everything. I try to do what's right—but I never can. I think I'm working it all out—but I'm not. I'm just getting in deeper and deeper. It's too much for me, too much. . . ."

When the hour ended, I rose and held the door open for her.

"I'll see you Monday," I said.

Her eyes were glistening. "Have a good time," she sighed.

On the train to New York I thought about Laura and the hour just ended, reviewing it word for word and wondering just where I had made my mistake. That I had committed a serious error I had no doubt, and it hardly needed Laura's abrupt change of mood to bring this to my attention. To mobilize guilt and anxiety just prior to a recess in therapy is in itself unwise. In this instance I had compounded the blunder by losing control over myself and responding, as I seldom do in the treatment situation, to criticism and provocation. I asked myself—had she touched some peculiarly sensitive chord in me? Am I so susceptible to faultfinding? Have I, all unaware, become especially tender on the subject of my incessant smoking? my cough? my responsibility to my patients? my appearance? Or was it, as I suspected then and am sure of now, that I had made the decision to contrive a directional change in Laura's analysis but had been incited to violate the timetable of therapy by an unexpected display of the fatuousness that had become her prevailing defense?

That evening I had dinner with friends and conducted the scheduled seminar, after which many of us gathered for a series of nightcaps and further discussion in a colleague's home. I had forgotten all about Laura by the time I returned to my hotel, and when the desk clerk gave me a message to call a certain long-distance operator in Baltimore, I thought it could concern only something personal at home or a communication from my office. I was surprised when Laura's voice came over the wire.

"Dr. Lindner?"

"Yes, Laura. What is it?"

"I've been trying to get you for hours."

"I'm sorry. Is something wrong?"

"I don't know. I just wanted to talk with you."

"What about?"

"About the way I feel. . . ."

"How do you feel?"

"Scared."

"Scared of what?"

"I don't know. Just scared, I guess. Of nothing in particular—just everything. . . . I don't like being alone."

"But you're alone most other nights, aren't you?" I asked.

"Yes . . . but somehow it's different tonight."

"Why?"

"Well, for one thing, you're not in Baltimore."

The line was silent as I waited for her to continue.

"And then," she said, "I think you're angry with me."

"Why do you think that?"

"The way I acted this afternoon. It was mean of me, I know. But I couldn't help it. Something was egging me on."

"What was it?"

"I don't know. I haven't figured it out. Something . . ."

"We'll talk about it Monday," I said.

More silence. I thought I heard noises as if she were crying.

"Do you forgive me?" she sobbed.

"We'll review the whole hour on Monday," I said, seeking a way out of this awkward situation. "Right now you'd better get to bed."

"All right," she said meekly. "I'm sorry I bothered you."

"No bother at all," I said. "Good night, Laura"—and hung up with relief.

I gave the lecture on Friday afternoon, and when it was over returned to my room for a nap before beginning my holiday with dinner in a favorite restaurant and a long-anticipated evening at the theater. In the quiet room, I bathed and lay down for a peaceful interlude of sleep. Hardly had I begun to doze when the phone rang. It was my wife, calling from Baltimore. Laura, she said, had slashed her wrists: I had better come home—quick. . . .

The doctor and I sat in the corner of the room, talking in whispers. On the bed, heavily sedated, Laura breathed noisily. Even in the dim light the pallor of her face was discernible, and I could see a faint white line edging her lips. On the blanket her hands lay limply. The white bandages at her wrists forced themselves accusingly on my attention. From time to time her hands twitched.

"I doubt that it was a serious attempt," the physician was saying, "although of course you never know. It's harder than you think, trying to get out that way. You've really got to mean it—you've got to mean it enough to saw away hard to get down where it counts. I don't think she tried very hard. The cut on the left wrist is fairly deep, but not deep enough, and the ones on the right wrist are superficial. There wasn't a hell of a lot of blood, either."

"I understand you got there awfully fast," I said.

"Pretty fast," he replied. "What happened was this: Right after she slashed herself she began screaming. A neighbor ran in and had the good sense to call me immediately. My office is in the same building, on the first floor, and I happened to be there at the time. I rushed upstairs, took a look at the cuts and saw they weren't too bad——"

"They were made with a razor blade, weren't they?" I interrupted.

"Yes," he said, and then continued, "so I slapped a couple of tourniquets on, phoned the hospital that I was sending her in, then called the ambulance. I followed it here to Sinai. In the Accident Room they cleaned her up and had her wrists sutured by the time I arrived. She was still quite excited, so I decided to put her in for a day or two. I gave her a shot of morphine and sent her upstairs."

"Who called my home?" I asked.

He shrugged. "I don't know. Before the ambulance came, her neighbor called Laura's sister and told her what happened and what I was going to do. I think the sister tried to get hold of you."

"I guess so," I said. "She knows Laura's in treatment with me."

"I don't envy you," he said. "She's a lulu."

"Why d'you say that?"

He shrugged and motioned toward the bed with a wave of his hand. "This kind of business, for one thing. Then the way she carried on until the shot took effect."

"What did she do?"

"Oh," he said vaguely, "she kept screaming and throwing herself around. Pretty wild." He stood up. "I don't think you've got anything to worry about as far as her physical condition goes, though. She'll be fine in the morning. Maybe a little groggy, that's all."

"I'm very grateful to you," I said.

"Not at all," he said on his way from the room. "There'll be some business with the police tomorrow. If you need me, just call."

Laura had her hour on Saturday—in the hospital. During it and many subsequent sessions we worked out the reasons

157

for her extravagant, self-destructive gesture. As the physician had observed, her act was hardly more than a dramatic demonstration without serious intent, although in the way of such things it could well have miscarried to a less fortunate conclusion. Its immediate purpose was to recall me from my holiday and to reawaken the sympathetic attention she believed herself to have prejudiced by her hostile provocativeness on Thursday. But the whole affair, we learned subsequently, had much deeper roots.

The motivation behind Laura's attempt at suicide was twofold. Unconsciously, it represented an effort to re-enact, with a more satisfying outcome, the desertion of her father; and, at the same time, it served the function of providing extreme penance for so-called "sins" of behavior and thought-crimes between the ages of twelve and twenty-four. So far as the first of these strange motivations is concerned, it is understandable how Laura interpreted my brief interruption of therapy as an abandonment similar to that abrupt and permanent earlier departure of her father. This time, however, as indicated by the phone call to my hotel on the night I left, she believed herself to have been at least in part responsible for it, to have driven him (in the person of the analyst) away. To call him back, her distraught mind conceived the suicidal act, which was nothing less than a frenzied effort—planned, so it appeared, but not executed, more than a decade before—to repeat the original drama but insure a different and more cordial ending.

The mad act was also powered dynamically by the fantastic arithmetic of confession and penance that Laura, like some demented accountant, had invented to discharge her guilty memories. As I had feared when the pattern became clear to me, the mental balance sheet she was keeping with her hourly testaments of culpability and the increasing asceticism of her life could never be stabilized. Self-abnegation had to lead to a martyrdom of some kind. My effort to prevent this miscarried—not because it was misconceived, but because it was so sloppily executed. My own unconscious needs—the residual infantilisms and immaturities within me—in this case subverted judgment and betrayed me into the commission of a timing error that could have cost Laura's life.

We both profited from this terrible experience and, in the end, it proved to have been something of a boon to each of us. I, of course, would have preferred to learn my lesson otherwise. As for Laura, she made a rapid recovery and returned to the analysis much sobered by her encounter with death. Apart from all else, the episode provided her with many genuine and useful insights, not the least of which were those that led her to abandon her false asceticism and to stop playing the role of the "well-analyzed," "adjusted" paragon among her friends.

The events just described furnished us with vast quantities of material for analysis in subsequent months. Particularly as it referred directly to the situation in psychoanalysis known technically as the "transference neurosis"—or the reflection in therapy of former patterns of relationship with early, significant figures in the life of the patient—the suicidal gesture Laura made led to an even deeper investigation of her existing neurotic attitudes and behavior. And as we dealt with this topic of transference—the organic core of every therapeutic enterprise; as we followed its meandering course through our sessions together, Laura rapidly made new and substantial gains. With every increase in her under-

159

standing another rich facet of personality was disclosed, and the burden of distress she had borne for so long became lighter and lighter.

The metamorphosis of Laura was a fascinating thing to observe. I, as the human instrument of changes that were taking place in her, was immensely gratified. Nevertheless, my pleasure and pride were incomplete, for I remained annoyingly aware that we had yet to find the explanation for the single remaining symptom that had so far evaded the influence of therapy. No progress at all had been made against the strange complaint which brought her into treatment: the seizures of uncontrollable hunger, the furious eating, and their dreadful effects.

I had my own theory about this stubborn symptom and was often tempted to follow the suggestion of a certain "school" of psychoanalysis and communicate my ideas to Laura. However, because I felt—and still feel—that such technique is theoretically unjustified—a reflection of the therapist's insecurity and impatience rather than a well-reasoned approach to the problems of psychotherapy— because I felt this way, I determined to curb my eagerness to bring Laura's chief symptom into focus by testing my interpretations on her. In adherence to methods in which I have been trained, therefore, I held my tongue and waited developments. Fortunately, they were not long in appearing; and when they did arrive, in one mighty tide of insight my patient's being was purged of the mental debris that had made her existence a purgatory.

Laura was seldom late for appointments, nor had she ever missed one without canceling for good cause well in advance. On this day, therefore, when she failed to appear at the appointed time I grew somewhat anxious. As the minutes passed, my concern mounted. Finally, after a half hour had sped and there was still no sign of Laura, I asked my secretary to call her apartment. There was no answer.

During the afternoon, caught up in work with other patients, I gave only a few passing thoughts to Laura's neglect to keep her hour or to inform me she would be absent. When I reminded myself of it at the close of the day, I tried, in a casual way, to recall her previous session and examine it for some clue to this unusual delinquency. Since none came readily, I pushed the matter from my mind and prepared to leave the office.

We were in the corridor awaiting the elevator when we heard the telephone. I was minded to let it ring, but Jeanne, more compulsive in such matters than I, insisted on returning to answer. While I held the elevator, she re-entered the office. A few moments later she reappeared, shrugging her shoulders in answer to my question.

"Must have been a wrong number," she said. "When I answered all I heard was a funny noise and then the line went dead."

I arrived home shortly after six o'clock and dressed to receive the guests who were coming for dinner. While in the shower, I heard the ringing of the telephone, which my wife answered. On emerging from the bathroom, I asked her who had called.

"That was the queerest thing," she said. "The party on the other end sounded like a drunk and I couldn't make out a word."

During dinner I was haunted by a sense of unease. While attending to the lively conversation going on around me, and participating in it as usual, near the edges of consciousness something nagged uncomfortably. I cannot say that I connected the two mysterious calls with Laura and her absence from the hour that day, but I am sure they contributed to the vague and fitful feelings I experienced. In any case, when the telephone again rang while we were having our coffee, I sprang from my place and rushed to answer it myself.

I lifted the receiver and said, "Hello?" Over the wire, in response, came a gurgling, throaty noise which, even in retrospect defies comparison with any sound I have ever heard. Unmistakably produced by the human voice, it had a gasping, breathless quality, yet somehow seemed animal in nature. It produced a series of meaningless syllables, urgent in tone but unidentifiable.

"Who is this?" I demanded.

There was a pause, then, laboriously, I heard the first long-drawn syllable of her name.

"Laura!" I said. "Where are you?"

Again the pause, followed by an effortful intake of breath and its expiration as if through a hollow tube: "Home . . ."

"Is something wrong?"

It seemed to come easier this time.

"Eat-ing."

"Since when?"

". . . . Don't—know."

"How d'you feel?" I asked, aware of the absurdity of the question but desperately at a loss to know what else to say.

"Aw-ful . . . No—more—food . . . Hun-gry . . ."

My mind raced. What could I do? What was there to do?

"Help—me," she said—and I heard the click of the instrument as it fell into its cradle.

"Laura," I said. "Wait!"—But the connection had been broken and my words echoed in my own ears. Hastily, I hung up and searched through the telephone directory for

162

her number. My fingers spun the dial. After an interval, I heard the shrill buzz of her phone. Insistently, it repeated itself, over and over. There was no answer.

I knew, then, what I had to do. Excusing myself from our guests, I got my car and drove to where Laura lived. On the way there, I thought about what some of my colleagues would say of what I was doing. No doubt they would be appalled by such a breach of orthodoxy and speak pontifically of "counter-transference," my "anxiety" at Laura's "acting out," and other violations of strict procedure. Well, let them. To me, psychoanalysis is a vital art that demands more of its practitioners than the clever exercise of their brains. Into its practice also goes the heart, and there are occasions when genuine human feelings take precedence over the rituals and dogmas of the craft.

I searched the mailboxes in the vestibule for Laura's name, then ran up the stairs to the second floor. In front of her door I paused and put my ear against the metal frame to listen. I heard nothing.

I pushed the button. Somewhere inside a chime sounded. A minute passed while I waited impatiently. I rang again, depressing the button forcefully time after time. Still no one came to the door. Finally, I turned the knob with one hand and pounded the panel with the flat of the other. In the silence that followed, I heard the noise of something heavy crashing to the floor, then the sibilant shuffling of feet.

I put my mouth close to the crack where door met frame. "Laura!" I called. "Open the door!"

Listening closely, I heard what sounded like sobs and faint moaning, then a voice that slowly pronounced the words, "Go—away."

I shook the knob violently. "Open up!" I commanded. "Let me in!"

The knob turned in my hand and the door opened. I pushed against it, but a chain on the jamb caught and held. In the dim light of the hallway, against the darkness inside, something white shone. It was Laura's face, but she withdrew it quickly.

"Go—away," she said in a thick voice.

"No."

"Please!"

She leaned against the door, trying to close it again. I put my foot in the opening.

"Take that chain off," I said with all the authority I could muster. "At once!"

The chain slid away and I walked into the room. It was dark, and I could make out only vague shapes of lamps and furniture. I fumbled along the wall for the light switch. Before my fingers found it, Laura, who was hardly more than an indistinguishable blur of whiteness by my side, ran past me into the room beyond.

I discovered the switch and turned on the light. In its sudden, harsh glare I surveyed the room. The sight was shocking. Everywhere I looked there was a litter of stained papers, torn boxes, empty bottles, open cans, broken crockery and dirty dishes. On the floor and on the tables large puddles gleamed wetly. Bits of food—crumbs, gnawed bones, fish-heads, sodden chunks of unknown stuffs—were strewn all about. The place looked as if the contents of a garbage can had been emptied in it, and the stench was sickening.

I swallowed hard against a rising wave of nausea and hurried into the room where Laura had disappeared. In the shaft of light that came through an archway, I saw a

164

rumpled bed, similarly piled with rubbish. In a corner, I made out the crouching figure of Laura.

By the entrance I found the switch and pressed it. As the light went on, Laura covered her face and shrank against the wall. I went over to her, extending my hands.

"Come," I said. "Stand up."

She shook her head violently. I bent down and lifted her to her feet. When she stood up, her fingers still hid her face. As gently as I could, I pulled them away. Then I stepped back and looked at Laura. What I saw, I will never forget.

The worst of it was her face. It was like a ceremonial mask on which some inspired maniac had depicted every corruption of the flesh. Vice was there, and gluttony; lust also, and greed. Depravity and abomination seemed to ooze from great pores that the puffed tautness of skin revealed.

I closed my eyes momentarily against this apparition of incarnate degradation. When I opened them, I saw the tears welling from holes where her eyes should have been. Hypnotized, I watched them course in thin streams down the bloated cheeks and fall on her nightgown. And then, for the first time, I saw it!

Laura was wearing a night robe of some sheer stuff that fell loosely from straps at her shoulders. Originally white, it was now soiled and stained with the evidences of her orgy. But my brain hardly registered the begrimed garment, except where it bulged below her middle in a sweeping arc, ballooning outward from her body as if she were pregnant.

I gasped with disbelief—and my hand went out automatically to touch the place where her nightgown swelled. My fingers encountered a softness that yielded to their pressure. Questioning, I raised my eyes to that caricature of a human face. It twisted into what I took for a smile. The mouth opened and closed to form a word that it labored to pronounce.

"Ba-by," Laura said.

"Baby?" I repeated. "Whose baby?"

"Lau-ra's ba-by. . . . Lo-ok."

She bent forward drunkenly and grasped her gown by the hem. Slowly she raised the garment, lifting it until her hands were high above her head. I stared at her exposed body. There, where my fingers had probed, a pillow was strapped to her skin with long bands of adhesive.

Laura let the nightgown fall. Swaying, she smoothed it where it bulged.

"See?" she said. "Looks—real—this way."

Her hands went up to cover her face again. Now great sobs shook her, and tears poured through her fingers as she cried. I led her to the bed and sat on its edge with her, trying to order the turmoil of my thoughts while she wept. Soon the crying ceased, and she bared her face again. Once more the lost mouth worked to make words.

"I—want—a—baby," she said, and fell over on the bed—asleep. . . .

I covered Laura with a blanket and went into the other room, where I remembered seeing a telephone. There, I called a practical nurse who had worked with me previously and whom I knew would be available. Within a half hour, she arrived. I briefed her quickly: the apartment was to be cleaned and aired: when Laura awakened, the doctor who lived downstairs was to be called to examine her and advise on treatment and diet: she was to report to me regularly, and in two days she was to bring Laura to my office. Then I left.

Although the night was cold I lowered the top on my car. I drove home slowly, breathing deeply of the clean air.

166

Two days later, while her nurse sat in the outer room, Laura and I began to put together the final pieces in the puzzle of her neurosis. As always, she had only a vague, confused memory of events during her seizure, recollecting them hazily through a fog of total intoxication. Until I recounted the episode, she had no clear remembrance of my visit and thought she had dreamed my presence in her rooms. Of the portion that concerned her pitiful imitation of pregnancy, not the slightest memorial trace remained.

It was clear that Laura's compelling desire was to have a child, that her feelings of emptiness arose from this desire, and that her convulsions of ravenous appetite were unconsciously designed to produce its illusory satisfaction. What was not immediately apparent, however, was why this natural feminine wish underwent such extravagant distortion in Laura's case, why it had become so intense, and why it had to express itself in a manner at once monstrous, occult and self-destructive.

My patient herself provided the clue to these focal enigmas when, in reconstructing the episode I had witnessed, she made a slip of the tongue so obvious in view of the facts that it hardly required interpretation.

It was about a week after the incident I have recorded. Laura and I were reviewing it again, looking for further clues. I was intrigued by the contrivance she wore that night to simulate the appearance of a pregnant woman, and asked for details about its construction. Laura could supply none. Apparently, she said, she had fashioned it in an advanced stage of her intoxication from food.

"Was this the first time you made anything like that?" I asked.

"I don't know," she said, somewhat hesitantly. "I can't be sure. Maybe I did and destroyed the thing before I came

167

out of the fog. It seems to me I remember finding something like you describe a couple of years ago after an attack, but I didn't know—or didn't want to know—what it was, so I just took it apart and forgot about it."

"You'd better look around the apartment carefully," I said, half joking. "Perhaps there's a spare hidden away someplace."

"I doubt it," she replied in the same mood. "I guess I have to mike a new baby every . . ." Her hand went over her mouth. "My God!" she exclaimed. "Did you hear what I just said?"

Mike was her father's name; and of course it was his baby she wanted. It was for this impossible fulfillment that Laura hungered—and now was starved no more. . . .

168

:
destiny's tot

ANTON

"If you want a picture of the future,
imagine a boot stamping on a human face
—forever."
—George Orwell, *Nineteen Eighty-
four*.

There is no better place to study and observe the psychopath than in a prison. Here, in a microcosm bounded by four stout walls, in a situation where his smallest activities are noticed, who he is and what he does emerge in glaring detail. His effect on others, too, is less subtle here than it is in the free world, and the very nature of the restraints placed upon him magnify his essential patterns. In a prison the masks psychopathy wears fall away; the meaningless distinctions that in the free world separate or classify men fade; and the remaining sediment is the pure stuff, the elemental ore, which requires no involved procedure of diagnostic chemistry to reveal what a person is.

I met Anton in the Federal Penitentiary in Lewisburg, Pennsylvania. For some years previous to our meeting I had been hearing of him, had seen his name and picture in the newspapers. I knew him as one of the corner Catalines and

171

gutter-führers the unrest of the 'thirties had vomited forth, and at that time I could only despair of his breed, feeling an impotent rage that they should be permitted to sell their rotten fruit. Therefore I was glad to learn from a news broadcast that Anton was being sent to prison, but, I confess, somewhat disappointed to discover that he was going, for a relatively short term, to such a model institution as the penitentiary where I was stationed. I had little notion then, as I listened to the radio, that Anton and I would soon find ourselves involved with each other in that curious minuet of psychotherapy called psychoanalysis; and I am sure I would have rejected any suggestion that I would ever be anxious to offer such a person my help.

The earliest word I had of Anton's arrival in Lewisburg came by "grapevine"—that curious, almost mystical channel of communication which often makes the interoffice telephone system of institutions an anachronism. Within an hour after he had been admitted I knew enough about him, his behavior, his manner and appearance to have picked him out from a crowd. When he appeared for routine examinations in my clinic the following week, I recognized him at once. He had remarkably black hair, which he had obviously tried to train so that it would fall across his forehead in emulation of his idol. His face was of a somewhat Slavic cast, with high cheekbones and wide-set eyes. One eye was a little off center; it gave his gaze a quality of thoughtful abstraction, useful in the pose he adopted. His body was large framed, but his hips narrowed athletically, making a fine swivel above thickly muscled legs and calves. His entire appearance was catlike, lithe, despite what at first glance seemed to be an unwieldy torso.

Anton merely grunted his presence when the inmate-clerk called off his name. During the group psychometric examination, which he took with the other "new fish" of that particular week's catch, it was obvious that he was eager to preserve a distance from his fellows. He neither spoke with them nor participated in the fraternization they practiced between the tasks set by the psychometrician. When the group gathered to leave the clinic and return to the Quarantine section, I noticed that he fell in at the rear. As they walked past the various offices and rooms where clinic personnel were working, he peered into each one, apparently making a rapid survey of his total situation.

Three days later Anton was scheduled for the individual psychiatric interview my colleagues and I performed with every new admission to the prison. By this time reports of various tests had been made available to us, and material from the courts and investigating agencies concerned with the conviction and sentencing of each prisoner had been collected. In bulky folders on my desk rested the complete criminal, social, physical, educational, employment and personal history of every man I had to see that day. As was customary, when Anton's turn for interview arrived, before pressing the button to indicate I was ready to see him, I hurriedly read through his file and made some notes about it.

As Anton took the few steps from the door to the chair into which I motioned him, I saw immediately that he was setting his face into a blankness, that he was obviously resolved to communicate as little about himself as possible. But his walk disclosed that curious litheness I have already commented upon, and the manner of his movement betrayed the contempt in which he held me and these proceedings. I knew I was in for a tough, unrewarding session.

The first few minutes of the interview were taken up by routine questions to which I already knew the answers.

173

As in all cases, I asked them not for the purpose of obtaining or even confirming information, but to establish the climate of the examination, to "feel out" the examinee as a boxer spars for a weak spot. Intuitively I knew that this man, more than most, would resent personal questioning, and that sooner than most he would tire of having to reiterate his answers in every office in which he was asked about himself in these weary weeks of Quarantine. I knew also that the only hope I had of breaking through the frosted front he was assuming for the examination was to arouse his anger. And, I must admit, I was also aware of my own hostility toward him, aware of the secret satisfaction I took in having him, an avowed fascist and anti-Semite, in this kind of authority-subject relationship with me, a Jew. I kept on, therefore, asking the kind of question I have indicated. He answered at first in monotonous mono-syllables, but after some minutes an edge of irritation began to appear in his voice. I continued until I was sure it was there, that my prodding had got beneath the shell he meant to be impervious; and then, with the following words, I brought the examination into focus.

"You don't like answering these questions, do you?"

He shrugged. "Go ahead," he said, "ask all you like."

"But you seem to resent it," I pressed him.

"You would, too, if everybody you met asked you the same damned things."

"Would you prefer it if I asked you different questions?"

He flared. "I don't give a damn what you ask," he said. "You got a job—go ahead and do it!"

"What do you think my job is?"

"They tell me you're the bug doctor. You're supposed to find out if I'm nuts."

"Is that why I'm asking you these questions?"

174

He shrugged again, but the slight quiver in his voice indicated the rage he was harnessing. "Everything you've asked me so far I've answered a hundred times." He waved toward the folders on the desk. "It's all in those files, anyhow. I don't see the sense of saying everything over and over."

"If my job is to find out if you're crazy——" I began. But he interrupted me with an impatient move of his hand.

"You can forget about that," he said. "I'm not crazy. I'm as sane as you are."

I indicated the folder. "According to the information there, you've done some mighty queer things."

"I've never done anything queer in my life," he responded hotly. "Everything I've done I've believed in."

"If you really *believe* all those things you've been saying and doing, I'd say you were really crazy."

"That's your opinion."

"Don't you think my opinion is valid?"

He snorted his contempt. "A Jew psychologist! What the hell else can I expect from you!" I saw I was through his shell now. "But go on," he continued. "Finish asking your stupid questions and let me out of here."

"You can go anytime you like," I said, "but I'd really like to know just why you think a Jew psychologist can't give a valid opinion on whether or not you're crazy."

"Because you Jews are all the same," he said. "You've wanted to get me for a long time. You put that crippled bastard in the White House and now you think you're in the saddle. Well, all right, so you got me in this joint and there's nothing I can do about it now. You can call me crazy and lock me up. That's just what a Jew psychologist would do. But," and here his voice rose, "you can't keep me here forever!"

"Oh, I don't know about that," I said. "It shouldn't be hard to get you committed to an insane asylum when your sentence expires. After all, we Jews have things pretty much our own way—according to you—and we can easily get a couple of Jew psychiatrists to certify you. . . ."

He saw through my baiting now and permitted himself a slight smile. "You're just trying to rile me up," he said. "Why?"

"To get beneath that mask you were wearing when you came in here," I confessed.

"I guess it worked," he admitted.

The atmosphere was more relaxed now and he accepted the cigarette and light I offered him.

"But you really do believe all the things you've said about the Government, the Jews, the Catholics and so on, don't you?" I asked when he had taken a few puffs.

"I guess I believe most of it."

"And the rest?"

He waved his cigarette expansively. "Political expediency."

"And do you expect to win like that?" I asked. "After all, look where it's got you so far."

A sneer curled his mouth. "Ah-h-h," he said, dismissing his surroundings airily, "these little setbacks don't mean a thing. Every leader goes through them . . . has to. Look at Mussolini, Hitler, Stalin. . . . It's part of the game. Means nothing."

"How do you intend to put in your time for the next couple of years?" I asked; and I couldn't resist adding,— "Writing your memoirs?"

My little piece of sadism escaped him. "You've got a good library here, I understand," he answered. "I intend to read and prepare myself for the future."

"And what will you do when you get out?"

"Same thing I was doing before," he said, "but more of it."

He now leaned forward confidingly. "By the time I get out of here the war will be over. Either Hitler will be in the White House or this country will be on its ass. My boys'll be waiting for me. I'll be needed. Meanwhile, I'm going to relax and build myself up."

Shortly after this I terminated the interview. I was, I admit, somewhat ashamed of the way I had conducted it. Certainly, no one could say it had been an objective examination—even the parts of it I have not described—and I had to acknowledge to myself that the man Anton, everything about him, everything he believed in and stood for, alienated me, repelled me. Curious, I reflected, how detached, understanding, even tolerant I could be with the murderers, thieves, procurers, forgers and bank robbers I saw and treated every day. But with Anton . . .

In any case, that afternoon I dictated my summary on him. More on the basis of his history than on the interview, I decided he was a psychopathic personality with paranoid, aggressive, antisocial trends. I recommended that he be quartered by himself under maximum security precautions to prevent him from spreading his ideas among the younger, more impressionable inmates, warned that he was a leader type who might easily become a focal individual for the unstable, psychopathically inclined elements in our institution, and, winding up my report, I suggested that he be assigned at his level of intelligence and in accordance with the high manual-skill index he had shown on our tests to one of the penitentiary shops. Then I promptly forgot all about him—or, at any rate, thought I had.

About a year passed before my next encounter with

Anton. In those days it was customary for the medical staff at Lewisburg to conduct a sick call directly before lunchtime. The inmates who answered it would line up at the hospital Admission Desk and be interviewed briefly by the Chief Medical Officer, who handled what he could on the spot and sent the rest to appropriate clinics. On the day I have in mind I was seated at my desk in the Psychological Clinic when Anton's sick card was brought in by a hospital runner. Beside the date stamped on the card there was a notation of the complaint in the scribble of our Chief: "Claims frequent black-out spells with slight amnesia, no falling, can't sleep, bad dreams." Attached to the card by a paper clip—indicating it was meant to be destroyed after reading—was a slip of paper with this message also in our Chief's handwriting: "Att: Dr. L.—Agitator and troublemaker—possible malingerer—looking for hideout in hospital maybe." After I read this I called for Anton's confidential psychiatric folder, skimmed it rapidly, and sent for him.

A glance at the dispirited figure who entered my office assured me that, unless this man was a consummate actor, he was no malingerer. By every line of his face and frame he expressed distress, misery and self-concern. Looking at him, it was hard to believe that this was the cocksure braggart, the offensive facsimile of a demagogue who had preened himself in this room a year before. Now he was just another sick inmate. And yet—yet there was something in his eyes to make one wonder if all this was not merely a variant pose of his, adopted for some self-seeking motive; a gleam, perhaps, of the old contempt he had shown so openly when last we met;—or maybe it was just that slight off-centeredness of his customary gaze. I decided to check the suspicion, awakened by my recollection of this man and

178

the warning note from the Chief, and to proceed with my job.

"What can I do for you?" I asked.

"I'm sick," he answered, "but that stiff-necked doctor downstairs don't believe me."

I let this pass and asked what was wrong.

"That's just it. I don't know. Can't put my finger on it. Maybe it's just that I'm tired. I can't sleep, and when I do I have nightmares."

I glanced at the card. "What about these black-out spells?"

"Yeah," he said. "That, too. I get a couple of them every day."

"Can you describe them?"

"Well—I don't know. I begin to feel a little sick in my stomach, and then for just about a few seconds it's like there was something black being pulled down over my head. I feel I can't breathe and can't see or hear anything, and then it's over."

"Is that all there is to it?" I asked.

He thought a moment. "No," he said. "When it's over I feel shaky inside and I can't remember what happened, what went on around me after this—this curtain I call it— came down over me."

He shook his head in negation when I asked him if he had ever before experienced anything like what he had described.

"Do you have these spells only in the daytime?" I asked.

"I think so," he said. Then, after a pause, "But wait! Something like it—but not the same thing—happens at night. I mean I feel like my jaws are locking together while I sleep and I'll never be able to separate them. I wake up scared and all sweaty. It's not the same as the other feeling in lots of ways, but it makes me feel the same when it's over."

179

Further questioning revealed that these spells of blankness were preceded by a sinking feeling. When I got to the matter of the "bad dreams," however, Anton's mood changed. Until now he had been entirely co-operative, but when the questioning involved the character of his dreams, he became sullen and the Anton of the previous year reappeared.

"I don't see why I have to tell you what I dream," he said. "This joint's like a fish bowl as it is. A man can't have any privacy at all except when he sleeps. Anyhow, my dreams don't worry me. It's not sleeping that's got me this way. I want some medicine to make me sleep."

"I'm not the kind of doctor who gives out medicine," I explained. "You were sent to me because the physicians didn't think it was medicine you needed."

"Then what the hell good can *you* do me?" he asked belligerently.

"That depends," I answered, "on how willing you are to co-operate with me. For example, when I ask you something I don't do it to pry but because I need the information to help you. I asked you about your dreams and you——"

"Yeah, yeah; I know," he broke in. "But I got no use for this psychology stuff. Anyhow, like I told you, I'm up to my eyeteeth with living like a goldfish."

I could feel my resentment against this man mobilizing once more within me, and to my ears came the echo-memory of his "Jew psychologist" of our last meeting. I was tempted, momentarily, to order him out of my office, to mark him down as a malingerer, and have done with the whole business. But, in time, I managed to recover my own balance by the self-reminder that this would not only be very unprofessional but, in a sense, tantamount to giving in before him and providing him with a satisfaction I knew he was seeking. Therefore, to gain some time and to re-establish

180

my position in this interview, I returned to the safer line of the initial approach.

"When you have these spells," I asked, "do you ever feel as if you're going to fall?"

He shook his head again. "No."

"Have you ever fainted in your life?"

"Yes—a few times."

"When?"

"Well," he began, "once I fainted when my old man . . ." He stopped, stood up, and glared at me. "Listen," he said angrily, "what gives here? I come in and ask for medicine and you give me a third degree. Screw you and your questions! Do I get something to make me sleep or don't I?"

"It's not medicine you need to let you sleep," I answered.

For a moment or two Anton stood and looked at me as if I were a thing he would like to grind into the dirt beneath his heels. Then, with a curse, he stalked from the room, closing the door behind him with a loud bang that expressed only a fraction of his fury.

That afternoon I reported this interview to my Chief. I told him I was sure the symptoms Anton expressed were real, that the man was not malingering. As regards my further impression diagnostically, I said I was not yet sure if the blackouts, preceded as they were by the shadow of what might be an aura and appearing during sleep as a tonic contraction of the facial muscles, were a neurotic phenomenon or an indication of epileptiform seizures of a neurogenic order. We would not be able to tell without a full examination, including many tests and a complete neurological work-up. But, I suggested, I felt it was in order to observe Anton's behavior more closely, to obtain reports on him from his work and quarters supervisors, and to await further developments. He (Anton) was angry now and not likely to be amenable to the kind of examination that would allow of differential diagnosis: to demand his return to the hospital for this purpose would only increase his resistance. I was sure he would return of his own accord and requested that on all subsequent appearances at sick call he be sent directly to my Clinic.

Within a few days, Anton was back. When the Chief marked his card to the Psychological Clinic, he turned on his heel and walked out of the hospital. About a week elapsed, and the same performance was repeated. Finally, at his third appearance on sick line, Anton made a scene. When the Chief once more sent him to my Clinic, Anton shouted that he was a sick man and this was a conspiracy to "bug" him; he hadn't slept through the night for months; he needed medicine, not any goddam psychology; he was going to have the whole hospital brought up on charges; we (the doctors) were a bunch of quacks anyhow; this was the last time he would ever ask for anything around here; to hell with the whole Jew-loving crew of us. And he ran from the hospital like a maddened animal.

But on the day following this demonstration there was a note awaiting me on my desk when I arrived for work. It had been sent through regular channels of intra-institutional mail and was from Anton. It said, simply: "I've got to see you. Please send for me." I immediately put his name on the list of inmates I was to see that afternoon.

When Anton came into the office this time, it was no longer as an antagonist but as a petitioner. Without even the preliminary of a greeting, he asked, "Can you help me?"

"I don't know," I answered. "I've got to find out what's wrong with you first."

"It's these spells," he said. "They scare the bejesus out

182

of me. And I feel all wound up inside, like soon something's going to snap and I'll go nuts."

"You say you've never had anything like them at all before?"

"No. Nothing like them."

"Why do you think you're having them now?"

"I don't know. That's something you've got to tell me. All I know is that ever since I came in here it seems something is growing bigger and bigger inside of me. I'm getting to the point where I think I could start screaming and never stop. The spells began a few weeks ago and they're getting worse. I'm getting more of them . . . each one is worse than the one before. It gives me the creeps. I'm scared. I don't want to die. Please help me!"

I didn't answer until I had thought the matter through as carefully as I could. There were two ways of disposing of this. The first was by way of a simple routine. I could examine Anton, have the necessary tests conducted by the various physicians on the staff and the outside consultants who visited from time to time, and in this manner obtain a diagnosis. If it was then determined that Anton had some organically based form of epilepsy, that his attacks were epileptiform in nature due to any one or a combination of physical causes, the whole thing would pass from my hands. The medical department would take over. If the condition was correctable, what was necessary would be done; if it was not, then a controlling medication would be prescribed. On the other hand, if our opinion after the tests was that these attacks and the accompanying distress were psychogenic, I would be faced with another decision. In this latter case I would have to decide whether to have Anton placed on the same medication and then forget him, or arrange that I or one of my colleagues administer psycho-

183

therapy. The question of value entered here and must be understood. There was not a member of the hospital staff who was not already burdened with far more than he could handle. Attending to one man meant depriving another of attention, and the most salvageable and worth-while cases were naturally selected from the mass that required intensive treatment. Would I be doing wisely by devoting as much energy and time as psychotherapy requires to a person like Anton? Approached this way the answer was patently no. But there was another point of view. If I could discover *why* Anton was a fascist, the real source of his beliefs and actions, where the fountainhead of his social psychopathy lay—perhaps, I thought, in some vague way this knowledge would be useful and important. So the value question was answered.

And there was yet something more involved that seemed to make it imperative that I study and treat this man. He had been diagnosed as a psychopathic personality. He belonged to a class of individuals who notoriously work out their conflicts and frustrations on others. Theoretically, the psychopath does not suffer out his problems as the neurotic does, but discharges them through acting. Theoretically, too, it was known that there existed some relationship between the so-called epilepsies and the psychopathies. Here, now, was a case where it was just possible that a bridge was being constructed from the behavior into the motor field. It was the first such instance I had run across; there was no description of anything similar in the literature that I then knew of: I wanted to know if this was really happening with Anton and why. Fortunately, I didn't fool myself into thinking that any offer of my services to Anton would be for his sake. Indeed, as I look back now, it strikes me that there may even have been a little sadism in my "altruism," for

I think I nourished a slight and not too unconscious hope that the process of psychotherapy would be painful to him.

During the minutes I speculated thusly, Anton was regarding me anxiously. He was greatly relieved when at last I spoke.

"The first thing we have to do," I said, "is to put you through a series of tests. I'll ask the doctors to go over you carefully here, and then we'll call in our consultant. If these symptoms of yours are physical, we'll try to correct what's wrong. If we can't correct it, we'll see if it's possible to give you some relief with medicine."

"Fine," he said. "When do we start?"

"Right away. But don't jump so fast. Offhand I'd say the doctors aren't going to find anything wrong with you. In that case, we'll have to treat you by psychotherapy."

"What's that mean?"

I told him.

"Will that do me any good?" he asked.

"It may and it may not," I answered. "But it'll be the only thing left to try."

He considered this briefly. Then he stood up and, with a sigh that expressed resignation, said, "I'm not going to say that I'll like doing what you said I have to do if the doctors don't find anything wrong. But I'm afraid of this thing and I want to get over it. So my answer is 'O.K.'"

Two weeks after this conversation Anton began psychoanalysis.

Anton was the only boy, the youngest in a family of five children. His father was a grocer and butcher in a suburb of an inland Eastern city, a heavy, chunky man whose flat hand was quick to be raised in anger and whose vigor constantly demanded—and got—replenishment from the jug

185

he kept on a shelf behind him in his store. Anton's mother, on the contrary, was a weak and sickly person. After the birth of her youngest child she began to show the strain of hard life, and for longer and longer periods of time took to her bed. From here she would fill the house with her groans and complaints, giving orders or directions in a voice that contrasted oddly with her pale face and fragile frame, and calling the children to her bedside to lavish upon each in turn her dammed-up affection. Anton especially recalled her wet kisses and her hasty, feverish hands as she would run them over him to pat his clothing into place.

Although the family lived in a neat frame house in a middle class neighborhood where all of the houses were alike and the lawns kept trim, it did not ever "belong." Mothers would caution their children not to play with Anton and his sisters and they, in turn, kept to a pretense that their loneliness and friendlessness were of their own making. Among themselves they developed a kind of snobbery that protected them from the disregard and the occasional slights or taunts of their neighbors.

This social ostracism was due to the behavior of the butcher, Anton's father, who became something of a legend in that district. Often after work at night, with the contents of the jug under his belt, he would stagger toward home singing raucously, shouting challenges to his neighbors, or calling out huge obscenities in a voice that shattered the quiet respectability of flower beds, trimmed hedges and antimacassars. Sometimes, too, he arrived at the corner in the company of an equally besotted woman; and then doors and windows would close decisively, while curtains parted and outraged eyes followed the pair down the street and into the frame house; at which point sharpened ears took over to record the sounds of revelry in the night, while

186

tongues clacked in sympathy for the children and the martyr on the bed.

In a haphazard way, the children grew. Between the mother's illnesses and the father's rages, between the father's brawling sensuality and the mother's querulous self-pity, all were somehow fed, clothed and sheltered. But as they grew, all of them, and Anton in particular, came to hate both parents; his father for obvious reasons and his mother for her weakness. Cut off from ordinary social contacts and forced in upon himself, at a very early age he developed an imaginary playmate, another boy whom he called Fritzy. With this invisible creature of his own making Anton strove to achieve much that was denied him in reality, many of the satisfactions of which he was deprived, and some of the small joys that are the birthright of children. Chiefly, he used Fritzy to have someone to dominate, for in the pecking order of his home Anton was at the bottom, and until he invented Fritzy the chain of blame or anger or frustration had always ended with him. When Anton began school, however, Fritzy died; not literally and all at once, of course, but slowly, disappearing into a bog of memory where things forgotten dissolve in the acid of time.

The eight years of formal school were so many prolonged nightmares for Anton. In the classroom he was undisciplined and a focal point for trouble. To call himself to the attention of other children, he knew only techniques of which his teachers disapproved. Soon, among his fellows, he became a leader and won note for his daring and recklessness in their escapades and in the warfare many of them conducted against school authorities. He was a "demon" according to one of his teachers in the primary grades; "uncontrollable and vile in his habits" according to another. And yet, despite everything, and incredible as it was to these very teachers

187

as well as to the boy himself, Anton progressed in his work. He had an alert, eager mind, more than an ordinary amount of curiosity, and an appetite for knowledge. Without conscious effort, certainly without study, he absorbed what was required of him; had his deportment been closer to average, he would have been his school's prize scholar.

When Anton was not busy disrupting classrooms or dodging his father's hand and his mother's complaints, he spent most of his time in vengeful, retributive daydreaming. Out of voracious and romantic reading (for he had early acquired a habit of reading anything he could find), he constructed gory fantasies of "getting even"—with the children who dressed in laundered clothes and wouldn't play with him; with neighbors who turned their backs when he passed; with his father and mother; with his teachers. One of his daydreams, recovered like Fritzy during psychoanalysis, is a model for all of them. In this, a wholesale plagiarism from one of the lush tales he read, he fancied himself an Eastern potentate, splendidly arrayed and seated on an elephant. This elephant had been trained as an executioner, and Anton saw himself directing the annihilation of his parents, his schoolfellows and, indeed, almost everyone in his world from its back. Slaves—so the fantasy ran—would capture and bind those whom Anton pointed out to them, and place the heads of the victims on a stone. Then Anton would order the elephant to raise its great leg and bring it down on the head so placed, squashing the cranium while he looked on with satisfaction. In this fantasy, two features are most interesting. The first is that it—and others like it—set the pattern for Anton's sexual life, for the brute aggressiveness with which he indulged his sex wants and the sadistic imposition of his will on others irrespective of their wishes in the matter; for these fantasies always took place as

188

a prelude or accompaniment to his masturbation. The second is that, in reality, Anton could not, even when I knew him, stand the sight of the blood with which these fantasies were filled. As a matter of fact, so averse was Anton to blood that he could not abide the color red and would not wear it, nor could he even bring himself to touch an object of that color without shuddering.

Red, for Anton, meant his father and his father's trade. As a child, during vacations and after school, he would sometimes have to help out in the store. Quick with his hands and at figures, Anton could handle the canned goods, the dairy products, the vegetables, the fruit; but he was filled with apprehension and became nauseated if he had to touch or even look at the meat. To watch his father prepare the carcasses for sale was literally unbearable for the boy. Knowing this, the butcher enjoyed forcing Anton to attend the meat counter, baited and tormented him and, for the pleasure of any onlooker, would imitate the shrinking fashion in which the child approached this work. One day, however, urged as usual by the jug on the shelf, the father carried his teasing too far. Enraged because Anton would not obey his order to cut a slice of raw liver, he grabbed the boy's hands, compelling them to hold the bloody meat. Then, exerting his strength against the boy's rigid arms, the butcher forced Anton to smear his face with his now bloody hands despite his crying and tearful protests. When he was released, Anton fainted. And from that day forward he never again went near the store.

At fourteen Anton left home. Without a word of farewell, taking nothing with him except the clothes he was wearing and some money he had saved from vacation jobs, he walked off. By this time a husky and strong fellow who looked older than his age and had the strength of a grown

189

man, he obtained a job as hod carrier with an itinerant construction crew that worked its way back and forth across the country. The work hardened him physically, and the rough, careless life of the men in his company was greatly to his taste. In the days he labored and sweated under his load; at night, with the others, he brawled and drank and exchanged some of his earnings for warmed-over love in the cribs of the cities where his job took him. Within a short time, because of his strength, his intelligence, his unscrupulous will, he became the acknowledged leader of the outfit. Now it was he, young as he was, who made the decisions for the others; and he rode the tide of this fortune as long as he was able. But the crew disbanded in 1931 with the slack in the building trades, and in a short while the taste of power he had had became a small memory.

In 1932, at the age of twenty, Anton found himself on the West Coast. He had been unemployed for some months and his small savings had vanished. He was friendless, embittered, angry. Within him was the same gnawing, betrayed feeling that had haunted his childhood years. Whatever he saw around him nourished his resentment. Out of the contrast between his shabbiness and the groomed neatness of people he passed on the streets; between what he had and what he was told by the advertisements he should have; between his loneliness and the chattering fraternity of others, he concocted within his vitals an acid brew. This flowed in his arteries and veins, a corrosive fluid, and ate away whatever remained in him of compassion and human warmth. And it was in such a frame of mind that he committed his first criminal offense, the theft of an automobile, which netted him a two-year sentence in a local prison.

In prison, after an initial period of sullen withdrawal from every hand held out to him in help or in the camaraderie of the exiled that in a prison passes for friendship, Anton began to think about the world and his place in it; to think twistedly and psychopathically under the guidance of a bogus "minister." This man, a forger and poseur whose only motive in living was gain, must have recognized in the vague-eyed delinquent an instrument by which his own mean ends could be served. He undertook, therefore, to become a mentor for Anton. Through bribery, this pair that was to become infamous arranged to cell together, and in the long prison days and nights the "minister" communicated to his mate all he had learned about the ways of men and societies, about power and the magnetism of the big lie, about the little seed of rottenness in everyone's soul that— with proper care—could be swelled to bursting in an odious efflorescence. There grew between them a close association, and in talk and exchange of ideas the months passed rapidly.

When Anton was released—his time expired soon after his associate was set free—he went immediately to join the "minister" in an organization the latter had recruited from among the dregs of the displaced. On the outside, in the free world, his education was continued. Under the tutelage of his friend he discovered that he had a voice which could carry and communicate accents of hatred, and the mission that now engaged him was such as to pour a balm on his frustrated soul. For about a year—actually as long as it took to squeeze from his associate all the latter had to give and to make the necessary plans—Anton accepted the subordinate place he was given in the scheme of the organization. Then, by a coup, he captured the group from his mentor and set himself up as Leader in his place. The "minister," perceiving that in such a case acquiescence to an accomplished fact was the wiser course, and regretting only that he had shaped his tool too well, now became second in command.

191

Indeed, he soon learned that his own talents were better suited to his new tasks, and to them he now devoted himself. With the team thus rearranged, the complexion of what was a disjointed and loosely organized group changed. It took on those characteristics for which it had been designed, and rapidly cohered into an organization with purpose and resolve. Somehow, somewhere, the funds were found to equip a goon squad with the infantile paraphernalia of colored shirts, boots, emblems and arms. A frame house in San Francisco was purchased and furnished in an appropriate style, and from its attic Anton conducted his operations. He sent his eager hirelings, recruited from the *lümpen*-proletariat and the pale fringes of the lower middle class, to deface churches and synagogues, to provoke riots at political meetings, to wreck union halls and perform close-order drill before audiences of children in abandoned real-estate developments. At first these activities were sneered or laughed at, but soon the sneers stopped, the laughter became an echo, and the columns of Anton's marching lines grew longer.

In a short time Anton's malodorous fame spread not only throughout the United States but across both oceans. Money to finance a scurrilous newspaper and to buy radio time came from devious sources—a screen star from Hollywood, a Midwestern columnist, an industrialist of note and a handful of businessmen. A curious thing developed: the man who could not stand blood now screamed for it;—from behind microphones in hushed studios; from rostrums in great, close-packed concert halls where flags were banked behind him and a band played anthems and hard-faced uniformed men stood with thumbs locked in their shining leather belts. His screams were effective, too; for to his standard of hate and the glorification of the brutal flocked economic and social and psychological frustrates by scores.

192

He had mobilized in them the resentment and disappointment of their narrow lives, and they came toward him as insects toward a lighted candle. What he offered was a share of what he had found: an outlet for pressures accumulated during thwarted years; and he indicated to them the ways in which their latent inclinations toward violent retribution could be channeled.

And Anton?—He loved it. He gorged himself on the adulation of his followers. He vibrated with an indescribable thrill to their shouts of welcome and their screams of assent to his every word. He reveled in dominating. He got a physical pleasure from observing his own glory and particularly from the moment to moment satisfaction of every whim, every want. In a uniform and shining boots he swaggered; and on his face was the sheen of a holy mission in process of fulfillment. But in his personal life, when he was not on display, he was ascetic. He lived alone and simply in the frame house, without friends, deliberately inaccessible, aloof from the mob. Thus he modeled himself on both of his gods.

This psychopathic idyll collapsed, of course, with Pearl Harbor. Anton went into hiding soon after the bombs fell, but the F.B.I. finally rooted him out and sent him off to the penitentiary. When they came upon him he was writing an editorial congratulating the Japanese for their astuteness and predicting an early and successful victory for the Rising Sun.

To treat a psychopath—at any time, in any place, or under any set of circumstances—is the most onerous and unrewarding job a clinician can undertake. Most therapists have an attitude of therapeutic nihilism regarding such persons. They start from the proposition that the psychopath is not amenable to treatment and that, in any case, few if any are worth the effort involved. Even the best and most conscientious practitioners of the therapeutic arts throw up their hands before this character malformation and become one with the census of opinion that would consign the whole group to the care of wardens of penal or mental institutions. They shake their shoulders in helplessness when questions of treatment are raised. Psychiatrists deplore their inaccessibility to therapy; psychologists regret their utilization of a special variety of intelligence that defeats clinical tests; psychoanalysts are chagrined by their usual impenetrability and disinclination to remain long enough in therapy for a working relationship between analyst and patient to be established. So the psychopath is a kind of therapeutic orphan who, even if he has enough insight (and few have) to realize the fact of his personality distortion, ordinarily finds it almost impossible to get the treatment he requires. To the individual psychopath himself this is usually not a very important matter since, unless his character is secondarily complicated by a distressful set of symptoms, he is either unaware of his need or resentful of interference in his affairs; but to harassed and shamed parents, to public officials charged with the protection and safety of the community, and to others who may be the victims of the psychopath, there are few things in life of greater urgency.

At the time I undertook to treat Anton I had worked out—if only to my own satisfaction—a therapeutic approach to the psychopath. The method I employed was hypnoanalysis—a technique combining psychoanalysis with hypnosis.* With this method I had been able to surmount many of the major difficulties involved in treating such persons and was even then in process of extending my proficiency

* See, *Rebel Without A Cause*, Grune and Stratton, New York, 1944.

and familiarity with the therapeutic tool. Anton's case, beside all else, represented for me a chance to apply the technique to an area it had not yet touched. Therefore, I was greatly distressed to learn soon after we started that I would have to abandon hypnoanalysis in this instance. . . . For Anton was not hypnotizable.

It was only after the expenditure of much effort that it was borne upon me that this man's inability to enter a hypnotic trance was due to a circumstance I had never before encountered. At first I thought it was simply resistance to me and to the process of treatment. My own attitude toward him, I reasoned, must be influencing this negative response. After all, he could not help knowing the way I felt about him and his activities. I was, so to speak, on the opposite side of the fence from him in almost everything. In our former contacts I had even obtained the satisfaction of some of my own secret desires, and I was convinced that my rejection and hostility were communicated to him by subtle means if not openly. Accordingly, I subjected myself to a rigid self-examination—the details of which are not pertinent here—from which I emerged unchanged in my feelings and attitudes about Anton and his activities, but better able to control them. Yet, although the situation between us improved, Anton remained unhypnotizable.

Having eliminated myself from the picture and observing that this made no remarkable change in it, I turned my attention to the other factors that make for lack of ability to enter the trance state. Foremost among these is simple (usually unconscious) resistance to being cured. I checked all the reasons why Anton should not want the help he was asking for—and had to dismiss them. There was, indeed, nothing that this man had to gain, at that time at least, by being ill. His relations in the prison, although not good,

195

were not markedly uncomfortable; his weakness was making him lose face among the followers he had there; undertaking psychotherapy in a prison is about the last thing an inmate in any case permits himself to do; the symptoms were most distressing and could not be employed for any conceivable kind of personal gain. Therefore, it must be something else. Well—there are numerous reasons why people can't be hypnotized. Among them are the presence of strong latent homosexual inclinations, reaction-formations and other defenses against dependence, a high level of distractibility, a low threshold of nervous excitation; and in addition to these and others are a whole catalogue of inhibitory factors derived from misinformation and fear. As far as the latter category was concerned, I felt I had eliminated most of them in the course of the training-in-hypnosis work that is a part of my routine with hypnotherapeutic patients. About the former, I could dismiss some of the points categorically but did not have enough information yet to act upon the others. Still, there were sufficient grounds for not crediting them with force enough to overcome the positive drive I knew Anton had toward recovery. In short, I had to look elsewhere.

Meanwhile, because the beginning of our work was marred by consistent failure, Anton's antagonism toward me grew. He charged the lack of success to me and my ineptness, castigating me, not only by word but also in his manner, for inadequacy. At the same time he showed a pronounced exacerbation of his symptoms: the attacks became more frequent, more prolonged, and accompanied by more apprehension.

During our sessions, as I strove desperately to obtain the trance I needed, I watched him closely. Eventually I became aware of a peculiar pattern in his reactions. As I repeated my monotonous suggestions, for the first few minutes he would appear to be falling under their sway. His limbs would relax, his eyelids begin to flutter, the pulse in his neck slowed perceptibly, and his breathing become more regular: indeed, he appeared about to drift off into sleep. But always, at the crucial moment when I thought he was on the lip-edge of the trance and only a small additional effort was required to send him into an hypnotic sleep, he would stiffen abruptly, a shudder would convulse his entire body, and his eyes would widen to a stare. After this had happened it was no use to go on; any additional attempts during a given period were in vain. Observing this time after time, it occurred to me that perhaps my voice or attitude was responsible;—maybe I was permitting something—an inflection, a movement, a tension in me—to reveal either impatience or a shadow of triumph at the immediate prospect of his succumbing: maybe he was interpreting this as a kind of "battle of wills," of personality strength. I checked this and made every possible effort to exclude such factors from my voice and manner. But again and again, failure. Finally, in exasperation and against all previous habits of procedure, I asked Anton what was wrong.

"You follow a curious pattern," I said. "It seems as if you're just about to go under, to fall asleep, and then for some reason either you pull yourself back or something automatically checks you and you become wide awake. Can you tell me what happens?"

"I don't know," he said. "It's like something clicks inside me. I feel drowsy while you're talking, I feel like going to sleep, and then all of a sudden I get panicky inside—scared—and before I can control it I'm wide awake."

"What d'you mean by panic, or scared?"

"It feels like I'm sinking, going down and down, and then

197

at a certain point I get a scared feeling. My heart begins to pound and I break out in a sweat all over. It feels like I'm going to die. I guess at that minute I sort of pull myself back."

"How do you know," I asked, "what it feels like to die?"

This puzzled him and he thought a moment before replying.

"I don't *know*," he said. "Wait! It's like the feeling I get just before I have one of those damned spells. Just the second before I pass out. Only I can't stop them like I can stop this."

"Is there any mental content present at that moment, any mental picture? Image? Memory? Idea?"

Now he paused for what seemed many minutes. At last:

"I never thought about that before," he said. "Maybe there is. I get the impression something's there—but it's very vague, just a kind of outline, hazy."

"Outline of what?"

His answer came rapidly, without thought and almost before the question had left my lips.

"Maybe of a body. Yeah—of a body. Just the outline . . ."

"Whose body?"

Anton twisted uncomfortably on the couch. "I don't know," he said. "I don't know." And in his voice there was now an overtone of anguish, as if to beg me to stop. But to this I paid no attention and went on.

"Whose body could it be?" I asked. "What occurs to you?"

"It's . . . it's . . ." And then, to my amazement, Anton's voice trailed off and he went into a convulsion right there on the couch. His body became rigid, his eyes rolled back until the pupils disappeared from sight, brief clicking noises came from his lips, and spittle rolled from his mouth in a

198

thin line. The whole thing lasted no more than perhaps forty seconds and terminated with the same abruptness with which it had begun. His limbs suddenly relaxed and his eyes came into focus. He raised a trembling hand to wipe his mouth: his chest heaved as if his lungs hungered for air. In a tremulous voice, after a little while, he said, "My God, that was one of the worst ones I ever had. What happened?"

I tried to describe what I had observed while Anton shook his head in confused surprise. Then he swung his feet from the couch and sat facing me, his head in his hands.

"Listen," he said. "Maybe we oughta stop this. What d'you think?"

"This attack was brought on by something," I answered. "It didn't just happen out of the blue. Why don't you see if you can describe exactly what went on?"

"All right. . . . It was something like this. I was trying to tell you something—what I was seeing when you asked whose body it could be. Just when I started to open my mouth it was like someone turned a floodlight on my face. I saw a hot white light and I felt like when you touch a charged wire, a kind of tingling all over me especially in my hands and feet and on my face. I wanted to say something but I couldn't. And next the light went out and I felt like I was being smothered, like a sack came down over my head. That's all I remember."

"What were you trying to say? Can you remember?"

He nodded but remained silent. Fear looked out from his eyes, big stains from sweat spread under the arms of his blue work shirt.

"You don't have to be afraid to tell me," I reassured him. "You've just had an attack; I doubt if you'd have another one so soon."

Slowly and deliberately, as if with each word he was expecting a blow, he said, "I started to tell you about the body I saw when you asked me whose it was. I—it was—it was my father!"

We sat in silence for some while after this, but soon Anton became calmer and with a sigh of relief settled himself on the couch.

"I don't suppose you know," I asked, "whether this same image of your father precedes every attack."

"I wouldn't know," he replied. "I have a feeling something like that's always there, but whether it's the old man I wouldn't know."

"Is your father alive?"

The answer to this came fast. "I hope not. The son-of-a-bitch shoulda never been born!"

"When did you see him last?"

"The night I ran away from home."

"Have you heard about him since?"

"No. I haven't heard about any of them."

"You never wrote to them?"

"What for? I got nothing to say to them and I don't care what they have to say to me. I just ain't interested."

"Do you ever think about them?"

"Not very often. Sometimes about my mother."

"What about your mother?"

Anton seemed much calmer now and the tone he used was indifferent and unconcerned. With the expression of hostility against his father he had released a load of venom, and when he spoke again it was as if he mused reminiscently.

"The things I think about my mother? Nothing very much. Just kid things from when I was small. Like one time before she was sick so much she took me visiting one of my aunts. We had to walk a long way in the snow to get there

200

and I was tired when we came to the house. My aunt gave me some hot chocolate, cocoa, I think, with a marshmallow in it. It was good. I can taste it right now. Good and hot. It made my insides all warm. I remember I fell asleep right there in the chair and didn't wake up until we were home. I could never figure it out—how I got home. Did my mother carry me all the way? Or did we go home in a cab or something? I always meant to ask her but I kept forgetting it. I wish I knew."

"Why?"

"I don't know. Just because, I guess." Here he paused slightly and then went on again. "That reminds me. I wasn't telling you the truth before. I did see my mother once. I guess I didn't want to tell you before. . . ."

"When was that?"

"About six months or a year after I ran away. We got on a job a few miles from where my family lived and one night I got this yen to see her. I don't know why. Anyhow, I got out to where they lived. It was pretty late by the time I got there so I didn't go in. I just walked up and down a few times in front of the house. Then a neighbor's dog began to bark at me and make a racket. My mother came to the window and looked out. I couldn't see much of her, but the way she opened the window and put her head out looked to me like she was O.K., so I went away."

"And that's all?"

"Sure."

"You didn't want to talk to her?"

"What for? It would only be the same stuff all over again."

"What do you mean by 'the same stuff all over again'?"

Anton shrugged. "I mean just what I said. Her crying and moaning and the old bastard shouting and swinging his fists.

201

I was fed up with it, didn't want no more of it. I had enough—all the years I was growing up. I knew when I left it was for good. To hell with all of that. Let the dames be the suckers. I was out of it and I was going to stay out of it."

"Which do you think affected you more," I asked, "your father's brutality or your mother's weakness?"

"About half and half," Anton answered. "Both of them made me sick. She with her crying all the time, slobbering all over me. She disgusted me. And the old man couldn't talk decent with you, always screaming or taking a poke or a kick at you. I don't know which was worse."

"But would you say you felt the same way about both of them?"

"I guess not exactly. I felt more sorry for her and disgusted by the way she acted. I never felt sorry for him. I just hated him." And now there was a new quality in Anton's voice. The calmness had disappeared. He spoke in a husky, low tone that rasped on the ear as if he were forcing the words over a barrier of choked feelings. One arm came up across his face, hiding his eyes, while the other, resting on the couch, showed his tension in a clenched fist. He continued, "I hated that bastard from the minute I knew him. I used to lie awake at nights playing he was dead . . . Hoping someone would kill him—that a building would fall on his head. I'd plan how to murder him. Sometimes I wouldn't sleep all night figuring out ways to kill that no good son-of-a-bitch!"

"And was it any better after you left home?" I asked. "Did you stop thinking about him?"

"Maybe it took me a little while to forget it," Anton said. "After a year or so I forgot about it."

"And you haven't thought of it since, until now?"

"I wouldn't say that. I probably thought about it off and

202

on. But it's only been since I came here that the whole thing's come back to me."

"Why is that?"

Anton waved his hand to indicate the entire institution. "This place," he said, "these people . . ." And his hour ended.

So the analysis of Anton began to take shape. Hypnosis was abandoned, for with the identification of the body, of the image that flashed before him in the moment preceding his attacks, and with the verbalization of his hatred for his father, the chief symptoms that had brought him to treatment disappeared. They were replaced by an occasional momentary blankness and a brief dizziness that would come upon him at irregular times during the next weeks. Had it not been for these remnants I am sure Anton would have abandoned therapy, for he found his hours with me increasingly disturbing as we probed deeper and deeper into forgotten memories, into the nether recesses of his twisted personality.

The first item that came to light with the arduous dredging we did was the further identity of the body on the floor. It was not only Anton's father, victim of his son's wishes and designs, but also Anton himself. The ancient talion law, eye for eye and tooth for tooth, demanded this payment in kind. For his father's life, Anton had to pay with his own. Thus it became clear that Anton had a fear of death so great, so overwhelming, that he could not permit himself to be hypnotized. To him, with the old hatred mobilized by the restraints and frustrations of imprisonment, hypnosis and sleep and the shattering of consciousness produced by the attacks were equated with death, the self-imposed capital punishment for parricide. The seizures, then, had a double meaning: they were expressions of the murderous impulses Anton had been charged with from the earliest days of his life, as well as punishment for the fantasied carrying out of his vicious intent. In them, he both killed and was killed. The fact that the body on the floor was representative of the two chief actors in this oedipal drama was neither novel nor surprising: in the unconscious, as shown in dreams, it often happens that a character or an object plays a dual role. How this came about with Anton, however, was a matter both of us were eager to investigate. Nor did it take long to resolve this problem. Stated in its simplest terms, the identification of himself with his father occurred by way of a simple, universal psychic mechanism. Layers beneath his hatred for this really brutal person was a core of longing, tenderness and admiration which Anton had for the alcoholic butcher. It dated far back into infancy and, despite everything, persisted as a small but bright glow in the deeps of his being. Perhaps it began in the first year of Anton's life when his father may have caressed him casually, have played with the infant, or fondled him: perhaps beneath the rough and vulgar exterior Anton at one time had been able to sense that pearl of human warmth even his father must have had. We never found out what it was that gave rise to this nucleus of love Anton denied until he came upon it in the analysis, but the fact of its presence could not be avoided. So, as we say, Anton was basically ambivalent toward his male parent, hating him and loving him. And as a consequence of this ambivalence there came about the identification of the boy with his father; a curious compound, of which the elements were love, the desire to emulate, and the understandable self-protective urge to invest himself with his enemy's cloak so that he could put himself out of harm's way.

Anton and I now believed we understood something of what went into the formation of his personality. I, at least, saw where his sadism, his brutality, his aggressiveness came from. He had identified with a person who had precisely such characteristics and, for the reasons just stated, had absorbed them into himself. For me, this understanding was a lesson in the perpetuation of the psychopathic character, a lesson as yet incomplete and only barely outlined. To fill it in, much more work was required; but we now struck a snag that held us up for many weeks.

Until this time, following our discovery of the double identity of the image preceding the attacks, few transference difficulties had been encountered and very little effort had been required to overcome resistances that appeared from time to time. My own feelings about this man were now well in hand and I had, fortunately for him, been diverted from my original rejection of him as a fascist by scientific curiosity about what went into the sculpturing of his personality. On his part, he was showing some respect for me as a person and a therapist. The attacks had faded to a mere shadow of themselves, and Anton was feeling particularly well. While I knew that we had a long way to go yet, I foresaw no difficulties along the road to a rapid completion of this analysis and was very complacent about its eventual outcome. Because I always proceed with a rough plan, I had set as my next target the uncovering of the meaning of his intense fear of death, after which I hoped to fit the details of his sexual life into the mosaic of his psychopathic structure and, lastly, to achieve the final synthesis. But in my complacency and self-satisfaction I neglected to take into account two factors that should have been stamped indelibly upon my own awareness: the fact that Anton was a psychopath, and the fact that I was working with him in a prison.

By now Anton had served a third of his sentence and was due for a parole hearing. We discussed this casually during our hours together, and I recall cautioning him not to place too much hope in receiving favorable consideration from the Parole Board. It was true that since he had begun his analysis he had given the prison authorities no cause for complaint. He had made a good record on his job, had lost some of his sullenness toward the custodial force, and had presented no disciplinary problems to the institution. Nonetheless, I reminded him, we were at war, and his history as a subversive and internal enemy would outweigh his prison record in the opinion of the examining officials. Anton, with the characteristic optimism of all psychopaths, discounted my warnings and began to anticipate an early release. One afternoon, shortly before the date scheduled for parole hearings, he paused during the recital of a memory to ask me if I had anything to do with his parole.

"I'll be asked for a recommendation," I answered.

"What will you say?"

"What I think . . . that you're not ready for it."

Abruptly, Anton's mood changed. He sat up and turned to face me. I could see a flush of anger rising from his collar and suffusing his face.

"You mean," he asked, "you're going to turn me down?"

"I have very little to do with it," I said. "All I'm asked for is a statement about you from a psychological point of view. I have to tell them I don't think you're in shape to go out."

"What's wrong with me? I'm better, ain't I?"

"Your symptoms are better," I said, "but your personality is about the same as it was when you came in."

206

"What's that got to do with it?"

"Everything, from where I sit."

His voice became cajoling. "Look," he said, "I don't give a damn about my personality. All I want to do is get out of here. I got a lot of work to do."

"What kind of work?"

"Organization, man!" he said impatiently. "My boys are waiting for me outside. They need me. I've wasted too much time already. I ought to be out there. There're a million things to do. In here I don't even know what's going on. I've got to get out and you've got to help me."

"The only thing I can do for you," I said, as deliberately as I could, "is to help you remake yourself. I'm not going to interfere in your parole. When I'm asked, I'll tell them that in my opinion your personality remains unchanged. You have the same rotten ideas and notions you had eighteen months ago. You're as impulsive, as reckless, as sadistic-minded and as antisocial in your acts as you ever were. You have the mentality of a storm trooper. If you continue to work with me, maybe you can become a decent person. You haven't been one and you're not one now. I won't help you get a parole because I can't take any responsibility for setting you free so you can spread your poison and infect others. When you're no longer a carrier of poison I'll do everything I can to get you out of here—but until then I won't lift a finger for you. I don't intend to tell the parole authorities any of this. But I *will* tell them that I don't consider you ready for parole now."

Anton stood and glared down at me. His lips were trembling and his face was dark.

"You son-of-a-bitch!" he said. Then he turned and walked out of the room.

For a week I held Anton's time open, hoping he would

return to work out the matter that had come between us and continue his analysis. I regretted our quarrel but knew I couldn't have done otherwise. Anton had to be told the truth for his own sake and the sake of the analysis. If his unconscious purpose in undertaking treatment was to enlist my aid in getting out of prison, this aim had to come into the open and be dealt with directly like any other. It was clear that our therapeutic aims—and this is something that happens regularly in every analysis everywhere—were different, except in the matter of his symptoms. Even at the risk of the whole business, this fundamental issue—the goal of treatment—had to be resolved.

When a week passed without a visit from Anton I regretfully gave his hours to another patient. But it was not long until he came back into my life in the dramatic and disturbing fashion so characteristic of psychopaths.

The Medical O.D. was suddenly taken ill one day and I was ordered to cover for him. The first duty I had to assume was the conduct of the sick line. I stood behind a rostrum, listened to the complaints of the men, and made routine assignments to the various clinics. The line was long; I was tired from standing, bored with hearing the same ailments described over and over again. Halfway through this chore, I looked up to receive the next inmate's request—and found myself confronted by Anton. There was hostility in his voice as he spoke.

"I want to see a doctor," he said sullenly.

"What about?" I asked.

"None of your business."

"You'll have to tell me what's wrong before I can send you to the proper clinic," I explained.

I could feel the eyes and ears of the rest of the men on the line, the two guards who stood by, and the clerks at the

Admitting Desk on us. "I don't have to tell you nothing," Anton said. "I'll do my telling to a real doctor."

"I'm sorry," I said. "If you don't tell me what's wrong I can't assign you to a clinic."

Then, in a voice that echoed through the whole building, he shouted, "You know goddam well what's wrong, you Jew bastard!" And with this he turned and stormed out of the hospital.

A hush as if everyone had stopped breathing fell over the men around me. I knew each was wondering what I was going to do. A guard hurried to my side.

"Should I bring him back?" he asked.

"No," I said. "Let him go."

I tried to think fast. I was expected to do something . . . but what? I had been insulted in the presence of inmates and officers. On the personal side this mattered nothing to me, but it was a serious breach of discipline toward an institutional official; if it were permitted to pass I would be criticized by my superiors. Moveover, if I did nothing about it, someone else—one of the guards certainly—would report it and Anton would be punished anyhow. Apart from this I had my reputation with the men to consider. In a moment the affair would be all over the prison. If I did not act, and act soon, I couldn't hope to hold the respect of the inmates. I could not afford to appear cowardly before them: I could not afford to risk their contempt, with all of its consequences for my work. On the other hand, there was Anton and our previous relationship to consider. I was—or had been—his analyst, and only I knew what was behind all of this. If I did what I was expected to do—enter a disciplinary citation against him—by this recourse to authority I would be complicating further our personal relationship, rejecting him utterly, adding fuel to his hatred of the world. Again,

209

if I did nothing, he, too, would regard me as a coward. All of my training and experience as a psychoanalyst pointed to one very definite fact: this incident was a function of the intimate therapeutic relationship between Anton and myself. It was a test, cleverly and purposely designed, to try me. There was only one thing I could do.

I called the Administrative Assistant and ordered him to take over the sick line. Then, accompanied by the stares, nudges and whispers of the men, I started for the dormitory where Anton lived.

As I walked through the prison corridors my thoughts were a turmoil of psychological and personal speculations. Anton was stronger than I. If it came to a fight I knew what would happen. I felt my knees go rubbery and my breath come fast. I was in no condition for a fight; apart from some boxing in the gymnasium at college I hadn't had a fight since childhood. I didn't want to be hurt. But I knew that what I was doing was psychologically and personally correct; that this was a risk I had to take.

I pushed open the door of the dormitory where Anton lived. About thirty men were scattered about the room. As one, they turned toward me, and I felt myself almost engulfed by the wave of their combined hostility as it reached me where I stood. I remember even now how I recoiled from it, how a living panic overspread my entire being.

Then I saw Anton. He was lying on his cot, hands clasped beneath his head, eyes fixed on the ceiling. I called his last name. He ignored me. I called again, more loudly; this time he turned in my direction. With my head, I beckoned him. Slowly, deliberately, he swung his feet from the cot and stood up. When I saw he was moving toward me, I walked out into the corridor. In a moment, he joined me, and we stood face to face.

210

"Well?" he challenged. "What d'you want?"

I tried to keep my voice low and even. "I want you to apologize for what happened on the sick line."

"Kiss my ass," he said and started back into the room.

I grabbed him by the shoulder and swung him around again.

"I said I want an apology."

He brushed away my hand and stood with his fists on his hips. "You keep your hands offa me," he said, "or you're gonna get hurt."

"Are you going to apologize?" I persisted.

Anton laughed contemptuously. "What're you gonna do if I don't? Call the hacks?" Then his hand shot out and he clutched at my shirt, his big knuckles digging into my chest. "If you didn't have that uniform on," he said, "you wouldn't be so brave."

I pushed his hand aside and reached up and pulled the insignia tabs from my collar.

"I don't have any uniform on," I said. "There's just the two of us here and I won't call the guards. Will you apologize or do I have to make you?"

We stared at each other for a long minute. Finally the anger went out of his eyes and a sheepish smile spread over his face.

"I guess I apologize," he said quietly.

As I turned to go he called me.

"Wait a minute."

I waited for him at the door. He seemed to hesitate, as if trying to find the right words.

"I'm—I'm sorry," he said finally. "If it's all right with you, I'd like to come over this afternoon for a talk."

"Sure," I said. "The usual time."

When we resumed treatment that afternoon, the mean-

211

ing of the incident just passed was clarified. My refusal to assist Anton to a parole was interpreted by him as a personal rejection. At that moment he saw in me his hated father, the one whose love he both sought and disparaged, the one by whom he had also been rejected. From this core, and by a series of further identifications, his feelings spread rapidly to encompass the whole of society. He saw himself as persecuted, a victim of injustice. This aroused in him an almost paranoidal fury which he nourished by bitter memories during the interval marked by our last meeting and the scene at the sick line. He wanted to strike back and I, as the living immediate representational figure of the childhood drama, was the aptest subject for his hostility. Further, through me, he could get at larger groups: the Jews, whom I represented, and the authoritarian world that restricted him, of which I was a symbol. My response to his challenge had impressed him not only because it indicated something personal about me, but because by it I had destroyed the illusory links and synapses by which he could connect the paternal image with the wide world: my individualization of the conflict had forced him to face the way he so mechanically ascribed his problems and frustrations to external groups or forces. By personalizing the encounter, by facing him man-to-man and stripping myself of everything that identified me with authority or with the ready stereotypes he had formerly used as focal points for psychopathic reactions, I had funneled his entire conflict and returned it to where it belonged—in the personal struggle with the ambivalently regarded father he still carried in his unconscious. Also, by degrees, it developed that I had correctly estimated this entire affair as a carefully arranged test which Anton was staging at this critical point in his therapy. Like all psychic infants of no matter what

212

age, he wanted to see how far he could go. On the one hand, he had been unable to trust my objective concern for his welfare; and, on the other, because of the old, secret and guilty love he had for his father (as the reverse of the hatred) he was compelled to try it. In this there was also the unconscious hope that I would return his hostility with hostility, thus allaying his hidden fears of homosexuality.

Homosexuality was a topic from which Anton wished to take full flight. But if he was to continue with his treatment, he knew that he must eventually come to grips with it. Actually, the inclination he had toward his own sex was merely part of the psychopathic character structure he possessed. Persons like Anton are neither homosexual nor heterosexual, but bisexual—attracted equally to both sexes. This lack of a clear orientation toward either sex is founded upon a failure of selectivity or discrimination between the sexes. It is due to their never having gone beyond the phallic stage in psychic development. They become, as it were, mired down in the oedipus conflict and remain there throughout their entire lives, or at least—as a clever colleague once put it to me—"until their gonads stop sizzling." Hence it is that psychopaths feel the need of sexual release in its most primitive terms, and use for purposes of relief any object, male or female, that presents itself. The greatest reason for failure in therapy with such characters is that this factor is not ordinarily taken into account, the oedipal drama not re-evoked. When Anton was forced to face it, the homosexual component in his personality came to light.

There followed, in succeeding weeks, the tale of Anton's sexual adventures. It was made up of the usual stuff and marked only by the transient, inconclusive nature of all of his contacts. At four he had been seduced into performing fellatio on an older boy, was shamed and embittered by the

213

experience and resolved to turn the tables when he got bigger and stronger. By the time he was twelve his greatest delight was in forcing smaller boys into his former position. He achieved much satisfaction from being the dominant one in these situations, and rarely hesitated to behave brutally with others to pay for his earlier submission and shame. His contacts with women, too, were fleeting, savage, and lacking even the pretense of tenderness. There was the prostitute who initiated him when he was eleven, and then a whole string of casual "lays," some bought with money, some with blows, the rest overborne in their defenses—if they had any—with a false ardor he assumed for the occasion. Every one of his sexual adventures was marked by the same set of circumstances and took the same course. No matter where Anton happened to be, nor under what conditions, the affair began with an acutely felt physiological need. He then set about finding an object *on* which (never *with* which) to satisfy the need. Anything that happened to come his way was welcome and usable—male or female, old or young, willing or unwilling. After the object had been used by Anton, it was summarily discarded. And this was the pattern of his sexual life, a stencil for the sex lives of all psychopaths, a consequence of the disrupted developmental course and its literal cessation, in psychic terms, in the phallic stage before the oedipus conflict has been resolved.

After therapy had penetrated to the homosexuality and laid bare the sexual core of the psychopathic state, it was but a short step to bring into focus the factor that lies at the very center of the psychopath's personality, so remote, so carefully defended, and so closely guarded that the knowledge of its presence is the very last thing to which he would admit. This is the special incestuous character of his relationship to his mother.

214

With justification it can be argued that something of incest enters into the relationship of all small children with their mothers. This fact is of the essence of the oedipus conflict, and as such it forms a dynamic for all neuroses as well as those developments which bypass neurosis to successful maturity. But in the case of the psychopath we find we are dealing with a special manifestation of this fact; and it soon develops that he has an added reason for his secret incestuous preoccupation. The reason, stated as simply as possible, is that mothers of psychopaths, consciously or unconsciously, overtly or covertly, seduce their children. Their seductions are not real in the sense of an act performed with or upon them; but they nevertheless behave in a seductive sexual fashion with a child and thus foster incestuous feelings. With such mothers the child is conceived of as a lover, and to all of her actions toward him she imparts an aura of sexuality. This stems from the fact that the mothers of psychopaths are usually unrequited in their feelings for their husbands—who are regularly strong, brutal, aggressive and domineering persons—or otherwise starved for love. The child is thus the recipient of mixed and forbidden feelings and desires, a stand-in or substitute for a lover.

I was led to an understanding of this factor of the special incestuous preoccupation in psychopaths when collecting data for a study on matricide.* During my years in prison work I had observed that one expletive, that referring to intercourse between son and mother (m-f), was at once the most dangerous and the most frequent on the lips of the psychopath. I had actually seen men killed for using it, and had learned that it was the single epithet with real potency

* "The Equivalents of Matricide," *The Psychoanalytic Quarterly*, Volume XVII, #4, 1948, p. 453.

and meaning among the many weary profanities of confined or regimented groups. Investigation soon disclosed that the power of this invective lay in that it touched a chord in psychopaths particularly, that for them it was true; in other words, that the expression gave voice to a basic fact which many of the psychopath's actions were aimed to keep hidden, and for the disclosure of which he was prepared to kill. Confirmation of this finding came from many sources; I recall an especially interesting letter from the eminent psychiatrist, Karl Menninger, reporting a similar recent case. Also, the opportunity I have had to analyze mothers of psychopaths bears out beyond doubt the proposition that they are unconscious seducers of their sons.

In Anton's case the unconscious (or, perhaps, scarce-conscious) seduction of the boy was carried on over the years when his mother was abed. Frustrated physically by her husband, but confronted with the sexual orgies he made no attempt to hide, the poor woman had expressed some of her craving through her behavior with Anton. In small or large ways she awakened, then kept alive, a desire for her in the boy. Her caresses were of a kind to kindle his passion, and her tempests of love were of a type that could not be misunderstood. In the analysis, Anton soon came to the realization that the chief reason he had run away from home was to put himself beyond the reach of temptation, that same temptation for which Oedipus lost his eyes and Hamlet his life. Nor was this all that Anton recalled and relived. Earlier—so early that to the unfamiliar with psychoanalysis it must seem incredible—there had been a series of literal rapes of the mother by her husband, with the infant lying on the same bed, a screaming witness to tableaux of violence. And, then, through the following years, there was the familiar tale of threat to his own organ by his calloused, care-

216

less father; a threat magnified and made more than usually plausible by the man's profession, by the ghoulish sense of humour he possessed—as indicated in the story of the bloody "facial" to which he forced Anton—and by other similar activities best left to the reader's imagination.

The many months of work that Anton and I spent collecting and collating the data he brought me at each session resulted in a rounded, comprehensible picture of the structure of this psychopathic personality. We emerged with an explanation of the making of a psychopath and the blueprint for the mentality of an entire class of humanity. For the ordering of Anton's own personality we achieved an almost one-to-one correspondence of internal dynamics, as they were arranged and motivated by his individual history, with external behavior. To begin with, the fear of death which Anton showed to such a pathological degree was at bottom a fear of castration. This arose in consequence of his forbidden sexual love for his mother, a love which she herself called forth and made palpable by her partially conscious sexual seduction of him. It was intensified by his father's undisguised threats to his genital, and also by the real possibilities the character and occupation of his father presented. The witnessing of sexual congress between father and mother also affected Anton profoundly. Despite the early age at which it took place, it became the basis for two conflicting identifications: one with the mother who was victimized by it and at the same time the recipient of the father's attentions; the other with the father who showed in this manner his strength and ability to harm, and who also enjoyed such a (to Anton) forbidden favor from the mother. Throughout the years thereafter, the temptation of Anton by his mother continued; but added to it, made more evident every day, was the living threat of his father.

217

The relationship to the father also became unclear and involved because of its characteristic ambivalent nature. One side of it was positive and attractive, an identification with the butcher's force and strength and dominance, to which Anton became attached and which he began to emulate. The attachment from this side, too, gave birth to the homosexual element in his later sexuality and determined the kind of erotic life he was to lead. But the other side of the relationship was a hostile hatred so forceful, so malignant, so vengeful, that the most ardent lifelong desire of Anton was to see his father dead, and, if possible, to kill him himself. As a child the destructive wish against his father was the most constant fact of his psychic life and the hoped-for result of all his actions. Nevertheless, because of his unconscious identification with his father, as well as the residue in him (as in all of us) of the ancient principle of talion, to kill his father meant his own death. It thus became necessary for Anton to do two things; to run away from home in order to place himself out of the range of the temptations of incest and murder; and to find targets for his hatred and aggression, targets that would permit him continuously to work out their pressures and so avoid self-destruction.

The fringe fascist party that Anton joined provided the adjustments he required to maintain a precarious balance between the warring parts of his personality and, above all, to drain the destruction in him. Because his discontent was greatest, he was able to mobilize similar discontent in others. For him, Fascism was the perfect adjustment. As the Communist Party substituted for Mac's neurosis,* so did Fascism perform for Anton's psychopathy. It provided everything for which a psychopath could ask: a whole world to hate, in extension of his primary hatred of the father; targets on

* See "Come Over, Red Rover."

which to exercise brutality and revenge, both as expressions of identity with the father's strength and dominance, and in retaliation for the hurts of childhood; symbolic trappings and uniform reminiscent of cherished infantile wishes and proclaimers, at the same time, of the homosexualism beneath the super-masculine pose.

In Anton's case the adjustment he had made through Fascism was destroyed when he came to prison. Under conditions of confinement there, the old conflicts were mobilized; symptoms that had been held in abeyance overwhelmed him. The festering evil, hidden beneath the pretense of fascist faith, showed through, proving this faith to be shallow and false. When psychoanalysis stripped it to the bone, the decay was revealed, the rotten underpinning had to crumble.

We terminated treatment when it was agreed that analysis had taken Anton as far as he could go while in prison. His symptoms had disappeared and his personality was altered to the extent that I, at least, would no longer have diagnosed him a psychopath. How permanent the "cure" was, I will never know. After all, time is the test—and in Anton's case time ran out on us.

Shortly after the conclusion of his analysis he was given a parole into the Army. I had a couple of letters from him, one from a P.O.E. on the West Coast, another from an undisclosed Pacific island. Two years later I learned he had been killed in action during the recovery of the Philippines. . . .

:
the jet-propelled couch

KIRK

> "No sound was there in that high presence chamber in Galing till in a minute's space the serving man returned with startled countenance, and, bowing before Lord Juss, said, 'Lord, it is an Ambassador from Witchland and his train. He craveth present audience.'"
>
> —E. R. Eddison, *The Worm Ouroboros.*

The chair behind the couch is not the stationary object it seems. I have traveled all over the world on it, and back and forth in time. Without moving from my easy seat I have met important personages and witnessed great events. But it remained for Kirk Allen to take me out of this world when he transformed the couch in my consulting room into a space ship that roved the galaxies.

My tale begins on a sultry June morning in Baltimore with a telephone call from a physician at a government installation in the Southwest. He said he was calling about a patient who had been sent to him and whom he, in turn, wished to refer to me. I asked him for details.

"The fellow I'm calling you about," he said, "is a man in his thirties, a research physicist with us out here. As far as I can tell, he's perfectly normal in every way except for a lot of crazy ideas about living part of the time in another world—

223

on another planet. Maybe this isn't so bad, but the trouble is he's really 'gone' so much—if you know what I mean—that his efficiency is way below par and the operation here is suffering because of it. As I say, he's a physicist. Washington sent him out to do a key job, and until a few weeks ago he was going great guns. But lately he's out of contact with the work so much and for so long that something's got to be done about it."

"How did you find out about his ideas?" I asked. "Did he complain to you—or what?"

"No," the doctor replied, "Allen—the patient's name is Kirk Allen—never said a thing about it. To him it's all perfectly natural. Of course, he's sorry about the drop in departmental efficiency. Apologizes all over the place and promises to do better. Says—get this!—says he'll *try to spend more time on this planet!*"

"And how did he get to you?" I persisted.

"Well, Allen's a section chief and the biggest part of his job is to evaluate and correlate reports of the research people under him and then send on digests of his section's work to the divisional head. His digests kept coming in later and later, and when they did get to the division head, Bagby—that's the division chief—not only noticed they were below standard for Allen, but some of them were incoherent and a few of the papers were covered with funny symbols or . . . pictographs, I guess you'd call them. . . ."

"—So Bagby called him in," I urged.

"Yes. He called him in and asked for an explanation."

"And what did Allen say?"

"Well, he really didn't say much of anything the first time. Just that he'd been away a lot lately and that he'd try to spend more time here from now on."

"Had he been away?" I asked.

"No. You see, it's really as hard to get out of here as to come in. Allen couldn't leave without all sorts of security red tape and Bagby knew he hadn't been off the premises for months and months. But then Bagby thought maybe Allen meant he'd been ill in his quarters or something. Well, Bagby checked, but the records showed that Allen hadn't missed a day. Then he called in some of the people Allen works with and got them to talk about him."

"Did he learn anything?" I asked.

"Nothing much, except that a few of the ones Bagby talked to said they'd noticed Allen seemed vague and distracted lately."

The doctor paused.

"Just lighting my pipe," he apologized. "Well, the whole thing hung fire for a few days—until the next batch of reports came in late again and covered over with the same kind of . . . doodling. So Bagby had another session with Allen."

"What happened this time?" I pressed.

"Well, the outcome of it was that Bagby sent Allen over to me. Seems that all he could get out of the boy was a lot of regretful apologies. Then Allen made this crazy statement about spending more time on this planet. He told Bagby it might be hard to arrange, but he'd do it somehow. Bagby tried to pressure him on this but couldn't get anywhere. It was all very vague, crazy talk. Bagby told me he thought the boy was pulling his leg at first, but when Allen persisted in what he said, Bagby realized the fellow must be off his rocker."

"Did Bagby ask about the doodling on the reports?"

"Oh, yes," the doctor said. "Seems all Allen had to say was that those symbols were notes he intended to transcribe into his diaries. Said he never got around to it and wanted

225

Bagby to give the reports back so he could catch up with his back entries!"

"You said Bagby sent Allen to you."

"Yes. Matter of fact, he's in my waiting room right now."

"What have you decided?"

"Only that I can't handle this," he replied. "I'm just an ordinary medical man. When it comes to stuff like this—psychiatric stuff—all I know is that I shouldn't fool with it. That's why I'm calling you."

"I couldn't possibly come out there. . . ."

The doctor chuckled. "We wouldn't have you if you could. . . . I'm sure you understand. . . . No; if you'll agree to take the fellow as a patient we'll get him to you in Baltimore. Incidentally, we'll be responsible for his fees."

"Why don't you use regular government facilities?"

"Because none are available to us," the doctor replied. "You see, Allen is with us under contract. We're required to provide medical services for him, but we're not set up here for his kind of case—I guess it just didn't occur to anyone that scientists might blow their tops like other people. So in a case like this I'm obliged to use my discretion and make the best disposition I can."

I hesitated. The doctor's voice recalled me from my speculations. "What d'you say?"

"I'm thinking it over," I said. "Tell me; is it your impression that Allen requires hospitalization?"

"Oh, no," he replied quickly. "I'd say this what-ever-it-is—fantasy, I guess you'd call it—is a perfectly innocuous business. I mean, Allen appears to be completely unaffected by it most of the time."

"But from what you say he's involved in it more and more," I pointed out.

226

"That's why I think something should be done right now. Maybe if we get him under treatment at once we can block it here."

"That's possible," I agreed.

"I really can't explain how it works exactly," the doctor continued, "but I have the impression his psychosis—I suppose that's what it is—doesn't interfere with his ability to take care of himself or get around in a normal fashion. At least not at this point. I'd say from what he's told me that he has a certain control over it—can get in and out of it when he wants to, I mean. And he's really one of the mildest, nicest chaps ever. I can assure you he'll be no custodial problem."

"I'm glad of that," I said.

"Then you'll take him?" the doctor asked eagerly.

"I can't say for sure," I answered, "but I'll be glad to see him and let you know."

"That's good enough for me," he said.

Kirk Allen arrived in Baltimore three days after my talk with the doctor. Any speculations I had had about him as a "mad scientist" evaporated when I saw him in my office. A vigorous-looking man of average height, clear-eyed and blond, his seersucker unwrinkled despite the long trip and the humidity, his panama encircled with a gay band, he looked like a junior executive. His manner, as he introduced himself and we made some initial small talk about the weather and his flight east, was charming. He spoke with just enough diffidence to let me know that the situation he now found himself in was slightly embarrassing. His pleasant, well-modulated baritone voice intrigued me from the first. Although his speech was unmistakably American, it had a vaguely foreign, musical lilt. This observation I

227

chose as the point of entrance for my clinical examination of him.

"You were not born in the United States, were you, Mr. Allen?" I said.

"No," he answered, "but how did you know?"

"Your voice, the way you talk. There's something about it. . . . I would suspect you spoke a softer language at one time. What was it?"

"You're right," he said. "My first language was a Polynesian dialect, but I thought it was pretty well hidden. Does it annoy you?"

"Not at all," I said. "As a matter of fact, I find it quite pleasant. Tell me, how did it happen?"

"My father," he answered, "was a naval officer. I was born in Hawaii, where he was stationed when the First World War broke out. My nurse until I was six years old was a Polynesian woman, and it was her dialect I learned to speak as a small child. Later my father was Commissioner on one of the mandated islands, and we remained there until his death, when I was fourteen. All that time I spoke English with no one except governesses who came out from the States to take care of me, and my parents, whom I hardly saw. My playmates, of course, were all native children and . . ."

Kirk Allen was the only child of his parents' marriage. His father, already an old man when Kirk was born, had been married previously and was even then a grandfather. Kirk recalled him as a man of imposing presence. A commander of fighting vessels under sail, and later of coal-burning men-of-war, he seemed always to have a deck beneath his feet. He was proud, taciturn, stern, and kept his more tender emotions rigorously in check. From those

228

about him he exacted absolute, immediate obedience, for which the only reward was a gruff monosyllabic acknowledgment or, in Kirk's case, a tousling of the boy's hair with his heavy hand. To cross this old man was dangerous. The walking stick he carried was never out of his grasp; there was no one on the island, except his wife and the transient white governesses, who did not at some time feel its weight. And yet, Kirk said, something about his father was warm and kind, something indefinable was softer. That quality was remembered in later years chiefly through the boy's sense of smell; a blend of tobacco, whisky, leather and salt air would evoke, for Kirk, a poignant picture of the aging gentleman who was seldom seen out of naval uniform, who conducted his home and "his island" like the wardroom of a battleship.

Why his mother had married the Commodore—as Kirk's father was called—was a mystery. She was at least thirty-five years younger than he and temperamentally his opposite. Her father had been a wealthy diplomat who had served his country in most of the European capitals and died under tragic, somewhat scandalous, circumstances in Italy. She had been educated in France at a convent that specialized in the care of girls from similar backgrounds, but her high spirits and audacity had led her into many amusing and—for those times—daring escapades. When her father died, her mother, who could not tolerate the revelations following his death, retired to Honolulu, where she felt more secure from gossip. Kirk's mother, then eighteen, went with her. The two women lived quietly there. The girl was under constant supervision, her innate gaiety severely suppressed and her social nature restrained. For about five years she devoted herself exclusively to her mother. Then, at a diplomatic function, she met the elderly widower. After a brief courtship she married him, perhaps, Kirk thought, as a desperate means of escaping her mother.

Immediately after marriage Mrs. Allen recovered her natural ebullience. The Commodore was indulgent with his beautiful young wife, proud of her in a fatherly fashion, and rejuvenated by her zestfulness. Their home rapidly became Honolulu's social center and remained so throughout the war years, although the Commodore was not often present to play his accustomed role of benign observer.

Kirk was born in 1918. Immediately after his birth the family went to Paris, where his father was assigned for duty at the peace negotiations. The Allens remained there about a year, and then the Commodore was reassigned to Hawaii. Shortly after their return to the Pacific area the old man was appointed Commissioner over a mandated island. There was, Kirk later heard, some question about accepting this assignment and much debate over whether his mother and he should accompany the Commodore. His parents were reluctant to exchange the comfortable life of Honolulu, where they were the undisputed leaders of society, for the rigors of existence on a remote outpost. They agreed, however, to accept the appointment for one year in order not to prejudice a long record of excellent government service. After this demonstration of loyalty, they felt they could reasonably request assignment back to Hawaii or Stateside. However, life did not work out according to their plans.

The first year of their stay on the island passed rapidly. Both the Commodore and his wife were busy, he with administrative duties and she with welfare projects for the natives. When the year ended the Commodore put in for replacement as planned. His still very young wife joyously anticipated the return to more civilized society and lived

230

only for the day when a new Commissioner would take over. But none came, and the days of anxious expectation stretched into weeks. Finally, the Commodore was informed that his application for replacement had been denied.

At the collapse of her hopes, Kirk's mother reverted to her premarital apathy: she lost her sparkle, became lethargic and melancholy, and went into a decline of spirits from which she did not recover for ten years and more. For a time she spent her energies in quarreling with her husband over their future, vainly urging him to resign. His concept of duty, however, was rigid, and although he indulged her in everything else, this he refused to do. Nor would she listen to his suggestion that she and her child return to Hawaii. Obviously needful of his paternal protection, and fearful to face the world without it, she chose to resign herself resentfully. She abandoned the projects she had begun with such enthusiasm only the previous year and withdrew from all social intercourse. Whereas she had formerly taken at least a supervisory interest in Kirk, she now left him completely in the charge of his Hawaiian nurse, native servants, or the governesses who came and went as the years passed. Her relations with the Commodore became merely formal: she would emerge from her room only at dinner time and retire as soon as the meal ended. What she did during the long days, Kirk never knew. She became a shadowy, mysterious figure in his life—someone unknown and apart.

The only other significant, hence formative, human relationships Kirk had during childhood and early adolescence were with his Hawaiian nurse, the native women who took charge of him after her death, and the few white women whom his father employed from the States.

Myna, the Hawaiian nurse, was the first and most im-

231

portant influence on Kirk's development. She had come to the family as a wet-nurse for the infant and remained to mother him until the end of his sixth year. Kirk's recollection of her as a person is unclear, but the feelings evoked by her memory are sweet and strong. She was a dark-skinned, buxom young Polynesian matron who came down from the hill country to seek employment in Honolulu just at the time Kirk was born. She could speak only a few words of English but was bright and intelligent and took over the mothering of the infant the moment she saw him. He was left in her complete care and loved her with an absoluteness which she returned. Not only was he nourished from her huge bosom, but from her vast placidity and comforting presence he obtained everything his real mother denied. He slept with her, ate with her, played with her. During the day she was hardly separated from him for a moment, and at night her warm nakedness engulfed him. In every way Myna treated Kirk as her child and reared him according to her own tradition. His first language was hers, and his early habits were determined by her native culture. Because his mother was busy, during that time, becoming the island's social queen, Myna had her own way with Kirk. Indeed, only when a trivial incident suddenly recalled the boy's presence to his parents did they bother to interfere with her charge. One day a visitor expressed surprise that Kirk prattled only in the dialect he had been taught by his nurse and vigorously ventured an opinion that the child was old enough to begin learning a "white" language. That brought the situation to the attention of Kirk's mother, and for a few months Myna was given other duties. As a result, Kirk learned the rudiments of English and was slowly—but only slightly—transformed from a "little savage" into a passable facsimile of a "civilized" child. When Kirk recalled this

232

period of re-education, he remembered it as a painful experience.

"Maybe it wasn't that way," he said, "but I think of it only in terms of constraint—if you can understand what I mean. The world seemed to close in on me somehow, to box me in. The worst part was shoes and clothing. I think I was used to being free—physically, I mean. Then everything became—well—tight . . . A matter of buttons and laces, things to put on and take off. And I had to worry then—about keeping clean and such things." But his mother could not maintain enthusiasm very long for the new regime, and she rapidly tired of her unaccustomed role. Gradually, Myna recovered her place. After that, however, the nurse kept a weather eye on the amenities of speech, clothing, manners and habits of her charge, and was careful to insure that Kirk—when his parents were about, at least—appeared to be a child of their culture rather than hers.

Participation in this conspiracy only deepened the love between Kirk and his nurse. By the time the family went to the island which was to be their home for many years, the bond between these two was absolute and enduring. On the island, Kirk was entrusted to Myna. Except for a few hours each day when the boy attended a school organized by his mother for the native children and taught by the wife of an Army officer, he never left Myna's side. She died suddenly when he was six years old, and the space in his life left by her death was never filled.

There were no other white children on the island. The Americans who came and went through the years were childless, so until he was fourteen Kirk did not see another boy or girl like himself. While outwardly this curious condition seemed to have no significance, it led to internal perplexity, fashioning a psychic predisposition that did not

233

reveal its consequences until, decades later, his mental estrangement became obvious. Throughout childhood and early adolescence he was haunted by the difference between himself and his companions, a difference not solely of skin color but of social heritage and the innumerable subtleties of life. While he could communicate with his playmates more directly and more fully than he could with white adults even of his own family, he was still set apart from them and different. There was always something, some invisible screen, between him and them, some barrier he could not bridge. And this produced a split in his personality that generated two contradictory views of self and world. On one side, a lowering of self-esteem developed— a feeling of inferiority and a sense of having been rejected for good cause. The native world, with its warmth and communal cohesiveness, opened to him only in part, admitted him only halfway. While he longed to share in it totally, he could not; and he naturally attributed this to some defect in himself, some profound but undiscoverable fault.

On the other side Kirk developed an internal sense of superiority. Because of the deference accorded him as a white boy, the son of the Commissioner, and because he was not permitted to take the final step toward total community with his native associates, a conviction of difference and special election was born in him. A private sense of distance between himself and all other inhabitants of the world grew: he *was* different and better, he told himself; more, he was therefore entitled to special treatment.

Between six and nine Kirk was cared for by a succession of native women. These women, he remembers, were cut from the same pattern as his lost Myna, but with none was he as close. Unlike her, they had other preoccupations, often

234

children of their own, and they cared for him dutifully rather than from love.

At nine began the parade of governesses. Like the native women, they tend to merge in Kirk's memory. Only two were important: one because she increased the boy's sense of isolation; the other because she introduced him to sex.

The governesses were brought out to educate Kirk. There were four or five of them: each remained the better part of a year; all but one left because of boredom. Life on the remote island, so romantic in prospect, in actuality proved disappointing. Since none happened to be an unusual person who could find entertainment or interest in that oneness with Nature which the natives made into an art of life, the experience was dull and devastating. The job of educating Kirk was the single responsibility of each governess: nevertheless, it was onerous. He had an overwhelming curiosity and, even then, an insatiable intellectual appetite. By nine, despite a slow start and casual teaching, he was far advanced in ability to read and comprehend. Forced in upon himself and constrained to seek substitutes for significant interpersonal relationships and experiences, he found in reading his only way of apprehending the world. Carefully, painfully, but later with amazing ease, he ploughed his way through everything readable on the island. The sorry textbooks used in the school, the religious tracts sent by missions, the volumes in the library of a resident Catholic priest, the paperbacks discarded by sailors from vessels that put in for various reasons, the novels brought out by wives of transient island personnel, his father's naval, engineering, navigational and gunnery manuals—all of these were devoured by Kirk, not once but many times over as the years of isolation mounted. Merely to keep up with his sponge-

235

like mind demanded more of the governesses than they were prepared to give. The best they could do—and in some areas they did that well—was to organize and discipline what he already knew.

I have said that only two of these women made any real impression on Kirk. One was his first governess, a middle-aged widow from a Far Western state, whose passion for cleanliness was pathological and whose hatred and mistrust of the natives amounted to hysteria. From the moment she arrived until the day she left Kirk's life was a hell of prohibitions and negative commands. This miserable person tried to foist on the boy her compulsions, her fears, her prejudices. She insisted on physical cleanliness to a degree beyond reason. At least twice each day he was scrubbed with scalding water; the slightest spot on his shirt was made the occasion for a complete change of clothing. She imbued Kirk with such dread of contamination from his familiar, innocuous surroundings that he literally threaded his way through the world like a cat on a sideboard. Because this pasteurized virago considered the native children "filthy niggers," Kirk was forbidden even to converse with his friends and disbarred from any fellowship except hers. After she went, he was again free to consort with the children, but he could never recover his former sense of easy naturalness with them.

While this woman—"Sterile Sally," Kirk called her during his analysis—did not remain long on the island, she affected the boy profoundly. Because of her, he was pushed more deeply inside himself. As a consequence of this added isolation, his fantasy life—until then of a fashion and degree usual among lonely children—increased sharply. Daydreaming now came to occupy much of his time, and there appeared those lavish, imaginative reconstructions of the

236

world which were to be so significant for him and so characteristic of his life up to the day we met.

The details of the initial fantasy that Kirk toyed with during Sterile Sally's residence and for some while thereafter need not concern us here. It was a childish hodgepodge, constructed from odd remnants of reading. He identified himself with characters from the *Oz* books, for example, and mentally played out a cordial existence in a friendlier, more exciting world. This primary experience unfolded the imaginative facility and the technique of mental detachment which he developed to astonishing proportions in adulthood.

At eleven a new governess entered Kirk's life, and opened for him another category of experience. She was a young woman whom Kirk recalls as quite attractive, who remained only long enough to introduce the boy to sex—and run off with the schoolteacher's husband. Here is Kirk's story of his sexual seduction:

"You must remember that life on the island was very different from life as you know it. Kids mature more rapidly there and sex is treated in another way. Sex play, for example, is not only open but encouraged by adults of the native community. The natural curiosity of kids is unchecked and the exploration of each other's bodies—which here children do in secret—is conducted openly. Matter of fact, the adults, if they attend to it at all, do so with amusement. Later, of course, the whole thing is surrounded with odd taboos because of their involved kinship regulations, but none of these apply before a certain age. Things like masturbation are carried on in public. The loin cloth or breech clout is the only article of clothing worn by men, while the women wear only a skirt or, if they work around whites, a loose dress. Practically the first thing anyone does

237

when he enters his own hut is to discard whatever he's been wearing and go about naked. Until ceremonial initiation for boys and marriage for girls, children ordinarily wear nothing except when they go to school or church. I imagine things are different now, but when I lived there that's the way it was.

"Anyhow, this much was true and probably still is: kids know all about sex from the beginning, and except for the few taboos about who can do what with whom after initiation there's almost absolute freedom. Parents copulate in front of their children, lovers conduct their affairs in the bush where kids occasionally run across them and think nothing of it, and so on.

"Like any other child, I knew what there was to know about sex and it never bothered me in any way. Although adults showed a certain restraint when I was around, in this area the kids accepted me wholly and I participated in their sex play. There was no difference between me and my playmates except that I was a shade lighter than the lightest of them and my hair was softer and blondish and I usually wore shorts.

"When Miss Lilian arrived—that was her name I now remember—I was, at least by her standards, a sexual sophisticate, although I hadn't actually had intercourse. Though I was not capable of ejaculation, my genitals were well developed and I even had a sprinkling of pubic hair. She noticed this and commented on it when she gave me my first bath. I paid no attention to her comment or her obvious interest in my sexual equipment at that time; but as the days passed she behaved in such a fashion that it was impossible, even at my age, to ignore her preoccupation with the whole matter of sex. Not only did she question me closely about the sex behavior of the natives; she also asked

238

me many questions about my own experience. Maybe it was my casualness that led her on. . . . I don't know. At any rate, it wasn't long before she took to undressing before me—exhibiting herself, I guess you'd call it—and being provocative in a way I had never seen any woman behave. Native women and girls certainly never acted that way. Even in their complete nakedness there was a kind of modesty—or maybe it was just unconcern. But I soon understood that Miss Lilian was urging me on—and she succeeded. She didn't just take her clothes off those nights when she undressed in my room; she peeled herself like a strip-teaser, standing in front of the mirror of my bureau where she could see me lying naked on my bed.

"Well, it worked. One night after she had been there a few months she did her little act in front of the mirror and, watching her, I got an erection. I remember I tried to hide it—not out of shame, you understand, but because of some vague feeling that it was somehow not right to have her see it. It couldn't have been shame because shame and sex, then, had nothing to do with each other. Among the natives you'd often see kids walking around with erections, and sometimes even grown men; but nobody paid the slightest attention. Shame among the natives was connected with other things— eating in the presence of others except at ceremonial banquets, failure to pay a debt, neglecting to employ the correct form of address to someone, doing anything taboo; these things occasioned shame, not things connected with sex. So what I felt when I got an erection watching Miss Lilian wasn't shame. Now I think it might have been a feeling of wrongfulness, a sort of prescience (if you like) of danger that this revelation of sexuality would betray me into behavior I should avoid. Let's put it this way: something in me revolted at the prospect of having any kind of

239

sex with Miss Lilian and I tried to hide my erection to keep from doing it."

(Later Kirk understood this feeling he so painfully tried to describe during our first interviews. Both the feeling and its significance became clear when, during analysis, it was revealed that Miss Lilian was the first and only woman with whom Kirk had had intercourse. She was, of course, taboo for him, as were all white women—a consequence of his deeply unconscious incestuous fears. So the feeling Kirk was talking about is really connected with guilt—which explains not only this incident but its drastic immediate as well as long-term consequences.)

"Needless to say, Miss Lilian spotted my aroused state before I could hide it—and that was that. Her eyes got big and her chest heaved, and the next thing I knew she was crawling all over me.

"Well, that first attempt was unsuccessful for me—and so were the next few. But before long—probably because the hormones increased under such stimulation—I was able to have ejaculations. After that happened Miss Lilian was insatiable. She initiated intercourse two or three times every night and often during the day. I became a sort of sex toy for her. In this respect she had an inventive mind. I guess there wasn't a position or act she didn't experiment with.

"How did I feel about this? Well, I was of two minds. I'd be lying if I said I didn't enjoy some of it; but I'd be lying even more if I said it was all pleasure. It wasn't. There were times when I had to run away from her lust, lock her out of my room, or even threaten to tell the Commodore. Later, when I found out about her affair with the schoolteacher's husband, I'd threaten to tell him. But even worse was the physical debility from so much sexual activity—remember,

I was only eleven years old. I grew vague and listless, haggard, run-down—maybe not from sex but certainly from loss of sleep and muscular fatigue. When I was unable to respond she would get furious. Sometimes she would beat me, claw at me with her nails, bite me. And when that wouldn't work—how she expected it to is beyond me!—she'd demand I satisfy her somehow, if not with some part of my person then with something artificial—a hairbrush, maybe, or whatever was handy. . . .

"If she had remained on the island much longer than she did, Miss Lilian, I think, would have headed into real trouble. However, the schoolteacher's husband, an Army officer, came along. I don't recall much about that. She sneaked off to see him a few times, and then one morning both of them were gone. Apparently they bribed the master of one of the merchant vessels and were smuggled aboard just before the ship sailed. She didn't even say good-by and I can't say I was very distressed about her going."

With Miss Lilian gone Kirk returned to his usual pursuits with an even greater sense of isolation. Brief as her stay had been, she had brought about an almost complete severance of the boy from his playmates, for she had been not only sexually possessive but jealous of attention paid to anyone other than herself, and had demanded his constant presence, his total preoccupation. After she left, there was no way of closing the gap his absence from the group had created, no way of resuming intimacy.

Other factors, also, now alienated Kirk. His experiences with the nymphomanic governess had catapulted him into premature adulthood beyond the range of his friends and he could not have achieved fellowship with them even had they been willing. But most important was the fact that he

241

assisted his own alienation unconsciously. It became his self-punishment for an awful, ever-present sense of guilt, and this, in turn, exacerbated the inferiority he already suffered. In a dim and at that time inexplicable way the boy became plagued with a kind of horror of his actions, a horror that can be compared with what the natives of his island felt when they trespassed the boundaries of taboo. His relationship with the native culture in which he was reared had deeply affected him; in his soul he was an islander. Therefore, his sexual behavior with the white woman, to whom he was related psychologically by common color and origins, was tantamount to incest, to a crossing of the invisible line no person of that culture could cross without punishment, sometimes inflicted by the group, more often by the person on himself. So, feeling that he had "sinned," Kirk, like any islander, was covered with guilt, which he chose to expiate by separation from society in the same manner as a native might by disappearing into the jungle.

In his isolation Kirk returned to his books, now his only friends. The fantasies which he had largely abandoned during Miss Lilian's residence once more claimed his attention. While outwardly engaged in reading, exploring the island, or studying with his new governess, he was inwardly living a full and exciting life. From the stories he read he constructed another and different universe, peopled with characters from the tales of his favorite authors and infused with vivid movement, dramatic event and colorful detail. In the beginning such fantasies were random, fitful, inconsistent and loosely constructed as most daydreams tend to be. He did not concentrate on any given set of characters, events, or places, but freely developed whatever took his fancy—which then followed rather closely the book or story he happened to be reading. But all that changed in his

242

twelfth year when a trivial coincidence altered the boy's life.

One day a large crate of books was delivered to the mission house. Kirk, whose appetite for books was well known to the missionary, was invited to borrow whatever he wished. Unlike most such deliveries, this turned out to be a windfall. Instead of the usual collection of sermons, dog-eared children's books, sets of inspirational essays, and biographies of characters unknown to anyone but the biographers, this shipment contained many novels, including a whole set of books by a highly imaginative and prolific writer. Gleefully, Kirk took his pick and settled himself for a season of pleasure.

The first book Kirk chose to read was a novel by a famous English author. He had already made this writer's acquaintance through other books, which he had enjoyed immensely, and now looked forward to a tale whose interest was guaranteed. He had hardly begun reading, however, when he suddenly became aware of the fact that the name of the hero of this novel was the same as his own. Momentarily, this gave him pause. As he describes it, "a kind of shock ran through me: for a minute I felt completely disoriented." This feeling dissolved rapidly and Kirk returned to the book. But now he read with greater interest, and as the story unrolled he found himself intent and involved as never before. When he finished the book—the same day he had begun it—he turned immediately to the first page and read it through again. After a third reading he finally set the book aside.

Several days later the experience of encountering a fictional character bearing his name was repeated—this time in a volume of semiphilosophical reflections by an American stylist of the 'twenties. The discovery once more shocked

243

Kirk: it led him into passionate participation in the book, followed by so many rereadings that parts of it were automatically committed to memory.

It was not long after these two experiences that Kirk again came across his own name applied to a character of fiction. This time, however, the experience caused no shock of surprise: Kirk says, "I think I expected it somehow, and when it happened it was as if I had known it all the time and was finding something that had been lost." On this occasion the character who bore his name was the protagonist in a long series of fantasies by another American author. Through volume after volume of strange and adventurous tales this figure weaved a perilous way as all-conquering hero—a prototype for the modern Superman. Fascinated, Kirk followed. And soon there came about in him an uncanny transformation which can be described only in his own words. . . .

"As I read about the adventures of Kirk Allen in these books the conviction began to grow on me that the stories were not only true to the very last detail but that they were about *me*. In some weird and inexplicable way *I knew that what I was reading was my biography*. Nothing in these books was unfamiliar to me: I recognized everything—the scenes, the people, the furnishings of rooms, the events, even the words that were spoken—recognized all this with a sense of familiarity that one has when he sees a house in which he has lived or a friend from years gone by. The whole business, if you like, was one long, almost interminable, *déjà vu* experience—as you psychologists call it. My everyday life began to recede at this point. In fact, it became fiction—and, as it did, the books became my reality. To daily affairs, to the task of staying alive, eating, studying, moving about on the island, I gave little attention—for this was dream. Real life—*my* real life—was in the books. There I lived: there I had my being."

Kirk read the numerous volumes of his "biography" over and over again until he was as familiar with them as with his own reflection in the mirror. Soon he no longer needed the books "to refresh my memory," but was able to recapitulate them entirely in his mind. While his corporeal body was living the life of a mundane boy, the vital part of him was far off on another planet, courting beautiful princesses, governing provinces, warring with strange enemies. But it should not be thought that he was content during this period after the books were discarded merely to rehearse the experiences recorded in them. Now, using "his biographer's" material as a base, he took off on his own. Assisted by the maps, charts, diagrams, architectural layouts, genealogical schemes and timetables painstakingly worked out while using the books for his guide, he filled in spaces between the volumes with fantasy "recollections" of his own; and when this was done, he began the task of his life: that of picking up where his "biographer" had left off and recording the subsequent history of the heroic Kirk Allen. Of this immense undertaking I shall have more to say later. Now it is time to return to our sketch of the pedestrian existence of our subject.

When Kirk was fourteen his father, the Commodore, died. Almost immediately his mother awakened from her ten-year apathy and prepared to leave the island. She arranged for Kirk to be admitted to a preparatory school in the eastern part of the United States, accompanied him there, and when satisfied that he had settled in the school, she left to begin a restless Odyssey. For fifteen years thereafter, until she died on an island off the Greek coast, she moved about the world. Only occasionally during these

245

years did she visit Kirk, and then but briefly; nor did she write to him except when it became necessary to discuss financial matters.

Meanwhile, Kirk entered a new type of existence, very different from the one he had known, yet marked as before by loneliness and isolation. He found it all but impossible to relate to his school fellows casually; and although he made a few friends there—and later at the University— he was unable to enter into real companionship with any- one. He devoted himself to his studies, in which he progressed with amazing rapidity, and to the development of his fantasies. During holidays he either remained at school or visited the homes of his stepbrothers. Occasionally he went on solitary walking tours.

At nineteen Kirk entered one of the great Eastern univer- sities. Here his interests solidified and he pointed his effort toward a career in science. Three years later he matriculated for advanced study. His scientific talents were immediately recognized by his professors. After the first semester he was given a research fellowship under the joint auspices of the University and the United States Government. When he completed the requirements for his doctoral degree he was mustered into military service and assigned to a special proj- ect then approaching a significant conclusion. When the Second World War ended (in a manner that had something to do with Kirk's work) he was discharged. There followed a year of study abroad under a much-coveted grant. When he returned he was invited to join the project at X Reser- vation.

Throughout the years between the discovery of his "biography" and his appearance in Baltimore, a large seg- ment of Kirk's time and a portion of his mind were devoted to the detailed development of his abiding fantasy. Whenever he was not totally preoccupied with scholastic or scientific work—and often even then, since his fantasy and his research interests (and assignments) coincided in certain ways—he was engaged in weaving an ever more closely knit imaginative mental life, the main lines of which were dictated by the recorded "biography" he had consumed so avidly on the island before the age of fourteen. But, over the years, some remarkable changes were made in his mode of fantasying, changes which brought him always closer to the breaking point signalized by his arrival in Baltimore. Here is how Kirk describes it:

"As you know, I became convinced the books were about me, that somehow the author had obtained a knowledge of my life and had written its story. So the first thing I had to do was remember, and it seemed to me that I actually recalled everything he described. It was, of course, a curious position to be in—an adolescent boy remembering the adventures of himself as a grown man. But I got around this difficulty by convincing myself that the books had been composed in the future and had been sent back by some means into the present for my instruction. It's hard to explain, but I soon developed the notion—now a favorite one with science-fiction writers—of the co-existence of temporal dimensions so that the past and the future are simultaneous with the present. This made it possible to live a current life but, all the same, to *remember the future.*

"My first effort, then, was to remember. I started by fixing in my mind, and later on paper in the form of maps, genealogical tables, and so on, what the author of my 'biography' had put down. When I had this mastered, by remembering I was able to correct his errors, fill in many details, and close gaps between one volume of the biography and the next. It took some years and an enormous amount of effort to accomplish this; but when it was done I had the tremendous satisfaction of knowing that I possessed the complete story of my life up to a certain point, and I was able to review it—actually live it in my head—while I carried on my everyday business. At any time of the day or night, with hardly any effort, I could select an incident or adventure and, while appearing to be doing what was expected of me at that moment, I would actually be living a completely different life by a simultaneous process of recall of the past and experience in the present. I know it sounds complicated, but it wasn't; and if it was, it was not nearly so complex as what happened next.

"After some time I became bored with reliving my future life and intrigued with the question of what was going to happen to Kirk Allen—or, from where I sat, what *had* happened to him—after the place at which the writer's 'biography' ended. You will recall that when the series of volumes ends, Kirk Allen is still a young and vigorous man. So I set myself the task of remembering what was going to happen to me beyond the point reached by my 'biographer.' There were no guide-lines for this, so the job became terribly difficult. One of the great difficulties, by the way, was to distinguish between imagination and re-call. I knew how easy it would be merely to imagine a future for Kirk Allen and fool myself into believing it. But I wanted truth—curious as this may seem to you—and I determined doggedly only to remember. The mental disci-pline this required was terrific. I found it was so easy to fool myself that many times I abandoned the job in disgust and returned to the now simple process of recalling what had been recorded. But I always turned back to the task and soon developed a technique for distinguishing between—

don't laugh!—imagination and recall. I discovered that always, when I imagined, some small detail, usually an insignificant thing—a color, a view, a costume, a name . . . something—was out of place; but when I *remembered*, everything fit. Pursuing this technique, I became remarkably adept at distinguishing between the reality of my recollections of the unrecorded future and the imaginative excursions to which I was so liable. For many years I devoted myself to this operation—indeed, until I returned from abroad and began work on the project I was on when I came here. And as I continued this process of—what?— predictive recall?—I kept careful records of it, writing down and preserving every detail.

"When I got back from Europe the whole business took a new turn. Here's what happened.

"One night soon after moving to the X Reservation I was preparing a map of a territory Kirk Allen had explored during an expedition to a planet in another galaxy. I won't stop to explain this—you'll find it in the papers I'm going to give you. Anyhow, I was working on this map very determinedly, stopping only now and then to refresh my memory. Somehow the details refused to come clear, although I had a vivid memory of flying over the territory at a fairly low altitude and taking stereoscopic photographs of it. I also remembered that when I arrived back at my home planet from this adventure, I gave a set of the pictures to the proper scientists at the Intergalactic Institute, but kept copies of the originals for myself, planning to study them more closely later. I even remembered exactly where they were—in a filing cabinet in a secret room in my palace. I tried to recall whether I had ever looked at the photos after filing them, but I could not and concluded Kirk Allen had simply put them away and forgotten them. Well, the un-

249

finished map lay before me on my drafting board, while the information I needed to correct and complete the map was more remote from me in space than the furthest star I could see, and far ahead of me in time. It was the first time I had encountered such a situation—ordinarily my memory served me perfectly—and I was perplexed and angry, as frustrated as I have ever been. I thought of those blasted photographs stuck away there in a place no one but I could get to. I wracked my brains trying to recall the landscape I had flown over, and the pictures I had glanced at casually before putting them away. No use. I was furious. I cursed myself for not looking at them more closely when I had them. And then I thought: 'If only . . . if only I were there, right now, I would go directly to those files and get those pictures!'

"No sooner had I given voice to this thought than my whole being seemed to respond with a resounding 'Why not?'—and in that same moment I *was* there!

"How can I explain this to you? One moment I was just a scientist on X Reservation bending over a drawing board in a clapboard B.Q. in the middle of an American desert;— the next moment I was Kirk Allen, Lord of a planet in an interplanetary empire in a distant universe, garbed in the robes of his exalted office, rising from the carved desk he had been sitting at, walking toward a secret room in his palace, entering it, going over to a filing cabinet in a recess in the wall, extracting an envelope of photographs, leaving the room and retracing his steps, sitting again at his desk, and studying the pictures with intense concentration.

"It was over in a matter of minutes, and I was again at the drawing board—the self you see here. But I knew the experience was real; and to prove it I now had a vivid recollection of the photographs, could see them as clearly as
250

if they were still in my hands, and had no trouble at all completing the map.

"You can imagine how this experience affected me. I was stunned by it, shaken to the core, but excited as I had never been. In some way I could not comprehend, by merely desiring it to be so, I had crossed the immensities of Space, broken out of Time, and merged with—literally become— that distant and future self whose like I had until now been remembering. Don't ask me to explain. I can't, although God knows I've tried! Have I discovered the secret of tele-portation? Do I have some special psychic equipment? Some unique organ or what Charles Fort called a 'wild talent'? Damned if I know!

"From that night on I have spent more and more time being the Kirk Allen of the future. At any time, no matter where I am or what I am doing, I can will to be him, and at once I am. As him, as my future self, I live his life; and when I return to this present self, I bring back the memories I have of that future and so am able to correct the records I am keeping. Now, you see, I no longer have to depend on memory: I actually live what the future Kirk Allen lives; and return here to amend or add to the biography, to the maps and tables and other stuff I will give you to examine. Please don't ask me how I get back to this present self— I can't tell you any more than I can tell you how I *become* him by merely wishing. When I am him, I don't seem to know of this earthly self—I guess I've forgotten it some-how—so I could not wish to return. It just happens—that's all. . . .

"But there is one thing more I should tell you, and that is that I am aware of a great disparity in the passage of time between events in the lives of these two selves. My existence here, in this present, goes at a pace you'd call normal; while

251

as Kirk Allen of the future time goes fast, seems compressed. What I mean is that the time I spend as *him*—although as him I experience it at a normal pace—compresses into only minutes on the clock my mundane self keeps. So I live perhaps a year or more as *that* Kirk Allen in a few minutes of *this* Kirk Allen's time. But what got me into trouble, I think, and led to my being sent here, is the fact that I've been spending more and more of my time as the other Kirk Allen, leading more and more the life there, going more frequently and staying longer. I don't think I can be blamed for this—his is such an exciting life compared with mine; but of course I have a job to do here. . . ."

The life history of Kirk, as I have set it down here, took some days to obtain. Although always polite and co-operative he was reluctant to part with its intimate details and they had to be extracted from him by careful, some-times subtle, questioning. The chief difficulty, however, was that he regarded himself as completely normal, was thor-oughly convinced of the reality of all that he experienced, and could not comprehend its significance in terms of his sanity. He acknowledged, of course, that his experiences were extraordinary, that they were, to put it mildly, fan-tastic; but he believed, as he said, that they were due to some unknown psychic quality or ability with which he had been somehow endowed. And toward this unknown factor he had a casual attitude: if it was there—and it evidently was—he would make the most of it, he would exploit it, he would enjoy it. Why it should interest anyone else, especially why it should cause such a fuss, he could not understand. When I asked him if he ever intended to share his secret with the world, he replied that he could not. He felt, he said, incapable of communicating it to others

252

since he was totally ignorant of why or how he was able to do what he did. However, he had thought someday to publish the material he was collecting. He would do this, perhaps, as fiction—since he could not expect the world to acknowledge it as fact. Maybe he would release the information as "biographical romances," as his "biographer" had done, as tales amending the errors of the available volumes and continuing them beyond the point at which they left off.

"Then why," I asked him, "are you so compulsive about getting every detail absolutely correct? If you merely intend to present all of this as fiction, does it really matter if an occasional comma is misplaced?"

"You don't seem to understand," Kirk said with a small sigh for my obvious stupidity; "you don't seem to understand that this is *my* life I'm investigating. I want to know everything about it. I'm careful—compulsive, you say—for *my* sake. It matters to *me*. It has to be right for *me!*"

From our initial talks—devoted chiefly, as I have said, to gathering the history outlined—I received two impressions. The first was of Kirk's utter madness; the second, of the life-sustaining necessity of his psychosis. As regards the former, what was of paramount significance to me as a therapist was the fact I have already mentioned: Kirk's inability to comprehend, to admit even to himself, his mental abnormality (or, to put it another way, the abnormality of his experiences). Now the lay reader may be surprised at these statements: he perhaps thinks that a conviction of sanity is an element in every instance of psychosis, that the person involved is so "far gone" that he does not know he is mad. But this is not so—or at least it is only so in that proportion of cases where brain and central nervous system

253

have been debilitated by toxins or disease. For the most part psychotics are aware of their disturbance, aware either because they suffer somehow through it or are made to suffer for it by others. In only the rarest circumstance does a mentally afflicted person escape suffering, and hence an acute knowledge of his own disorder. But such a one was Kirk: his madness was a private one, an insanity nourished in and by the isolation he had known since early childhood, an insanity that had been slow to reveal itself, slow to affect his external relationships, slow to cause him any distress. And what he experienced now that his psychosis had, so to speak, been made public, was not of a distressful nature: the shock expressed by his supervisor, Bagby, and the doctor at X Reservation, only amused him. Against the wall of Kirk's absolute conviction of sanity—a phenomenon so rare—I was, at first, completely helpless.

The second impression—that Kirk's very life was sustained wholly by his madness—rendered his case even more difficult to handle. While it is true that every psychosis represents a life-saving maneuver on the part of the individual, is his way of solving the conflict between the world and himself, in practically every instance there remains some area of life that—through therapy or otherwise—can be made to yield satisfactions comparable to those available to the person through his madness. In the case of Kirk, it seemed, there was none. What, after all, could compete with the unending gratifications of his fantasy? What could I or anyone offer him in exchange for this elaborate edifice of imagination that, stone by stone, he had reared over the long years? I knew, in short, that without the fantasy Kirk could not *be*—that he *was* only in his dramatic imaginative life. How, then, could he be restored to sanity and yet remain alive?

254

I pondered these and other questions for many days. Meanwhile, Kirk turned over to me all of his records. By now his trunks had arrived in Baltimore, and while he busied himself finding a suitable place to live, and then settled in for what promised to be a long stay—for I had decided by this time to treat him despite the difficulties of the case—I began my study of the material he had collected over the years.

It is impossible to convey more than a bare impression of Kirk's "records." In the space at my disposal here I can hardly do more than itemize. There were, to begin with, about twelve thousand pages of typescript comprising the amended "biography" of Kirk Allen. This was divided into some 200 chapters and read like fiction. Appended to these pages were approximately 2,000 more of notes in Kirk's handwriting, containing corrections necessitated by his more recent "researches," and a huge bundle of scraps and jottings on envelopes, receipted bills, laundry slips, sheets from memo pads, etc. These latter were largely incomprehensible since they were written in Kirk's private shorthand, while some of them were little more than hasty designs or sketches, mathematical equations, or symbolic representations of something or other: each, however, was carefully numbered and lettered with red pencil to indicate where it belonged in the main script.

Apart from the bulky manuscript with its appendix and notes there were:

a glossary of names and terms that ran to more than 100 pages: 82 full-color maps carefully drawn to scale, 23 of planetary bodies in four projections, 31 of land masses on these planets, 14 labeled "Kirk Allen's Expedition to ————," the remainder of cities on the various planets: 161 architectural sketches and elevations, some colored, some drawn only in ink but all carefully scaled and annotated: 12 genealogical tables: an 18-page description of the galactic system in which Kirk Allen's home planet was contained, with 4 astronomical charts, one for each of the seasons, and 9 star maps of the skies from observatories on other planets in the system: a 200-page history of the empire Kirk Allen ruled, with a 3-page table of dates and names of battles or outstanding historical events: a series of 44 folders containing from 2 to 20 pages apiece, each dealing with some aspect of the planet over which Kirk Allen of the future ruled, with life in his imperial city, or with a phase of existence on this planet or elsewhere in the system; typical titles, neatly printed on these folders, were, "The Fauna of Srom Olma I," "The Transportation System of Seraneb," "Science of Srom," "The Geology of Srom Olma I," "The Metabiology of the Valley Dwellers," "The History of the Intergalactic Scientific Institute," "Parapsychology of Srom Norbra X," "Economic Foundations of the Valley Society," "Sociology on Srom Olma I," "The Application of Unified Field Theory and the Mechanics of the Stardrive to Space Travel," "The Unique Brain Development of the Crystopeds of Srom Norbra X," "Anthropological Studies on Srom Olma I," "The Religious Beliefs of the Valley Dwellers," "Manufacturing Processes and Dye Chemistry," "Fire Worship and Sacrifice on Srom Sodrat II," "Food Distribution in Seraneb," "Sex Habits and Practices of the Crystopeds," "Plant Biology and Genetic Science of Srom Olma I," and so on: finally, 306 drawings, some in water colors, some in chalk, some in crayon, of people, animals, plants, insects, weapons, utensils, machines, articles of clothing, vehicles, instruments and furniture. . . .

Such was the material Kirk Allen placed at my disposal for study at the beginning of his therapy. The reader can imagine for himself my dismay at the sheer bulk of this matter: I do not know if he can appreciate with what misgivings I approached the task of weaning this man from his madness.

The atmosphere in which Kirk's therapy commenced was a poor one to begin with. As I have said, he was assured of his sanity and regarded the whole thing as a joke. More than this, he was here with me in Baltimore under the most inauspicious conditions for treatment, since he had not come of his own volition. The authorities had sent him, demanding he be treated not only for his sake but because they feared that in his disturbed condition he was a poor security risk who could neither be kept on the job nor discharged so long as he remained the way he was. As for him, although he resented the implications of what was happening, he obeyed with a faintly grudging good grace. In his behavior toward me he acted the part of a noble opponent who courteously permits his antagonist to choose the time, the place, even the weapons of their encounter. Unfailingly polite, respectful almost to the point of burlesque, he submitted to my ministrations, attempted to follow my instructions to the letter, and gave me every possible scope for my activities. For my part I saw at once that all his politeness, his courtesy, his respectfulness, was little more than the mask for a deep antagonism. Beneath this mask—betrayed, indeed, by its very presence—lurked hostility and, perhaps, even fear. In a dim way, I saw, Kirk too appreciated the necessity of his psychosis, appreciated that his very life depended upon its maintenance. And despite his outward show of unconcern, his forceful defense of his sanity, and his stubborn insistence on the validity of his experiences—despite these, the small doubt implanted by the action of the authorities as well as my decision to treat him threatened the structure essential to his existence. My declaration that I would accept him for treatment could only mean I considered him mad, and the fear this provoked induced hostility, which Kirk disguised, in these early days, as excessive politeness.

The situation between us was thus a very tense one when, the history having been collected, the "records" inspected, and the therapeutic scenery set, I prepared to begin the treatment of this patient in earnest. So far as I could, from the beginning I ignored the aspect of "challenge" implied in Kirk's attitude: I tried, that is, to avoid giving in any way the impression that I was entering the lists with him to prove that he was psychotic, that this was to be a tug of war over the question of his sanity. Instead, because it was obvious that both his temperament and training were scientific, I set myself to capitalize on the one quality he had demonstrated throughout his life, the quality that had inspired his first attempts to deal with his loneliness, the quality that urged him toward a scientific career: his curiosity.

It will be recalled that while Kirk was untroubled by the question of the validity of his para-psychic experiences, he acknowledged ignorance about the mechanics of their operation. He talked vaguely of "teleportation," a special in-built psychic "organ," a highly developed "telepathic" sense, or a "wild talent" of some kind. On the pretext of discovering just how he did all the remarkable things he reported and, beneath this, just why it was he, Kirk Allen, to whom these special gifts were given, I strove to enlist his active participation in treatment. This meant, of course, that at least for the time being I "accepted" the validity of his experiences, the "truth" of the material in the records,

258

the "facts" of Kirk's curious reports of travel through time and space.

When Kirk appreciated that we had achieved a common ground where we could work together on a problem that intrigued him so; when he understood that I was not out to prove him "crazy" and that, therefore, I constituted no threat to the careful but unstable structure on which his entire existence was based; he dropped his defenses and fell to the mutual task with enthusiasm.

For many months, motivated thusly by his curiosity and given tremendous impetus by the security he felt in our relationship, Kirk and I progressed swiftly toward the goal we had set ourselves. Always holding in abeyance the primary question, always suspending decision on it—indeed, always ignoring that such a question existed—we concentrated on the problem of the moment, the problem which may be phrased as: What had happened to Kirk to render him "sensitive" to the extraordinary experiences he reported? Our emphasis was, of course, on his actual biography, on the formative events, relationships and associations of his childhood and adolescence. Nevertheless, so that he should not lack the assurance that no detail was being overlooked in our pursuit of an answer to this problem, I consented to—as a matter of fact, even urged him toward—the exploration of additional means to discovering the source or sources of his "sensitivity." Accordingly, from time to time Kirk submitted to various examinations I arranged for him. Under an assumed name he put himself through the Diagnostic Clinic at the Johns Hopkins Hospital, received a thorough-going neurological examination including electroencephalogram, air-injection engrams, and X-ray studies of his cranium from an outstanding neurologist of my acquaintance, was surveyed thoroughly by an endocrinologist, and even studied in meticulous detail by a physical anthropologist. Needless to say, the outcome of all these elaborate tests and measurements was nil: in every respect save the psychological Kirk was distressingly average.

Since it is not my intention here to deal at length with Kirk's analysis—particularly with the dynamics of his disturbance—but rather to tell a more personal tale, I shall attend only briefly to the findings arrived at during the early months of treatment. Suffice to say that by the end of this period I was in a position to formulate, at least to my own satisfaction, the underlying psychic factors accounting for his psychosis. Briefly, they were as follows:

As the reader has suspected, it all went back to the very earliest years of his life when the child was isolated, cut off, and forced to live in an arid emotional waste wherein his deepest needs were left unsatisfied. Quite likely the incident that was to prove traumatic for him and determine, to a great extent, his future pattern, occurred when his family so abruptly severed his almost symbiotic relationship with the Polynesian nurse, Myna. Until then he had lived in her protecting and nourishing shadow, with all his needs, biological and emotional, gratified. After that event, however, a most radical alteration took place in his world; not only was he denied access to what had by now become for him the fountainhead of his security, but with this enforced separation the pivotal point of his contact with the universe was lost. He could not, that is to say, even communicate with others, nor could he employ any of his former techniques of behavior to obtain that which he— or any child—required for normal development. And while the period of his separation from Myna was brief, the experience was poignant enough to induce anxiety to such a degree that his infant mind, threatened with permanent engulfment, strained to master it by the only means available at that stage: fantasy.

The first world Kirk built for himself was constructed at an age when most children are consolidating the gains of infancy and passing into a childhood in which the chief mental operation is the testing of reality. This was a phase through which Kirk, then, never went; and it left him with a stunted capacity to distinguish between the real world and that which was the product of his own mental functioning. So far as the details of this first interior world are concerned, we have little to inform us because of Kirk's hazy recollection. We can assume, however, that its characteristics were determined by the same factors that were always to underwrite his fantasying. Converting his loneliness, his littleness, his feelings of rejection, his childish helplessness, and his miserably deprived and inferior state to their opposites, then (as later) he was undoubtedly the obverse of these in his fantasied person: the master rather than the victim of events and things.

So much for the first manifestations of Kirk's disorder and their determinants. There followed then the generation of those elements responsible for the two most intriguing and characteristic qualities of Kirk's fantasying: the qualities of time and distance.

Myna, it will be recalled, was restored to Kirk, but not until the separation damage described had been done, and not to the degree of intimacy that had obtained prior to the rude divorce of the child from this one person who mattered. Moreover, her return and the removal of the Commodore's family to the mandated island coincided, and were followed in relatively swift succession, by Kirk's mother's virtual retirement and the subsequent death of

261

the faithful Polynesian nurse. These events had also to be mastered by the boy, and so they were by the imaginative manipulations now familiar to him. But during this period, produced both by the events themselves and by normal processes common to all children there entered into Kirk's psychological development more and more the elements of aggression and hostility.

Frustrated in all of his affectional aspirations, isolated and turned in upon himself, Kirk began to nourish intense feelings of hatred which rapidly declared themselves in destructive fantasies. Because he could not tolerate the devastating emotions to which continual denial of his natural needs gave birth—emotions that provoked urges to aggress, to hate, and to destroy—he adopted a defense designed at once to discharge the accompanying feelings while protecting him from their effects. This he did, at first, by employing distance, and later time, as the central features of his fantasies. Now, removed from him by these convenient mechanisms, both instinctual and frustration-provoked impulses were rendered more tolerable. That is to say, he could tolerate his inner turmoil and the accompanying negative feelings by converting them to the stuff of fantasy and then projecting such fantasies to distant scenes and other times. Accordingly, in the years between Myna's death and his discovery of the books of his "biography," Kirk's fantasies acquired three new aspects: they became less innocuous in content, were removed from his immediate neighborhood to progressively further places, and tended more and more to be set outside his present time.

When the books came into Kirk's possession he unconsciously seized upon them as a perfect vehicle of defense. The premature sexual experiences with Miss Lilian, especially their intensive, guilt-laden, animal-like character, had increased his burden of inner hostility, his smoldering aggressiveness, and his destructive urgings. The capacity to divert these thoughts and feelings through fantasy projection was breaking down, not because he lacked imaginative invention but simply because no fantasy structure he could then envision with his limited reality resources was powerful enough to carry the tremendous weight of his negative impulses. The discovery of the books, then, was a life-saving accident.

It needed no more than the fortuitous correspondence of names to create the bridge across which Kirk traveled from painful reality to all-satisfying fantasy. Through vistas evoked by the books, the endless scope for his impulses, urges and needs became available. With boundless universes of space and endless maneuverability in time at his immediate command, he could no longer be threatened by inner ragings. Within the limitless cosmos and its temporal infinitude, no matter how strong these became they could be—and were—absorbed totally, leaving him unaffected. And in the years to come, it goes without saying, he needed these light-years of distance, these eons of time; for, after his father's death and during the lonely period that followed, the inner rage, bitterness and fury grew to frightening proportions.

The first strange shift in the mechanics of fantasying that Kirk reported—the shift from merely recalling what had been written in the "biography" to amending it by imaginative excursion beyond the confines of the books—was revealed by analysis to have been a natural psychic consequence of his strange development. Apparently the "biography" was unable to supply all of Kirk's requirements for discharge of anxiety and mastery of experience, and when he reached this point he was forced to invent new material—or alter the old—so that it would take account of his needs more adequately. To discover this mental "gimmick" was one of the simpler tasks of Kirk's analysis. Its disclosure carried us far along the path of reconstructing his life in its finest details, for with this insight employed as a skeleton key to his past, it became possible to show him, eventually, how (and why) an almost one-to-one correspondence existed between his fantasy constructs and his actual past experiences. That is to say, in order to master his past and relieve its anxious consequences, each event was *transformed* to a bit of fantasy and, in that guise, assisted by the time and distance factors, was more easily handled.

The second shift in technique—that from recall of the future beyond the "biography's" scope and amendation of detail to correspond with real experience—was again a natural defensive psychic maneuver, but a maneuver necessitated by a new element that entered Kirk's life soon after he settled in his job at X Reservation.

As I have written, the Miss Lilian episode had been Kirk's first and only venture into sexual activity. It was, the reader will remember, a devastating transaction for the boy, awakening in him remote incestuous longings and their consequent effects of fear and guilt. These emotions, indeed, may be said to have precipitated Kirk's flight into the more serious reaches of unreality: it is even likely that had there been no Miss Lilian there would have been lacking that special sensitivity required to respond so drastically to the stimulus of the "biography" and Kirk might have developed more normally. In any case, following his shattering encounter with the nymphomanic governess, Kirk shunned sexual experience in reality and avoided, as much as he could, all relationships with women. In his fantasy life, however, where it was safe, he was not only sexually alert but a notorious and successful lover. This was the situation when, on taking up his assignment at X Reservation, Kirk found himself once more threatened by sex.

Among the scientists working with Kirk on the project at X was an attractive geologist who had recently been divorced. She was slightly older than Kirk, an intelligent, vivacious, witty woman of wide social experience who was also internationally famous for her work. The only unattached female member of the scientific staff, she was in great demand among the men, most of whom were bachelors. Nevertheless, it was Kirk who interested her and on him that she exerted all her charm. Of this quality she must have had an abundance, since she succeeded where many other girls had failed and rapidly developed a close association with the preoccupied young physicist. Soon they were meeting frequently, attending occasional social functions together, and sharing as a couple whatever entertainments the isolated community had to offer. Kirk, however, regarded this association otherwise than his friend: for him it was a pleasant companionship in which the gender of his partner was incidental, and it was his intention to keep it that way. The girl had other plans. She soon began to behave in a manner that distressed him, that awakened once more his dread of sex. The more reticent he acted, the bolder her advances became, until a point was reached where her demands for sex were overt and unequivocal. When this happened Kirk attempted to dissolve the relationship, but she would not have it so and pursued him relentlessly. Employing every wile at her command, she attempted to seduce him; and he, thus threatened, sought desperately to escape.

On the night Kirk achieved for the first time what he was thereafter to regard as the most crucial experience in his life—the illusion of actual tenancy of the body and being of the future Kirk Allen on another planet—his problem with the fair geologist had reached a climax. He had dined with her in her apartment and after dinner she had made a frank sexual overture which literally scared him out of his wits. In great agitation he fled to his own room and, in an effort to calm himself, turned to his "records." In his pre-occupation with them, it seems, the solution of complete flight into unreality appeared as the best available means whereby his threatened self could be preserved, and he un-consciously seized upon it. Thereafter, it became his "escape hatch" from intolerable actuality.

What is of great interest to the psychoanalyst, of course, is the fact that this solution of total flight into fantasy occurred to Kirk while he was consciously engaged in the preparation of a map. It is notorious that maps, charts, architectural plans and other similar material often have the unconscious symbolic significance of the human form, especially of curiosity or perplexity regarding sexual details. In the incident that precipitated the new pattern of Kirk's fantasying, then, it can be seen with unusual clarity how remarkably effective fantasy is as a defense against unconscious pressures: not only are problems or strains relegated to a time and place that render them harmless, but there, in addition, they are solved or relieved.

By the end of the first year of analysis, although we had moved rapidly and accumulated much information, Kirk and I found ourselves in a most curious position. By this time we had been able to work out the entire mechanics of the gigantic fantasy, we had traced its sources to their roots, and we had even elaborated, in meticulous detail, the one-to-one correspondence of experiential fact with imaginative feature. But none of this affected my patient's

266

behavior to the slightest degree. Although he conceded that the foundations of his psychosis (which we still avoided calling by this name) rested in the past, although he recognized it as the self-salvaging maneuver of escape from reality it was, although he understood as well as I the why and how of its operation—nevertheless, he showed no inclination to abandon it. Almost daily he entered the strange realm of his elaborate preoccupation, returning therefrom each time with some exciting bit of news or some colorful item to add to the "records." Outwardly he maintained the façade of an integrated and well-functioning person. Since he was free to dispose of his time and energy as he pleased, and had no other obligation than to keep his appointments with me, he was in an enviable position to lead a leisurely and uncomplicated life. To keep himself busy he attended lectures at the universities in and near Baltimore, made acquaintances among the scientists here, and participated casually in the intellectual life of the community. In sum, he was quite content.

I, on the other hand, was not. More than this, I was downright unhappy over the situation and perplexed as I have never been before about a patient. For I saw that the gains we had made against Kirk's madness were more apparent than real, that the only success I had had—if, indeed, this paltry accomplishment could be attributed to the analysis— was the minor one of holding my patient in treatment and keeping his condition relatively stable. By this I mean that, at least, Kirk had not gone further into his psychosis, that there had been no increment in the extent of his involvement in the weird fantasy, that he was fixed in it at approximately the same place as when he arrived in Baltimore the previous year.

For weeks I wrestled with the problem of what to do.

In rapid succession I ran through every technique, device, even trick of therapy I knew or had heard of or read about. Nightly I pored over my notes, thinking long and hard about this strange case. More and more, between the times we met for his hours, I found myself preoccupied with Kirk's analysis, and less and less with my other patients.

Readers who are unfamiliar with my previous writings will wonder here why I did not admit failure and refer Kirk elsewhere, say to a psychiatrist who might employ one of the more drastic methods such as shock treatment. This I could not do, not only because I was then and still am reluctant to admit defeat until every possible psycho-therapeutic avenue has been explored, but because I could not conscientiously expose this patient (or, indeed, any other) either to the experience of such treatment or to its possible negative effects. I am one of the more vocal antagonists of such "heroic" measures as convulsive "therapy" and the psychosurgical methods, believing most sincerely that they violate every progressive canon of therapy and convinced they do more harm than good, either immediately or in the long run. It seems to me the height of absurdity to blast or cut the very portion of the brain on which both the individual's and the species' welfare depends, to say nothing of the fact that all our evidence points to the temporary nature of the "cures" achieved and the irreversible damage done to the personality thus treated. Especially in Kirk's case would I regard the employment of such methods with abhorrence. His psychosis notwithstanding, he had a fine brain, a basically well-motivated personality, and showed promise of being—when freed from the debilitation of his disorder—one of those valuable persons on whom the future of our civilization depends. No; I could not, if there was any way to prevent it, consign him to the new kind of vegetable kingdom being created by so many of my well-intentioned but mistaken colleagues.

Why, then, it may be asked by other readers—this time readers acquainted with my work—did I not employ hypnosis? The answer to this is obvious: Kirk's hold on reality was tenuous enough as it was, and I frankly feared to break the thin thread by which his connection with this world was maintained. I cannot say for sure whether hypnosis would have had this effect, but I confess I was afraid it might.

It was during one of Kirk's hours at the time of my deepest despair over being unable to help him that I suddenly decided there remained but a single unexplored way to handle his case. In a sudden flash of inspiration it came to me that in order to separate Kirk from his madness it was necessary for me to enter his fantasy and, from that position, to pry him loose from the psychosis.

The idea of participating in the psychosis of a patient is anything but new. Therapists have been doing it for many years, but it was such brilliant workers as John Rosen, Milton Wexler, and others who formulated the principles of the technique and described its mode of operation. Their fascinating accounts of the method had already appeared in the literature by the time I came to treat Kirk, and I had read their papers with more than usual interest. But I had never utilized the method myself, nor had I as yet observed the work, as I was later to do. Equipped, therefore, with only a handful of general propositions to prepare me for this enterprise, and only vaguely aware of its hazards, but driven to it by necessity, I took the first steps toward personal involvement in the weird yet magnificent fantasy that had heretofore belonged solely to Kirk.

I began by steeping myself in the "records." For days on

end, employing every spare moment, I studied the mass of material Kirk had given me until I knew it so well that the most insignificant detail was engraved in my memory. Naturally, such intensive study brought to light many inconsistencies, and it was with these that I started my new assault on Kirk's psychosis. What I did was confront him with an error in logic, a mistake in calculation, or a difference in description between one part of the "record" and another, and demand that he "fix" it. Often this required that Kirk make another "trip" into the future, from where he would "return" with the necessary information and, together, we would correct whatever deficiency was involved. A good example of what actually took place during our meetings is the following:

On a morning some weeks after I had begun to use the new approach, Kirk arrived at my office for his regular appointment. When he came into the room I was sitting at the desk studying the two astronomical charts and nine star maps Kirk had prepared, and the manuscript of a descriptive section of his "records" dealing with astronomical research. Since we were not using the couch in this phase of our work, he drew up a chair. For a few minutes he watched while I worked, glancing in turn at me, at the maps, and at the pad of scratch paper on which I had jotted down some figures. My silent concentration on the materials before me eventually produced—as I knew it would—sufficient tension to cause him to break the quiet.

"What's wrong?" he asked.

"Plenty," I replied, throwing down my pencil and lighting a cigarette. "These distances are all fouled up. Either your astronomical projection from Srom Norbra X is wrong or the star maps are way off. They just don't make sense. Look here . . ."

For the next quarter hour I reviewed an error in distance between certain suns in the fanciful galaxy where Kirk Allen's home planet was located—an error I had happily discovered the previous evening—and showed him that his maps could not possibly be correct in view of this mistake. He was very upset by this, took a pencil from his breast pocket, and made many rapid calculations on the back of one of the maps. When he finished he frowned and leaned back in his chair.

"I don't understand it," he said. "I could swear I copied those maps exactly from the originals at the Institute."

"Maybe," I suggested, "you made your mistake in translating from Olmayan measurements to miles."

He shook his head. "I doubt it," he said.

"How were the distances measured in the first place?"

"Well, until we had the Stardrive and could actually get close to some of these suns we used ordinary methods—you know, spectroscopic analysis of light and so on. But after the 'Age of Interstellar Flight' the errors were corrected by direct instrument readings."

"How are the instruments calibrated? In miles, kilometers, or what?"

"The basic unit," he said pedantically, "is the 'ecapalim,' an Olmayan word corresponding to our mile, actually about a mile and five sixteenths. But because of the immense distances, instruments on spaceships register in 'tonecapalim,' or units of about one hundred and sixty thousand miles." He thought awhile, then, "Here, let me see if it's just an error in translating to miles." He worked rapidly and soon covered the back of the map with numbers. I watched him closely meanwhile, admiring his mathematical facility but noting carefully his growing tension. Finally, with a grunt

271

of disgust, he tossed his pencil on the desk and paced the room restlessly.

"That's not it," he said. "There's something fundamentally wrong."

"Well," I comforted, "it's not very serious, after all. . . ."

"Not serious!" he exploded, turning to me with anger flaring in his eyes and his face drawn into a tight mask of contempt. "Not serious! Why, man, these maps are used by my pilots. No wonder I've lost so many ships!"

"Have you lost very many?" I asked innocently.

He passed a trembling hand over his face and muttered some words I couldn't hear. Then he returned to his chair and collapsed on it like a discarded marionette. I, watching intently, felt a thrill of triumph as I realized what this episode had produced: the first small aperture in the fantasy, the first puncture in the magnificent pretense. Careful to control the eagerness in my voice, I repeated the question. "Have you really lost many ships?"

"I . . . I don't know," he faltered. "I'll have to check on it when I go back."

We sat in silence again, each of us busy with strange thoughts. I had the almost telepathic impression that Kirk's mind was a turmoil of questions about me. Heretofore, he had merely accepted my acceptance of the fantasy. Now, with his own faith in it slightly shaken and mine apparently unruffled, he was perplexed. Perceiving this, I quickly followed up my advantage.

I picked up the maps and charts from the desk and examined them closely, holding them directly under the desk light and turning each one over as if looking for something. When I felt his attention was aroused sufficiently, I asked, "You don't happen to remember when you made these, do you?"

272

"No," Kirk replied. "Why?"

"Well, it occurred to me you might have marked a date on them. It would have helped."

"How?"

"It's just an idea," I said casually. "I thought if they were dated you could find out when you examined the originals at the Institute."

"What good would that do?"

"Probably none," I said, "except that it's possible these maps are based on information obtained before the 'Age of Interstellar Flight.' That may be what's wrong. If you knew the dates of your visits to the Institute you could ask to be shown the stuff you saw then— I'm sure in a place like that they'd have a record of what you looked at."

His eyes brightened and his body tensed with alertness. "You mean," he said, "that maybe these maps are based on old ones and my pilots are using corrected charts?"

"Sure," I said. "After all, if you'd been losing many ships, you'd have heard about it long before this and the matter would have been investigated. But you just said you don't know how many vessels have been lost—which is rather odd, isn't it? So I'd suspect these are based on old stuff and your pilots have more up-to-date charts. I doubt if you'll find you've been losing ships at more than a normal rate, at least at a rate you can account for by the usual dangers of interstellar flight."

"That's easy to check on," Kirk said brightly.

"Of course," I agreed. "When you go back, get in touch with the Institute. I think you'll clear up this mystery in short order."

I rose to signal the end of our hour. As Kirk was about to depart he paused in the doorway, from where his eyes swept over me in a long, slow quizzical gaze. I knew then that I had, indeed, forced a slight crack in the apparently unassailable fantasy. I knew that my participation in it, the evidence I had just given of total acceptance—even of conspiracy to the extent of helping him sustain his defense when it was threatened—had, for the first time, made him question it. And on the following day, when he announced that during the night he had journeyed to Srom Olma to visit the Institute there and had found, as I predicted, that his maps were based on "calculations made before the Age of Flight," a new note was to be detected in his voice. It was, I thought, a hesitant note, lacking the old deliberateness and assurance, betraying a lessening of conviction or, perhaps, faith. Evidence that my impression was correct accumulated during subsequent days. Despite my urging, Kirk never got around to preparing new star maps. Although he declared his intention to do so, and agreed with me that the job had to be done for the sake of maintaining the completeness and correctness of the "records," he let the matter slide, putting it off with one lame excuse after another until it faded from his thoughts.

This incident reflects the pattern of my operational methods with Kirk following the decision to participate in his psychosis. While it was crucial, it is merely one of many such episodes, each of which contributed a little more leverage for prying my patient out of his madness. How it and others like it worked is probably obvious to the discerning reader. In nontechnical terms, one of the principles on which the whole performance is based can be described simply by reference to a commonplace: it is impossible for two objects to occupy the same place at the same time. It is as if a delusion such as Kirk's has room in it only for one person at one time, as if a psychotic structure, too, is rigidly circumscribed as to "living space." When, as in this case,

274

another person invades the delusion, the original occupant finds himself literally forced to give way.

This fantastic situation can also be represented by imagining an encounter between two victims of, let us say, the Napoleonic delusion. The conviction of each that he is the real Napoleon must be called into question by the presence of the other, and it is not unusual for one to surrender, in whole or in part, when such a confrontation occurs. Some years ago I observed exactly this while on the staff of a psychiatric sanitarium in Maryland. At that time we had a middle-aged paranoid woman who clung to the delusion that she was Mary, Mother of God. It happened that we admitted another patient with the same delusion some months after the first had been received. Both were rather mild-mannered people, both Catholics, both from a similar socio-economic level. On the lawn one day, happily in the presence of another staff member and myself, the two deluded women met and began to exchange confidences. Before long each revealed to the other her "secret" identity. What followed was most instructive. The first, our "oldest" patient, received the information with visible perturbation and an immediate reaction of startle. "Why you can't be, my dear," she said. "You must be crazy. *I* am the Mother of God." The new patient regarded her companion sorrowfully and, in a voice resonant with pity, said, "I'm afraid it's you who are mixed up; *I* am Mary." There followed a brief but polite argument which I was restrained from interfering with by my older and more experienced colleague, who bade me merely to listen and observe. After a while the argument ceased, and there followed a long silence during which the antagonists inspected each other warily. Finally, the "older" patient beckoned to the doctor standing with me.

"Dr. S.," she asked, "what was the name of Our Blessed Mary's Mother?"

"I think it was Anne," he replied.

At once this patient turned to the other, her face glowing and her eyes shining. "If you're Mary," she declared, "*I* must be Anne, your mother." And the two women embraced.

As a postscript to this story, it should be recorded that the woman who surrendered her Mother of God delusion thereafter responded rapidly to treatment and was soon discharged.

Participation serves another purpose which should not be overlooked. To paraphrase the astute Dr. John N. Rosen, when the therapist engages in the same behavior as the patient—and expresses the same ideas in the same language—the patient's own image and activities are projected before him as on a screen. He is thus, in one bold maneuver, thrust to the side of reality, forced to take up a critical position vis-à-vis what he observes, i.e. his own behavior, and compelled to adopt an attitude. This attitude is soon transformed into a therapeutic tool with which the clinician now refashions the psychic structure.

All three of these principles of "participation therapy"— and others that need not occupy us here—operated on Kirk. My direct involvement in the fantasy that had, until then, been his private preserve, constricted his "*lebensraum*," confronted him with his mirror image, and maneuvered him into the critical reality position. As a consequence, slowly but surely, he was being edged out of his psychosis.

But, meanwhile, strange things were happening to me, his psychoanalyst (or, better, his psychotherapist, since the method I was employing was no longer strictly that of psychoanalysis); and it is to these unforeseen personal effects—because they are, at least in retrospect, amusing and instructive—that I now wish to turn.

Kirk's case fascinated me from the very beginning. Like any other profession the practice of psychoanalysis has its share of drawbacks and dissatisfactions. While the adventure through the human mind is more often than not exciting, and for a person like myself no other conceivable occupation could be as intellectually and emotionally rewarding, nevertheless there are long plateaus of dullness, of routine, that tend to arouse all-too-human discontents. I have often thought that these occasional limbolike periods, when daily journeys through the unconscious seem so tame—appearing less like explorations through dangerous, trackless jungles and more like commuting on a suburban trolley—I have often thought these periods would be more tolerable were it not for the additional occupational discomforts of satiation and confinement.

In his work, moment after moment, an analyst lives intimately with the human passions. Lust, greed, envy, hate—the seven deadly sins and more; love, charity, faith—the heavenly virtues and all the beatitudes; these assail him endlessly. While he is not to be caught up in the emotional tempest that storms about him unremittingly, it is in such an atmosphere that he must exist. One consequence of this incessant exposure must be satiety, a feeling of fullness, of overripeness, the defense against which is the antagonistic feeling of monotony. Only a "surprise," only a sudden, unpredictable event, can restore to the analyst who has reached the satiation point that quickening of interest, of zest, necessary to refresh his senses and render him once more sensitive in the way he must be if he is to perform efficiently. Fortunately, such "surprises" are not lacking.

By confinement, I refer to the actual physical fact of enforced immobility that is the condition of work for people such as I. Everything we do takes place in the consulting room. Activity, movement, is denied to us. The great dramas of which we partake, the tremendous conflicts, the shattering experiences—these come to us, come to the rooms in which we sit and listen. Eternally, we are spectators—rather, auditors. Sometimes, it cannot be denied, one chafes against the sheer physical constriction of such a life; one longs for movement; one becomes physically restless, hungering for the air of the outdoors, for the vigorous employment of the limbs and for the distant use of eyes against horizons rather than walls. Finally, one tires of words, words, words. The long vacations habitual with analysts are one antidote, and it is to be observed how they drift to the mountains and the sea in an annual effort to feed their appetites for mobility and space.

I write about these conditions of psychoanalytic practice to explain something of the mood I was in when I made the decision to participate in Kirk's psychosis, and to account for what happened to me when I did. At that time I was in a period of emotional satiation, bored with my work, which seemed to me to be offering fewer and fewer satisfactions. I had not then the wit to comprehend that my boredom was a defense against unresolved personal conflicts, that I was drawing a defensive cloak about myself—better, placing a screen between myself and the emotional turmoil of my patients—in order to protect me from constant emotional stimulation. Moreover, I was then also restless in a physical way. Always a rather vigorous person who would rather run than walk, and provided with a body designed for activity, I contemplated the slow but progressive degeneration of flesh and muscle with angry disgust. The long hours of sitting, the stale air; the flabbiness of arms and legs, the pallid skin tones, the first suggestion of potty bulge beneath the waistline—against these and many other minor but telling symptoms of oncoming physical decrepitude I felt helpless and self-rejecting, blaming them, for want of more insight, on the implausible profession I had chosen to follow.

Yet these two contributory factors to my mood when the affair of Kirk took its unforeseen twist do not, by themselves, even begin to explain what transpired. Among others that account for my vulnerability, beyond a transient mood, there has to be mentioned my fondness for fantasy, my taste for science fiction, and certain temperamental qualities that contribute to the making of my personality.

I have always been given to an active fantasy life, to the weaving of pleasing imaginative interior romances. Without being too biographical, I can reveal that the roots of this tendency are to be discovered in a solitude during childhood comparable but not similar to Kirk's; more psychological, that is, than actual. Nor was my fantasying at all like Kirk's—obsessional, violent, and complex—but rather of the common Walter Mitty type. As a child and adolescent it offered gratifications withheld by the tedious reality of school, lessons and middle-class family life. As an adult it provided—and still does—those harmless outlets for life's ordinary frustrations that take from events their sting and that can, if employed properly, be creative. I have always delighted in this capacity for fantasying and have tried to bend it to my uses. Until the episode with Kirk, however, I had no idea what a double-edged tool it could be.

As for my taste for science fiction, I can only say that I have been, since learning to read, an *aficionado* of the genre. Introduced to *Amazing Stories* by a schoolmate, I rapidly acquired an insatiable appetite for the stuff, to the despair of my parents who regarded the dog-eared pulps that over-flowed our bookshelves with the kind of despair with which today's parents view a similar litter of comic books. Fortunately, my literary aspirations and tastes soon directed me toward authors representing the higher reaches of the art, and my passage from BEM's through Burroughs to Wells, Heard and Stapledon was swift. At forty I remain a rather reluctant addict, fighting the temptations of Van Vogt, Bradbury, and Co., but succumbing blissfully to the irresistible appeal of a new Orwell (alas! there will be no more from him), a Wylie, or a Huxley. Parenthetically, I owe to science fiction much more than gratitude for entertainment. Re-enforcing a native curiosity and an inclination toward science, such reading has led me toward the serious study of subjects like Semantics and Cybernetics, to say nothing of laying a foundation for intellectual hobbies like philosophy, higher mathematics and astrophysics.

Emotionally satiated, restive under confinement, given anyhow to the uses of imagination, and a devotee of science fiction to begin with—these are the obvious factors that entered into the interesting personal experiences I underwent in the closing phase of Kirk Allen's therapy. For, as the reader has anticipated, I, the therapist, became quite involved in the psychosis of my patient and for a time and to some degree shared his obsession.

From the moment I made its acquaintance Kirk's case, as I have said, fascinated me. The dictionary meaning of the word "fascinate" describes my state and tells the story better than I can: it means "to bewitch, to enchant, to cast a spell over, etc." This definition applies to the psychological state I soon found myself in when, as my participation in the grandiose delusion increased through the deliberate efforts
280

I have described, the sharply defined edges of reality began to fade and I entered part way into the incredible universe of Kirk's design.

In the beginning it was a game. My wholesale acceptance of the fantasy was no more than a pretense, a device I had seized upon that promised to pry loose a disturbed mind from its adhesive clutch on a foundering life raft. But eventually it ceased to be a game, and the moves, the maneuvers, the manipulations of the pieces, passed from the hands of this player to become the tools of forces of which he was then hardly aware.

That this could have happened to me I attribute to more than the precipitating factors I have already mentioned. Beyond these, it cannot be denied that other intimate temperamental characteristics played their parts. Among them, I have only to mention two I have always known to be determinants of my personality and motivants of my behavior.

There is first to be considered that I was intrigued by the prospect Kirk's fantasy presented for the realization of my dearest wish: the wish to have sufficient time to know, to do, and to be all the wonderful things denied me and all men by temporal limitations. I possess a curiosity beyond the average, an appetite for knowing and experiencing that is almost boundless. My life does not provide sufficient scope for the satisfaction of this hunger, but the intricate fabrication woven by my patient did. And in this sense it was enticing. By engaging in it, I could obtain the illusion of gratifying this immense curiosity and appeasing the chronic thirst of my seeking mind. With but a small step of an already lively imagination, I could escape from the prison of time: I could *be* geologist, explorer, astronomer, historian, physicist, adventurer and all those other enviable beings whose

281

roles I had, at one time or another, played in my own pallid fantasies and whose knowledge I have always wanted to possess. This was a potent allure.

Then there is another charm that Kirk's extramundane delusion held for me. To an ego that has more than a modest share of a need to assert itself in creative ways, the opportunities afforded by this unique situation were tempting. While the position of "Lord of a Planet" had already been pre-empted, my peculiar function once I had forced my way into Kirk's romantic creation gave free play to every inventive whim, every inspiration, every demiurgic notion I ever hope to have. For as the power-behind-the-throne, the prime mover of a universe unhampered by realistic restrictions, the possibilities to exercise creativity on a grand scale were inviting beyond description.

In view of such predisposing and precipitating factors I do not find it remarkable that my engagement as a participant in Kirk's psychosis disturbed somewhat that mental equilibrium on which I have always prided myself and brought me within sight of psychological distress. We all of us possess areas of lessened resistance, and somewhere on the psychic armor of the strongest there is a vulnerable place. In this case it happened that the materials of Kirk's psychosis and the Achilles heel of my personality met and meshed like the gears of a clock.

The early signs that I had fallen under the spell of Kirk's Utopian vision and was succumbing to it were innocuous enough and hardly such as to cause concern. They consisted, by and large, of an increased interest in the details of the fantasy and a mild but persistent anxiousness about them. Unlike before, however, this interest and anxiety were not for the sake of the therapy so much as in the service of the fantasy itself. I continued my intense pursuit of error and

282

inconsistency in the "records," but now with the obsessive aim of "setting them straight," of "getting the facts." When I discovered mistakes, where before I would employ them solely for purposes of treatment, in this phase I gave first consideration to their correction. Nor did I, on finding them, experience the thrill of satisfaction I had felt formerly when the unearthing of error meant more ammunition in the fight against my patient's psychosis. Instead, such faults aroused anxiety in *me*, made *me* uncomfortable, and created moderately distressful symptoms which could be relieved only when the correction was made.

There were occasions, moreover, when a problem about the "records" could not be settled in discussions with Kirk. When this happened, I seemed to be compelled by rising anxiety to work out a solution of my own. Soon I found myself devoting spare time to calculations and speculations designed to "solve" what perplexed or bothered me. When I managed such a solution, the relief it afforded was intense. No less intense was the pleasure I took in Kirk's liberal congratulations when I presented the explanation to him as a triumph of *my* ingenuity. Often, too, when neither discussion with Kirk nor the efforts I made on my own sufficed to clarify some point, I found it "necessary" for him to obtain the required information by "journeying" to the place where it could be discovered. On occasions of this kind, assigning him the role of cosmic errand boy, I actually ordered Kirk to make these excursions into the fantasy, then discovered myself awaiting his "return" with extraordinary eagerness.

At this point I find it necessary to assure the reader that, despite the foregoing, I was not myself psychotic either during the phase I have been describing or later when these strange manifestations increased in quantity and quality. My condition throughout was, rather, that of enchantment

283

developing toward obsession. I never lost sight of the fact that the "trips" Kirk made into a far future to a remote, nonexistent galaxy were impossible. But, in my preoccupation with the fantasy as such, I found it convenient to overlook, so far as *I* was concerned, the manner in which its wonderful details were made available to me. This is to say, I omitted from my concerns *how* Kirk collected "facts" and attended only to the "facts" themselves. That he employed the implausible vehicle of "teleportation" or some equally incredible and psychotic means to do what was required of him, I simply overlooked in my enthusiasm for the elaborate conceit.

As the days passed, however, the symptoms I have been writing about increased in number and intensity. They were all of an obsessional nature and, as such disturbances tend to do, they began to invade my thought and behavior to an ever greater degree. Whereas the fantasy and its delights had previously beckoned only when I was actually with Kirk or in spare time, it now intruded itself into moments when I was not fully engaged otherwise, and even, on occasion, when I was attending to affairs far removed from Kirk and his delusion. I found myself, for example, translating certain words, terms and names into the "Olmayan" language. Phrases in this weird tongue, unannounced and unbidden, often came into my thoughts and remained there to plague consciousness annoyingly like a haunting melody until I set them down on paper and transposed them to English. At a startlingly rapid rate, it seems, larger and larger areas of my mind were being taken over by the fantasy.

I have since questioned those who share my life to find out if, at the time of which I am writing, I betrayed in any way that I was prepossessed by a growing obsession. Apparently there was no change in my deportment, either toward them or in my work, for the state to which I am confessing here entirely escaped their notice. How this could have been I fail to understand, for I retain the impression of this as a time when happenings in the real world, events that would ordinarily have stimulated me, lost their appeal—of a time when I was abstracted and engrossed. The truth is that the state of calm I maintained outwardly was a false front behind which, uncannily, I was living the most exciting kind of life. With Kirk's puzzled assistance I was taking part in cosmic adventures, sharing the exhilaration of the sweeping extravaganza he had plotted.

When I recall this period now, it becomes obvious to me how I employed the rationalization of clinical altruism for personal ends and thus fell into a trap that awaits all unwary therapists of the mind. I remember clearly how, in those interim moments when I paused to ask myself what I was doing or to question the validity of my thoughts and feelings, I deliberately dismissed the evidence that I was succumbing to a fascination that could be fatal by referring my behavior to the therapeutic gambit necessitated by my patient's disorder. Today I cannot deny the fact that, in my psychic condition at the time, certain elements in the fantasy—some of which I have written about—appealed to me powerfully precisely because they fulfilled long dormant needs and desires. Then, however, because I was unaware of the strength of these desires, I fell prey to the mechanism of self-deception which was activated by the coincidental circumstance that Kirk's psychosis demanded exactly the kind of treatment I was offering.

Armed, then, with the rationalization I have described, during this brief but acute period I skirted the edges of the abyss. Although aware of the dangerous game I was playing, I seem to have been willing to play it to the limit for stakes of then unknown neurotic satisfaction. Like a swimmer who has made a wager with himself to test his endurance, it was as if I were determined to see how far I could go in order to try some unconscious conclusion with fate. Thus the game, at the height of my distraction, threatened to become a deadly one, a contest between dark forces of the mind that invited total surrender and the energies of a consciousness determined to maintain its integrity. This latter part of my mind remained, throughout, clear and analytically functional. Not only instinct with self-preservation, but experienced beyond most minds in such matters, it perceived the hazards. On it my destiny depended, for against the fascination of the fantasy that occupied the nether geography of that same mind it battled valiantly and, as it turned out, successfully.

There arrived a moment when I could not ignore the telltale signs of obsession, a moment when the ego realized the threat and allied itself with the forces of light. This crucial time was signalized by acute psychic distress, by an exacerbation of my symptoms to the point where they became painful. It was the pain, then, that informed me of the real peril I was courting and energized the machinery of self-preservation.

To describe what happened would necessitate presenting a clinical picture of the germinal stages of the obsessional state. Since this is hardly the place for such a description, let it suffice to say that, with the passage of time, all the manifestations of obsession I have mentioned intensified. The anxiety, for example, could no longer be passed off as inner excitement: it rose to a pitch of aching apprehension where it demanded recognition. To meet this rising tide, the obsessional demands increased and, in turn, the compulsive requirements from thought and action became more exacting.

Finally, the amount of my preoccupation with the fantasy, the time I had to spend on its details and the efforts I was forced to expend for its sake, enlarged to a point where other areas of my existence were invaded.

The transformation of fascination into psychic distress alarmed me sufficiently to take the necessary steps for extricating myself from this weird predicament. It acted, first, as a spur to self-analysis. Gradually, by the use of this accustomed tool, I was able to allay the more acute symptoms I have recorded and to initiate those insightful processes that lead to recovery from psychological disorder. But before I had completed this task, there occurred an amazing event which, in the space of one brief hour, not only broke what remained of the spell I was under, but marked the successful conclusion of Kirk's treatment. For it chanced that Kirk and I reversed roles and, in one of those startling denouements that make my work the unpredictable, wonderful and rewarding pursuit it is, the folly we shared collapsed.

The scene was the same: my office, high above the noisy streets of Baltimore. Outside there was a flurry of snow that melted as the flakes touched a surface. Through its soft screen the monument at Mt. Vernon Place and, beyond, the busy harbor, had the charm of an old print. Inside it was warm and quiet. Because of the grayness of the day, all the lamps were lit and soft shadows made subdued geometric patterns on the cocoa-colored walls. At the desk, I sat, preparing for my session with Kirk by studying some drawings he had made. From the next room I could hear my secretary at her typewriter. Suddenly, to the accompaniment of a pleasant tinkle of chimes, the door to the hallway opened and I knew that Kirk had arrived for his hour. I was eager to see him, for on the previous day I had sent him on a

287

"mission" and had since been awaiting his report. After an interval, I pressed the buzzer to signal him in.

Kirk entered and took his accustomed place in the chair by my desk. We grunted our usual greetings; then, without preliminary, urged by now familiar tensions, I began.

"Did you get the information?" I asked.

He nodded, and from his pocket took a leather-bound notebook which he opened and placed on the desk. Quickly I thumbed through the pages, observing with a swift sense of satisfaction that each contained a drawing and some penciled notes in Kirk's handwriting. Then I went back to the first page, extracted it from the binding, and set it beside a sketch I had already taken from the pile at my elbow. Disregarding Kirk, I gave my attention to the two papers. So absolute was my absorption in comparing the sheets and making notes that I failed to notice when Kirk left his chair and stood by the window. When I finally turned to him, intending to make some comment, I observed how he was staring down at me with an expression of concern.

"Something wrong?" I asked.

"No," he replied. "Nothing's wrong."

"Then why are you standing there? Don't you want to work on this with me?"

"Not especially."

"How come?"

He shrugged. "I don't know. . . . Just tired, I guess."

"That's odd," I commented. "This material on Olmayan ethnic types is particularly interesting. . . . Don't you find it so?"

Again he shrugged, but this time he resumed his seat.

For the next quarter hour we "worked" together; I with lively absorption, he in a desultory fashion which did not escape my notice. The situation was most unusual, for I

288

was accustomed to much more participation from him. This morning his "heart" was not in what we were doing. He answered my questions in a dispirited way, and when I raised a point for discussion his voice and manner lacked the enthusiasm I had come to expect from him. I could not ignore the strangeness of his manner when, finally, he again left his chair and began to pace the room.

"Kirk," I said, pushing aside the litter on the desk and lighting a cigarette, "what's wrong? What's eating you this morning?"

"Nothing," he said. "Nothing at all."

"Then why are you so . . . restless?"

"Oh, it's just . . ." and his voice trailed off while his arms described a gesture of weary despair.

"Just what?" I urged.

"Well . . . it's just that I've got something to tell you— and I can't seem to get it out."

"Something you haven't told me?"

He nodded.

"Something about yourself, or the work?"

"About both, I guess."

"Well," I said, "after all this time I shouldn't think you'd have any trouble telling me what's on your mind."

"I don't . . . usually. But this is different."

"Tell me anyhow," I urged.

Opposite the desk, he stopped and fixed me with anxious eyes.

"All right," he said. "I'll tell you—but you're not going to like it . . ." Then, "I've been lying to you."

"Lying to me? What about?"

He leaned across and picked up the note book. "About this," he said, "and this," indicating the papers on the desk, "and all the stuff I've been giving you these last few weeks.

289

It's all a lie, all of it. I've been making it up . . . inventing all that—that—nonsense!"

I tried not to show what I was feeling, to hide the mixture of emotions that surged through me—the disappointment and the triumph, the concern and the relief. With fingers I knew were trembling, I slowly crushed my cigarette.

"You've been making it all up?" I asked.

"Yes. All of it."

"It's all false?" I asked again.

"All false!"

"Even the . . . trips?"

"Trips!" he snorted. "What trips? Why it's been weeks since I gave up that foolishness. . . ."

"But you've been telling me——"

He seated himself on the edge of his chair, his whole body rigid and his face tight with tension. "I know what I've been telling you," he said earnestly. "But, believe me, I've been pretending for a long time. There've been no trips. I saw through all of that stuff—weeks ago. . . ."

"What do you mean—you saw through?"

"Just what I said. I realized I was crazy. I realized I've been deluding myself for years; that there never have been any 'trips,' that it was all just—just insanity."

"Then why," I asked, "why did you pretend? Why did you keep on telling me . . . ?"

"Because I felt I had to," he said. "Because I felt *you wanted me to!*"

The last words echoed and re-echoed in the silent room. For many minutes I seemed to hear them. Then they faded, to be replaced by the normal sounds of the morning—the asthmatic hum of the elevator, the tapping of a typewriter, the closing of a door down the hall, and the honking of horns from the street nine stories below.

I rose and walked to my chair behind the couch. There I seated myself and indicated to Kirk that he should lie down. When he had settled himself on it, I said, "Tell me about it Kirk."

. . . It had not been a sudden thing, this abandonment by Kirk of his psychosis, but the result of a dawning understanding that he had begun to develop from the moment he became aware I was sharing—or at least appeared to share—his delusion. From that time forward it had somehow lost its potency, and the gratifications it gave him lacked their former charge of excitement. With this reduction in the appeal of the fantasy, moreover, the insights gained but not employed during the long months of our dynamic exploration of the past at last came into their own. Kirk's former ability to enter the fantasy, to achieve that abnormal state of sensitivity to his needs that had catapulted him into his mythical universe, began to diminish. It was not long before the whole amazing defense—for such Kirk now recognized his obsession to be—collapsed or, better, decayed, to be replaced, item for item, by reality.

But in these latter weeks, although discovering himself each day to be more free of the abiding delusion, Kirk, so he now told me, was still obliged to concern himself with it for the strangest of reasons. Incomprehensible though it may seem, he felt it necessary to engage in a pretense *for my sake*. My enchantment with the fantasy, my preoccupation with its details, my literal involvement in it as a sharer of its exciting gratifications—these not only puzzled him with the recovery of his reasoning capacity and the extension of his hard-won grasp on reality: they created, in addition, a real dilemma. For while *he* no longer believed in the fantasy, he thought *I* did, and such was the nature of his friendly concern for me, and his devotion, that he could not bring himself to disclose his lack of faith lest he somehow "hurt" me. His position, incredibly, was similar to mine when I made the decision to participate in the grandiose obsession, but with this difference: his inability to "hurt" me was a purely emotional reaction, while my decision to employ a technical variant came from professional appreciation of a delicate psychological situation.

Moreover, Kirk was not able to appreciate the fact that when he abandoned his psychosis he had achieved my sole object for him; that to wean him from madness had been the conscious aim of my actions, and that this alone was important to me. As he saw and felt it, there had been a complete turnabout in our positions, a turnabout that confused and worried him, and one before which he remained helpless. As the reader now knows, it was not because I was such an excellent actor that Kirk believed so thoroughly in the apparent reversal of roles: it was, rather, that he sensed how I had been attracted by the stupendous fantasy and felt, in myself, its magnetic pull. . . .

Until Kirk Allen came into my life I had never doubted my own stability. The aberrations of mind, so I had always thought, were for others. Tolerant, somewhat amused, indulgent, I held to the myth of my own mental impregnability. Superior in the knowledge that I, at least, was completely sane and could not—no matter what—be shaken from my sanity, I tended to regard the foibles of my fellows, their fears, their perplexities, with what I know now to have been contempt.

I am shamed by this smugness. But now, as I listen from my chair behind the couch, I know better. I know that my chair and the couch are separated only by a thin line. I know that it is, after all, but a happier combination of accidents that determines, finally, who shall lie on that couch, and who shall sit behind it.

It has been years since I saw Kirk Allen, but I think of him often, and of the days when we roved the galaxies together. Especially do I recall Kirk on summer nights on Long Island, when the sky over Peconic Bay is bright with quivering stars. And sometimes, as I gaze above, I smile to myself and whisper:

"How goes it with the Crystopeds?"

"How are things in Seraneb?"